A MEDIEVAL MIRROR

Speculum humanae salvationis

1324-1500

A MEDIEVAL MIRROR

Speculum humanae salvationis
1324-1500

Adrian Wilson &
Joyce Lancaster Wilson

THE UNIVERSITY OF California PRESS

Berkeley   Los Angeles   London

Dedicated to Fernand Baudin
and to the memory of Willem Ovink

University of California Press
Berkeley and Los Angeles, California

University of California Press, Ltd.
London, England

Copyright ©1984 by Adrian and Joyce Wilson

Printed in Japan

Library of Congress Cataloging in Publication Data

Wilson, Adrian.
  A medieval mirror, Speculum humanæ salvationis, 1324–1500.

  Bibliography: p.
  Includes index.
    1. Books—Benelux countries—History—400–1400. 2. Books—Benelux countries—
History—1400–1600. 3. Speculum humanæ salvationis. 4. Typology (Theology)—
Bibliography. 5. Theology, Doctrinal—Middle Ages, 600–1500—Bibliography.
6. Printing—Benelux countries—History. 7. Scriptoria—Benelux countries. 8. Block-
books. 9. Illumination of books and manuscripts, Medieval—Benelux countries.
10. Illustrated books—15th and 16th centuries. I. Wilson, Joyce Lancaster.
II. Title.
Z8.B45W54 1984   002'.09492   83-24273
ISBN 0-520-05194-7

1   2   3   4   5   6   7   8   9

Contents

Preface

Speculum humanæ salvationis

Spieghel der menscheliker behoudenisse

Spiegel menschlicher Behältnis

Miroir de la Salvation humaine

Mirouer de la Redemption

Miroure of Mans Saluacienne

Under these titles was produced one of the most widely disseminated and influential works of the late Middle Ages. The word *speculum* means mirror or reflection and it was used in the titles of many medieval writings such as the famous *Speculum ecclesiæ* of Honorius of Autun, the *Speculum majus* of Vincent of Beauvais, and the *Speculum vitæ humanæ* of Rodericus Zamorensis. These works were indeed reflections of the pervasive religious concepts of the time. They inspired other writers as well as artists and craftsmen whose interpretations were found in miniatures, sculptures, tapestries, stained glass, and, by the early fifteenth century, in woodcuts.

The authors undertook the study of the *Speculum humanæ salvationis* because of its special relationship to their work on the history of the printed book, on the designing of books, and on manuscript models. The extraordinary metamorphosis of the *Speculum* from manuscripts to blockbooks, and into later incunabula, presents a unique opportunity for the study of the illustrated book of the late medieval period. In addition, there is not only the interesting variety of miniatures but also the fine quality of the woodcuts to encourage investigation. In the following work the focus is on graphic art and printing. References to the *Speculum* text are limited to elucidating those aspects of the venerable book, and only translations that originated in the Low Countries are described.

The *Speculum humanæ salvationis* was written anonymously and it is unique in portraying, more fully and dramatically than any other book of the period, the medieval concept of typology, or the thesis that all the events of the New Testament were prefigured by the events recounted in the Old. It was indebted to the earlier *Biblia Pauperum* or *Biblia Picta* manuscripts, which were also typological, but they were composed almost entirely of pictures, while the first *Speculum humanæ salvationis* had an extensive text to explain its miniatures.

From the first quarter of the fourteenth century to the end of the fifteenth, several hundred copies of it were made, nearly all illuminated, which followed the precise numerical pattern of the original manuscript and the subjects and iconography of its miniatures. The *Speculum humanæ salvationis*, therefore, holds a unique place in the study of medieval miniatures in providing an enormous variety of styles and visual interpretations of the identical sequence of subjects.

In its text and pictures the *Speculum* contains a vivid account of the religious and artistic forces at work in the fourteenth and fifteenth centuries, when the lessons in piety, the allegories, and all of the arts were devoted to instilling in the minds of the people the need for salvation and the dread of eternal damnation. The *Speculum* is entirely concerned with the Fall and Redemption and with their prefiguration in the Old Testament. It is difficult for the modern mind to project itself into this typological system in which, for example, the drunkenness of Noah and the derision of his sons are associated with the derision of the Son of God. But one can imagine the spiritual power of the concepts within the context of their time, and admire the wealth of ingenuity, thought, and imagination which is expressed in them.

The popularity of the *Speculum* caused it to be translated not long after it was composed in the early fourteenth century into German and later into French, English, Dutch, and Czech. There exists in Brussels, in the Bibliothèque Royale, an extraordinary manuscript, or *minute*, as it was titled, on paper, of the first French translation made for Philip the Good, Duke of Burgundy, by Jean Miélot in 1448, entitled *Miroir de la Salvation humaine*. It was this *minute* which lured the present writers into the study of the *Speculum*. Miélot also kept a workbook of his translations, trial pages of fantastic decorated initials, legends, sketches, and labyrinths containing his name. It is a unique record, preserved at the Bibliothèque Nationale in Paris, of preparatory exercises for the making of *de luxe* codices. In this library is an illuminated copy on vellum of the *Miroir* translation which was made in the *minute*. Photographs and diapositives made it possible to compare all the French translations and to relate them to the inventories of the Burgundian library.

The blockbook editions of the *Speculum* are unique in printing history for they are made up of hand-rubbed woodcuts combined with text printed with movable type in a press. They are still unassigned as to date, place, or printer. Generations of scholars have attempted to solve these riddles, but the anonymity of the artists, block cutters, type printers, and publisher has persisted. The mysteries are part of the fascination of the *Speculum*. Only through the paper watermarks, those mute beasts and symbolic devices, have new clues been found for the approximate dating of the printing of the books. The woodcuts, with their heritage of medieval iconography and costume, seem to be much earlier.

Manuscript copies of the *Speculum* were produced through the fifteenth century, and in addition to these and the blockbooks, there were sixteen incunabula, with type and woodcuts printed together, issued by eleven presses. But the changes caused by the Reformation and the Renaissance gradually decreased the interest in typological interpretations of the Bible, and no further editions were printed after the first decade of the sixteenth century.

There has proven to be a vast literature related to the *Speculum humanæ salvationis*: textual analysis, the art of the miniatures and woodcuts, the iconography, the prototypography of the blockbooks, the paper, and the printing. The questions of localization, dating, and inter-relationship with other manuscripts and printing continue to be explored and show no indication of being laid to rest. Our research in the great libraries (and a few private ones) has been a rewarding luxury, and our work has been facilitated by recent scholarly articles, facsimiles, and reprints, as well as by the ease of acquiring photographs, copies, and diapositives from sources all over the world. The encouragement and enthusiasm of scholars and friends has immeasurably helped us to hold up a new mirror to the venerable *Speculum humanæ salvationis*.

Acknowledgments

There is an old Dutch saying: "Oude vriendschap slijt niet" (Old friendship does not wear out), which has been demonstrated throughout our work on this book. Whatever language our friends spoke, Dutch, French, German, English (and some know all of them and Latin), they generously gave invaluable advice, clues and translations. The acknowledgment of our debts to them gives us the opportunity of retracing with great pleasure our research voyages in 1978 and 1979.

In Belgium, the book designer Fernand Baudin led us to countless sources in the literature on the *Speculum humanæ salvationis* and on the Brethren of the Common Life, and even to the sites of their communities in the Forêt de Soigne, near Brussels. He facilitated our studies in the Bibliothèque Royale, willingly searched out answers to our questions, and sent documents to us after we had returned to San Francisco. We extend to him our profound thanks. Also most helpful at the Bibliothèque were the distinguished scholars Elly Cockx-Indestege and Claudine Lemaire. In Louvain, at the Katholieke Universiteit, Bert Cardon shared with us his work on the Flemish verse translation of the *Speculum* and the French copies at Saint-Omer.

Among our friends in Holland, we are deeply grateful to the late Dr. G. Willem Ovink of the University of Amsterdam, who shared his knowledge of Dutch printing, history, and art with us; and to his son, Arnold, who translated a pertinent text. Dr. Ovink's critical reading of our work was immeasurably helpful and supportive. Another friend, Sem Hartz, former art director and type designer of Joh. Enschedé en Zonen, in Haarlem, joined us in our study of the City Library's copies of the *Speculum* blockbooks, in the elegant security of the Frans Hals Museum where they are housed. The Director of the City Library, Cees van Dijk, provided us with important unpublished material. We are indebted to Dr. Pieter F. J. Obbema of the Library of the University of Leiden, for reading the typescript and for his suggestions.

The extensive research and publications of Wytze and Lotte Hellinga have been extremely valuable in our study of prototypography related to the blockbooks. We are grateful also to

Lotte Hellinga, now of the British Library, for reading our text and for her perceptive comments. At the British Library also, Nicolas Barker, Head of Conservation, has been generous with advice. David McKittrick at the Cambridge University Library kindly assisted us in the examination of its examples of early Dutch printing.

In Germany, Hermann Zapf's enthusiasm and knowledge were helpful, as always. He photographed for us two extraordinary *Speculum* manuscripts at Darmstadt and, by happy chance, brought the slides to us in California. Dr. Peter Zahn, then of the University Library of Munich, examined with us its copy, the only dated example of a *Speculum* blockbook. Across the Leopoldstrasse at the Bayerische Staatsbibliothek, we explored a number of the many *Speculum* manuscripts in that rich collection. At the fabled Herzog-August-Bibliothek at Wolfenbüttel, the staff kindly brought us the relevant treasures, and in Nuremberg we were graciously assisted by Frau Elisabeth Becker of the Stadtbibliothek and helped by the staff of the Germanisches Nationalmuseum. At the Gutenberg Museum in Mainz, the Director, Dr. Hans Halbey, showed us the *Speculum* manuscript and related materials there. Later, in San Francisco, he and Mrs. Halbey helped us with translations.

During our research in France, Mme. Jeanne Veyrin-Forrer of the Réserve des Incunabules at the Bibliothèque Nationale in Paris received us most warmly and assisted us with the study of its copies of the blockbooks. We are also much indebted to Adele Lancaster of Paris, for research and obtaining photographs for us there.

At the Houghton Library at Harvard, with the kind help of Eleanor Garvey, we arranged for the reproductions from its early *Speculum* manuscript. Marjorie Wynne, at the Beinecke Rare Book and Manuscript Library at Yale, made it possible for us to compare its "girdle book" *Speculum* manuscript with several incunabula editions. At Wesleyan University we were generously supplied with photocopies of the rare facsimile of the blockbook through Ellen d'Oench of the Davison Art Center.

Thanks to the help of James Wells and Anthony Amodeo of the Newberry Library in Chicago, we were able to study at greater length, in our own workshop, the color slides of the Library's magnificent French translation, with unexpected results.

In California, Carey Bliss of the Huntington Library in San Marino made available to us the only copy of a *Speculum* blockbook in the Far West, that of the second Dutch edition, and there we were able to examine five of the incunabula printings. We are also indebted to the assistance of James D. Hart, Director, and the staff of the Bancroft Library of the University of California at Berkeley; to D. Stephen Corey of the Gleeson Library of the University of San Francisco; and to the staff of the Stanford University Libraries.

We wish to acknowledge, with gratitude, the cooperation and help of Bernard Rosenthal, scholar/bookseller of San Francisco; Professor Fredric J. Mosher of the School of Librarianship and Information Sciences at the University of California at Berkeley, who gave many valuable suggestions; Anne H. van Buren of the Department of Fine Arts of Tufts University for her information on miniatures; and Professor James H. Marrow of the Art History Department of the University of California at Berkeley, for his patient, analytical, and helpful examination of our text and illustrations, and for his enthusiasm.

A.W. and J. L.W.

A MEDIEVAL MIRROR

Speculum humanae salvationis
1324-1500

I–1.
Jean Miélot in his study.
Le Miroir de la salvation humaine.
Bibliothèque Nationale, Paris, Ms. fr. 6275, fol. 96 verso.

I

Medieval Book Production in the Low Countries

The period in which the *Speculum humanæ salvationis* was composed, the first quarter of the fourteenth century, was dominated by medieval religious concepts that affected every aspect of daily life from birth to death. They were reflected in art, architecture, sculpture, music, and drama, and the making of books was largely confined, from the fall of the Roman Empire, to monasteries, convents and ecclesiastical organizations for several hundred years. Religious orders had been established and spread increasingly all over the western world. Pilgrims and monks carried their manuscripts from one monastery to another across great distances, and because they had, in Latin, a common language, the production and exchange of texts by and for these centers flourished. Life in monastic communities provided the seclusion, the freedom from worldly concerns and distractions, and the focal disciplines that were ideally suited to the copying and to the decoration of books.

From Carolingian times on, scriptoria with illuminators also existed in the courts of royalty and nobility and produced countless beautiful codices with miniatures, not all of a religious nature, but including chivalric and historical texts. By the second half of the twelfth century the art of miniaturists and illuminators was so keenly appreciated that even fairly recent writing, such as the *Historia scholastica* of Petrus Comestor (d.1178), a combination of sacred and profane history, was luxuriously executed.[1]

In the thirteenth and fourteenth centuries, under noble and royal patronage, the French manuscripts were unrivalled, but the ateliers, which had nurtured miniaturists from Flanders, Holland, Bohemia, and Italy, declined after 1430 as a result of the impoverishment of the nobility by the Hundred Years' War. In the Low Countries, although the French influence was strong, miniature painting and illumination developed a brilliant independent vigor with

1. André Boutemy, "Medieval Illumination," in *The Book Through 5000 Years*, edited by H. D. L. Vervliet (London and New York, 1972), p. 222.

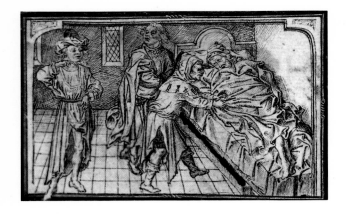

I–3.
Bishop Ambrosius with Mussels and Crab.
The Hours of Catherine of Cleves, c.1440.
The Pierpont Morgan Library, New York, M. 917, p. 244.

I–2.
The Shame of Noah, fol. 15 verso.
The Expulsion from Eden, fol. 9 verso.
The Vengeance of Lamech, fol. 11 verso.
Dutch Bible, 1439.
Bayerische Staatsbibliothek, Munich, Cod. Germ. 1102.

the support of the wealthy burghers, and particularly the powerful Dukes of Burgundy. Their vast domains, acquired by conquest, treaty, purchase, and marriage, included most of the present Netherlands and Belgium, the then extensive duchy of Luxembourg, and Picardy, Artois, Alsace, Lorraine, the Franche-Comté, Nivernais, and Charolais.

As an Episcopal See, Utrecht, in the North, became a center for the illustration of books between 1430 and 1450. The debt of its artists to the Ghent-Bruges school of the Van Eycks, in terms of both style and composition, can be seen in the work of many of the Utrecht miniaturists. In this period, a different and vigorous Dutch style appeared, notably in the work of the Master of Catherine of Cleves, whose magnificent Book of Hours (c.1440), divided into two parts, is now in The Pierpont Morgan Library, Mss. 917 and 945. This artist is also credited with some of the miniatures in the fine Dutch Bible now in the Bayerische Staatsbibliothek in Munich, dated 1439 (fig. I-2).[2]

By the middle of the century, however, some of the best of the Dutch miniaturists, such as Willem Vrelant, emigrated to Bruges when that town restricted in 1403, 1426, and 1457 the importation of detached miniatures made in Utrecht.[3] The passage of such strict measures indicated the importance of the sale of Dutch miniatures and the unusual practice of book-making in Utrecht. There, the scribes wrote the text continuously, leaving space for initials, but not for illustrations. These were painted on separate leaves and inserted into the text or, evidently in many cases, sent to Bruges, where the presence of the Burgundian court had established that city as a center of *de luxe* manuscript production. Vrelant and other Dutch artists appear in the official records as working for the court after the Bruges edict.[4]

Another and very different source of the Netherlandish books was the religious movement known as the *Devotio moderna* which originated in the teaching, sermons, and writings of Geert Grote at the end of the fourteenth century. His reformist concepts became the spiritual basis for the many religious communities called the Brethren of the Common Life. The first commune was actually that of Sisters, a group of pious women who dedicated themselves, without taking vows, to the conventual life in the service of God, in the house in Deventer given to them by Geert Grote. The movement spread, and communities of Brothers as well as Sisters were established with centers throughout the Low Countries and in Germany and northern Switzerland. It attracted intellectuals and deeply pious people by a commitment to sincerity, to simplicity, and to work.

Among the followers of the *Devotio moderna*, but in a more traditional monastic organization, were the Augustinian Regular Canons of the congregation of Windesheim. These retained a

2. L. M. J. Delaissé, *A Century of Dutch Manuscript Illumination* (Berkeley and Los Angeles, 1968), pp. 29–30, pls. 45–48. See also Sandra Hindman, *Text and Image in Fifteenth-Century Illustrated Dutch Bibles* (Leiden, 1977).
3. Delaissé, *op. cit.*, pp. 70 and 74.
4. J. Weale, "Documents inédits sur les enlumineurs de Bruges," in Le Beffroi, IV (1872–1873), p. 253. See also James Douglas Farquhar, *Creation and Imitation* (Fort Lauderdale, Florida, 1976), pp. 24–33, and "Identity in an Anonymous Age: Bruges Manuscript Illuminators and Their Signs, " in Viator, XI (1980), pp. 371 ff.

close relationship with the communities of the Brothers and the Sisters of the Common Life.[5] All were devoted to the establishment of schools and the teaching of religion to the common people. Producing manuscripts was at the core of their activities, including many in the vernacular tongue, and some with miniatures and illumination such as the fine five-volume Latin Bible inscribed by Thomas a Kempis in the Agnietenberg community, which is now in the Hessische Landes- und Hochschulbibliothek Darmstadt.

The rules for the regulation of daily work were posted in the communities and have been preserved.[6] They included scheduled hours daily in the copying, illustrating, and binding of manuscripts, both for their own use and as commissioned works to supplement the income of the community.

In scriptoria of monasteries in the Catholic orders, the texts were often richly illuminated and included Bibles, the lives and miracles of those saints to whom they had a special devotion, and the indispensable writings of the Fathers of the Church. Small portable Latin Bibles were produced in quantity, written in exquisite regular Gothic hands on the finest parchment, often containing miniatures and pictorial or historiated initials.[7]

In the actual work of making books, the medieval scribe must have begun, as would a modern designer, by determining the amount of text which would make a page when written in the chosen script and size and in the desired format. To this must have been added the space planned for miniatures, initials, headings, captions, and sometimes areas for glosses. This calculation would reveal the number of sheets of parchment or vellum needed. Sometimes the skins were prepared by the scribes themselves as evening work when the light was too poor for writing,[8] but probably it was more common to obtain them from the parchment maker. Once the scribe acquired them his next step would be to stack the sheets, possibly in threes, fours, or fives, for gatherings that would make, when the sheets were folded, from twelve to twenty pages. From his basic format plan, he would prick, through the parchment stack, the positions of the margins and the grid for the guide lines of the script. The points would then be connected by ruling lines in pale colored ink or by blind scoring.

Whether the scribe actually wrote in a sewn gathering, or even a bound book, as is so often shown in miniatures (fig. I–1), is difficult to determine. The practice may sometimes have been to inscribe a single four-page sheet of the text consecutively, turning over or replacing the pages to preserve the sequence.[9] There are examples of manuscripts in which a full skin was folded

5. R. R. Post, *The Modern Devotion: Confrontation with Reformation and Humanism* (Leiden, 1968), pp. 349, 367.

6. Pieter F. J. Obbema, "Van schrijven naar drukken," in *Boeken in Nederland*, edited by Ernst Braches (Amsterdam, 1979), p. 21.

7. Antoine de Schryver, "Gothic Manuscripts in Belgium and the Netherlands," in *The Book Through 5000 Years*, pp. 261–62, 266.

8. Fridolin Dressler, *Scriptorum Opus: Schreiber-Mönche am Werk* (Wiesbaden, 1971), p. 9.

9. Eric G. Turner, *The Typology of the Codex* (Philadelphia, 1977), p. 74.

twice to make eight pages, or three times to make sixteen, where the scribe wrote his text leaving the sheet uncut.[10] Scribes are also shown seated at steeply slanted, double-faced desks with the skin folded over the top in the direction of the animal's spine, but it must have been awkward to turn it around or upside-down for each new page. Probably this was the exception, and one may assume that the sheets were usually cut into bi-folios before inscription.

In the workshops of the Brethren of the Common Life, binding was clearly part of the activity, and a number of bindings from these workshops in different locations have been identified. Fifteenth-century metal book fittings were excavated in 1905–06 on the site of the Brussels house. All the known bindings of the Brothers are panel-stamped, many with a small name, "nazaret," stamped by hand, which identified the Brussels community.[11] Panel-stamped bindings were common in the fifteenth century, particularly in the Low Countries, and originated as early as 1250 in Flanders. The dies and panels were engraved in metal, like coins or medallions, and stamped into the leather, not by hand but by a screw press. The patterns and designs were copied from engraved playing cards, or models possibly disseminated in pattern books.[12] Binding work was done not only for the house itself but also for the same customers to whom devotional books were supplied, and for other convents.

The evidence of the blockbooks in which condensed text is carved on the same block as a religious picture also points to their production, in multiple copies, in the centers of the Brethren of the Common Life. The *Exercitium super pater noster* and the *Spirituale pomerium* could be attributed to the communities of Sept-Fontaines and Groenendael. These, and the other Netherlandish blockbooks, are discussed in our Chapter IV. The dates of their origins and their localizations are still controversial, but the communities of the Sisters and of the Brothers of the Common Life, with their dedication to educate and their exceptional tradition of producing and distributing books in the Low Countries in the fifteenth century, might well have been the centers for the creation and dissemination of this new means of popular communication.

Profound changes which affected the making of books had been taking place in the social, intellectual, and religious spheres since the end of the twelfth century. The instruction of laymen and the foundation of universities were taking place concurrently with the development of a wealthy and independent middle class. The conditions under which books were written, copied, distributed, and read were being secularized, and the centers of intellectual life began to shift away from the monasteries and toward a new constituency of readers. Most of these were clerics who retained a bond with the ecclesiastical establishments, but they and their professors had need of many texts, reference works, and commentaries. The universities also had to

10. Léon Gilissen, *Prolégomènes à la Codicologie* (Ghent, 1977), analyzes the subject at length.
11. Paul Needham, *Twelve Centuries of Bookbinding, 400–1600* (New York and London, 1979), pp. 96–98.
12. *Ibid.*, p. 92 and p. 87.

develop organized libraries. The *pecia* system of copying separate signatures was instituted in France, Italy, and Spain, but it was never adopted in the Low Countries.[13]

During the late fourteenth century, while the religious houses continued to produce manuscripts, lay scriptoria appeared around the universities and in the market places of the cities. Professional scribes were available to execute contracts, letters, accounts, and documents on commission. Probably few of these were capable of fine book work, but there may have been some that produced illuminated manuscripts. Books could be copied, of course, by anyone who could write, and the number of "occasional" scribes who made books for themselves as well as for others may well have been as great as the professional scriveners.[14]

The introduction of paper had important results in the making and the price of books. Paper did not, of course, replace parchment and vellum rapidly, and the difference in price at the outset was not great, but it promoted the specialization of vellum and parchment for use in official documents and *de luxe* books. The early papers were comparatively heavy and the surfaces did not lend themselves so happily to the pen or brush. While small handwritten Latin Bibles on fine parchment were readily portable, the early printed Bibles on paper required two large volumes. But gradually the use of paper permitted the introduction of ordinary school books to the market in a much greater quantity and at less expense than the vellum and parchment ones.

In Flanders, and particularly at Bruges, paper was in use from the first years of the fourteenth century. The *pampiermakers* are found in the accounts of the city from 1304.[15] These must have been merchants of imported papers and not papermakers themselves, for the first paper mill in Flanders was not established until 1405, probably due to the lack of rapidly flowing water.[16] The paper used in the Low Countries came from mills on rivers in what is now central and northeastern France: the Moselle, the Meuse, the Marne, and the Saulx. The rivers provided water power, the medium for pulping, and the downstream transportation to the shipping arteries of the Rhine and the Seine. The most important papermaking towns were Metz, Bar-le-Duc, Troyes, and Epinal, and their products were distributed primarily through Antwerp and Bruges.[17]

To return to the blockbooks, it seems that the number of lay woodcutters working at illustration in the middle of the fifteenth century was very small. According to an art historian of

13. Graham Pollard, "The *pecia* system in the medieval universities," in *Medieval Scribes, Manuscripts and Libraries: Essays Presented to N. R. Ker*, edited by M. B. Parkes and Andrew Watson (London, 1978), p. 148.
   See also Wytze Gs Hellinga, *Copy and Print in the Netherlands* (Amsterdam, 1962), p. 110; Jean Destrez, *La Pecia dans les manuscrits universitaires du XIIIe et du XIVe siècle* (Paris, 1935), also in Scriptorium, XI, 2 (1957).
14. Curt F. Bühler, *The Fifteenth Century Book* (Philadelphia, 1961), p. 20.
15. L. Giliodts-van Severen, *L'Oeuvre de Jean Brito* (Bruges, 1897), p. 385 fn.
16. A. J. J. Delen, *Histoire du livre et de l'imprimerie en Belgique des origines à nos jours*. Deuxième partie (Brussels, 1930), p. 29.
17. Allan H. Stevenson, "The Problem of the Blockbooks," unpublished notes of lectures given at the University of Amsterdam, 1965, now in the Haarlem Stadsbibliotheek.

Netherlandish woodcutting, not more than twenty-five were active in book illustration in the last quarter of the century,[18] and there must have been even fewer before 1475. Outside of the religious communities, the long-established guilds for painters, illuminators, and carpenters were strictly organized. In 1452 a trial took place in Louvain in which the guild of carpenters sued Jan van den Berghe, whose work was the cutting of letters and pictures (*letteren ende beelde-prynten*), maintaining that he must join the guild and conform to the prescribed obligations.[19] The engraver argued that his work was a unique art unlike any other in the city, and that it was concerned with the clergy. He seems to have been the only one to exercise his craft in Louvain at that time outside the monasteries.[20] Arthur M. Hind in *An Introduction to a History of Woodcut* writes, "it can therefore be inferred with certainty that he was engaged in the cutting of some book of a religious kind like the Netherlandish blockbooks."[21] In turn, the guild replied that its members were also cutters of letters and images, that this occupation required the same tools as the carpenters, barrel makers, etc., and that their guild would not allow Van den Berghe to invoke the liberty of clerics. The magistrate of Louvain granted the case of the guild but exempted Van den Berghe from the enrollment fees.[22]

However, as we have seen, there were certainly engravers of letters and images in the religious communities and attached to the courts of the nobility, over which the guilds had no control, and where woodcutting flourished. These craftsmen were still practicing long after the first printing presses were established in the Low Countries. They supplied woodcuts for early printed books at Louvain, Brussels, Utrecht, and Haarlem.

18. William Martin Conway, *The Woodcutters of the Netherlands in the Fifteenth Century* (1884; reprint Hildesheim, 1961).
19. Arthur M. Hind, *An Introduction to a History of Woodcut* (1935; reprint New York 1963), p. 83.
20. Hélène Verougstraete, *Un Incunabule flamand: Le Speculum humanæ salvationis.* Mémoire présenté pour l'obtention du grade de licenciée en archéologie et histoire de l'art (Université Catholique de Louvain, 1968, unpublished), p. 101.
21. Hind, *op. cit.*, p. 211.
22. E. van Even, *L'Ancienne Ecole de Peinture de Louvain* (Brussels, 1870), p. 101.

II

Latin Manuscripts of the Speculum

Compiled at the beginning of the fourteenth century for the use of preaching monks and clerics, the *Speculum humanæ salvationis* was a widely used volume in the late Middle Ages. There exist today more than 350 manuscripts in Latin and translations into Dutch, French, German, English, and Czech.[1]   Copies were made in religious houses, convents of all orders, as well as by lay scribes. Toward the end of the fifteenth century there was hardly a library in northern Europe that did not possess an example. Like the majority of religious texts of the time, the *Speculum* was a compilation made primarily from commentaries on and adaptations of the Bible. Almost all copies are illustrated, following the pattern of the manuscripts dated 1324, made from one which is presumably lost. In the Prologue is the statement that the learned can find information from the scriptures, but the unlearned must be taught by pictures, which are the books of the lay people.[2]

The text and pictures of the *Speculum* are devoted to the interpretation of the New Testament through prefigurations in the Old, the so-called typological system, which was the medieval way of relating the Old Testament to the life of Jesus Christ. Originating in Asia Minor with the Greek Fathers, it passed into Western thought and was greatly spread by the influence of St. Augustine.[3]

Typology appears in the writings of many medieval religious scholars and notably in the *Biblia pauperum*, written in the late thirteenth century, which contained in words and pictures

1. E. Breitenbach, *Speculum humanæ salvationis: Eine typengeschichtliche Untersuchung* (Strasbourg, 1930), pp. 5–43.
2. An English translation of the Prologue appears in M. R. James and Bernard Berenson, *Speculum humanæ salvationis* (Oxford, 1926), p. 7.
3. Emile Mâle, *The Gothic Image* (1913; reprint New York, 1958), p. 135, translated from *L'Art religieux du XIIIe siècle en France* (Paris, 1898) as *Religious Art in France of the Thirteenth Century*.

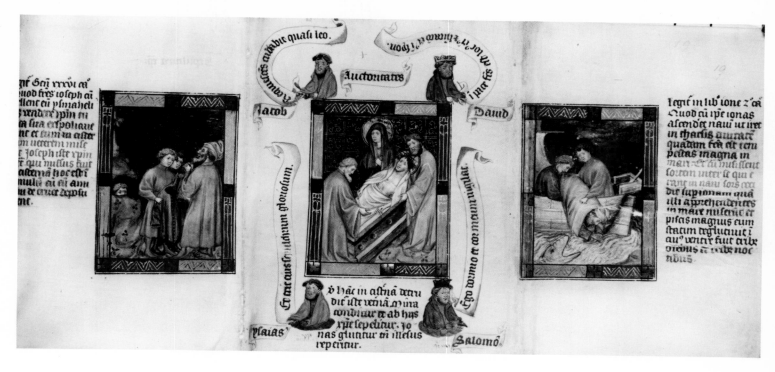

II–1.
Jacob Laments His Son Joseph.
Christ Placed in the Sarcophagus.
Jonah Thrown to the Whale.
Biblia pauperum. c.1400.
British Library, London, Kings Ms. 5.

a succinct interpretation of the Bible. To the medieval theologian every event in the Gospels had been announced in advance. For example, the entombment of Jesus was prefigured in the casting of Joseph into the well by his jealous brothers, and Jonah thrown into the sea and swallowed by the whale (fig. II–1).

The commentaries on the Bible were, in practice, as important as the scriptures themselves. The Church had never specifically recommended the reading of the Bible to the faithful, for a book so full of enigmas could be understood only with the help of the writings of the Fathers of the Church.[4] The major sources of the *Speculum* were the *Historia scholastica* of Petrus Comestor, the *Legenda aurea* of Jacobus de Voragine, the *Antiquitate Judaica* of Flavius Josephus, and the works of St. Thomas Aquinas.[5] Many of the events are drawn from the books of the Apocrypha, most of which were accepted parts of the Bible until their rejection by the Puritans in the seventeenth century as not originating in the Hebrew text. Later editions of the King James version and many modern Bibles omit the Apocryphal books.

The two chapters with which the *Speculum* begins, and which precede the chapters with Old Testament prefigurations, describe the Fall of Lucifer and his accomplices from Heaven into Hell, the Creation of Eve, the Admonition of God not to eat of the tree of the knowledge of

4. *Ibid.,* p. 172.
5. Paul Perdrizet, *Etude sur le Speculum humanæ salvationis* (Paris, 1908). See also
   L. M. Fr. Daniels, *De Spieghel der menscheliker Behoudenisse* (Tielt, 1949).

good and evil (sometimes interpreted as God uniting Adam and Eve in marriage), the Temptation, the Fall and Expulsion, and finally the Deluge, which ended the first age of the world according to medieval historiographers.

These are the events on which is based the doctrine of Redemption by the Savior. They have no prefigurations. Medieval authors also held that mankind was not saved from damnation by Christ alone but also by the life of the Virgin Mary, the associate of Christ in Redemption. That is why the account of the Redemption begins, in Chapter III of the *Speculum*, not with the Annunciation to Mary, but with the Annunciation to Joachim of the conception of the Holy Virgin Mary by his wife, Anna. One finds in the *Speculum* certain aspects of Catholicism which were contested during the Reformation, among them the Mariolatry which pervades the book and culminates in the last two chapters, XLIV and XLV, devoted to the Seven Sorrows and the Seven Joys of Mary.

As noted above, the *Speculum* was written sometime before 1324, the date which appears in two manuscripts in Paris (Bibliothèque Nationale, Ms. lat. 9584, and Bibliothèque de l'Arsenal, Ms. lat. 593). The Prohemium in each copy opens with the following lines, with the Latin contractions spelled out:

> Incipit prohemium cuiusdam nove compilationis edite sub anno domini millesimo ccc 24 nomen vero authoris humilitate siletur. Sed titulus sive nomen operis est speculum humane salvationis.

> (Here begins the prohemium of a new compilation published in the year of our Lord one thousand three hundred twenty-four although the name of the author is unstated out of humility. But the title or name of the work is Speculum humanæ salvationis).

It seems very probable that the reference to the anonymity of the author, because of his humility, was in his original manuscript.[6]

Line fifty-three, Chapter XXVIII of the *Speculum* states, *dicitur enim quod ubi est Papa ibi est Romana curia.* This could only have been written during the so-called "Babylonian Captivity" when the papal court was in Avignon (1309–1378). It follows that the manuscript must have been written between 1309 and 1324.

The authorship of the *Speculum* has been variously attributed to Conradus of Altzheim,[7] to Vincent of Beauvais,[8] to Henricus Suso,[9] and in the extensive work of Lutz and Perdrizet, to Ludolphus of Saxony.[10] There is also an inscription in a fifteenth-century hand in the margin of the first leaf of a *Speculum* which reads *Nicolaus a Lyra dicitur hanc compilacionem fecisse.*[11]

6. James and Berenson, *op.cit.*, p. 6.
7. *Catalogue of Manuscripts of The Hunterian Museum Library in the University of Glasgow,* edited by John Young and P. H. Aitken (Glasgow, 1908), pp. 68–71.
8. Sandra Hindman and James Douglas Farquhar, *Pen to Press* (College Park, Maryland, 1977), p. 233.
9. L. M. Fr. Daniels, "Ludolphus van Saksen en Henricus Suso," in Ons Geestelijk erf, XX, 1–2 (1949), pp. 138–150.
10. J. Lutz and P. Perdrizet, *Speculum humanæ salvationis:* Texte critique. Traduction inédite de Jean Miélot (1448). Les sources et l'influence iconographique principalement sur l'art alsacien du XIVᵉ siècle, 2 Vols. (Leipzig, 1907).
11. The Pierpont Morgan Library, M. 140.

As evidence of Ludolphus' authorship Lutz and Perdrizet cite several factors. Originally a Dominican monk, Ludolphus joined the Carthusian Order in 1340 and wrote the *Vita christi*, in which he included Chapter IX of the *Speculum* and other sections of the text without crediting his source. This was taken to show that he was incorporating an earlier work of his own, but it has since been shown that he borrowed twenty-three fragments of the *Horologium sapientiæ* by Henricus Suso, and portions of texts by other authors, without acknowledgment.[12] This was common practice in the writings of the Middle Ages and cannot, therefore, be clear evidence that Ludolphus wrote the *Speculum*.

There are, however, good reasons to place the origin of the text in a Dominican monastery. In Chapter III, the Immaculate Conception is described in accordance with the doctrines of the Dominican Order; Chapter XXXVII tells of the vision of St. Dominic; Chapter XXX includes the theory of the sanctification before birth expressed by St. Thomas Aquinas, a Dominican, and special honor is also paid to him in Chapter XLII.

The text in Chapter XXXIX tells of the knighting of Christ: his charger is the ass of Palm Sunday; his helmet is the crown of thorns; his gloves and his spurs are the nails of the Crucifixion; and his champion is the Virgin Mary. The ceremony is executed *more Alemannico* (in the German way) with sword strokes on the neck. At that period the wording would have indicated a location in southwest Germany, or Swabia. The text would seem to have been composed in a convent of the Preaching Brothers of Strassburg (at that time, within the borders of Swabia), by a Dominican of Saxon origin.[13]

Complete manuscripts of the *Speculum* include a Prologue of two pages, a Prohemium of four (both without illustrations), forty-two chapters with the miniatures above the four text columns (herein referred to as a, b, c, and d) followed by three chapters of double length with eight miniatures, requiring four pages each. After the two chapters devoted to the first age of the world, forty follow the typological pattern in which the first image from a New Testament event is accompanied by three prefigurations taken from the Old Testament or other sources mentioned earlier. In the last three chapters, devoted to the Seven Stations of the Passion and the Seven Sorrows and the Seven Joys of Mary, the miniatures are not typological. The complete work, then, would require fifty-one leaves.

The precise mathematical format of the *Speculum* is reflected in the linear scheme. The text of the first forty-two chapters has twenty-five lines to a column, two columns to a page; the bottom line of the first is rhymed with the top line of the second column. There are four columns or 100 lines to each chapter, filling a page-opening. The last three chapters are twenty-six lines to a column, eight columns to a chapter, filling two page-openings. The Prologue occupies 100 lines and the Prohemium, or table of contents of the chapters, has 300 lines.

---

12. Daniels, "Ludolphus van Saksen," *op.cit.*
13. Lutz and Perdrizet, *op.cit.*, p. 249. However, Marcel Thomas has proposed a
    Franciscan origin, or Franciscan influence, in "Zur kulturgeschichtlichen Einordnung
    der Armenbibel mit Speculum humanæ salvationis," in Archiv für Kulturgeschichte,
    LII (1970), pp. 192–223.

While most manuscripts follow this pattern, some include only forty-two chapters, omitting the last three, and some omit the Prologue or the Prohemium, or both. There are captions over the miniatures in some copies but these differ from one to another. The references which appear sometimes at the foot or at the head of the text columns, naming the book of the Bible or some other source, also vary or are omitted. In the text itself, copyists have made minor changes but retained the rhymed doublets.

It must have been of great value to the scribes, the blockbook maker, and the incunabulists that the earliest known manuscripts laid out such a specific format for the *Speculum*, which has been followed, with some variations, through the many copies.

The oldest *summa* listing the *Speculum* is not dated, but it was made about the middle of the fourteenth century by Ulrich, Abbot of Lilienfeld. It notes only forty-two chapters. It has been suggested that the last three chapters were added later.[14] However, the copies mentioned above, made from a manuscript dated 1324, which predates the *summa*, include forty-five chapters. The copyist of the manuscript in the *summa* must, therefore, have deleted the last three chapters, or worked from an abbreviated example.

Each chapter can be thought of as an inspiration for a sermon by preaching Brothers, to whom the pictures were as important as the text. The persons and scenes had religious significance which could be disseminated to the unlearned more dramatically through images than through words. In some manuscripts the typological lesson is emphasized by parallel compositions of the four pictures within each chapter.

In the minds of the theologians of the Middle Ages the religious symbolism of every flower, plant, animal, and form was determined, and this is reflected by the artists and miniaturists of the *Speculum*. We find also, in some of the finest manuscripts, their obedience to the traditional rules of a kind of mathematics as well, in which position, grouping, symmetry, and number have mystic meaning. These systems were transmitted through the Church to craftsmen, sculptors, painters, and miniaturists from one end of Europe to the other.[15]

No works of the late Gothic had more influence on artists working in all the media than the *Biblia pauperum* and the *Speculum humanæ salvationis*. The influence of the typological text and illustrations of the latter can be seen in the fourteenth-century stained glass windows of churches at Mulhouse, Colmar, Rouffach, and Wissembourg. The woodcuts of the blockbooks clearly appear in designs of the fifteenth-century sculptures of the church of Saint-Maurice at Vienne and in the famous tapestries of the Life of Christ at La Chaise-Dieu and the series at Rheims.[16] Mâle states that one could be sure that any Flemish artist of importance had in his atelier manuscripts of these two works. Jan van Eyck, in 1440, worked from a *Speculum* in the triptych for the church of Saint-Martin in Ypres. The typological treatment of the Nativity was traditional

14. Perdrizet, *Etude, op.cit.*
15. Mâle, *op.cit.*, pp. 1–5.
16. Robert A. Koch, "The Sculptures of the Church of Saint-Maurice at Vienne, the Biblia Pauperum and the Speculum Humanæ Salvationis," in Art Bulletin, XXXII (1950), pp. 151–55.

II–2.
a. The Fall of Lucifer. b. The Creation of Eve.
Speculum humanæ salvationis, Chapter I.
Bibliothèque Nationale, Paris, Ms. lat. 9584, fol. 4 verso.

and one might assume that Van Eyck could find it in other sources, but on the exterior of the side panel is the earliest example, in panel painting, of the Annunciation to Augustus and the Tiburtine Sibyl just as it appears in the *Speculum*. This subject entered the artistic iconography specifically through the *Speculum* text and image. There was a copy also in the atelier of Roger van der Weyden, as can be seen in the famous Bladelin triptych, where the same prefigurations of the Nativity are pictured.[17] The use of both books as sources, in a single work of art, is not uncommon.

While the artists of the *Speculum* created manuscript miniatures that are very different in style from one copy to the other, they are fairly consistent in the iconography and the symbolism suited to the subjects. A rewarding study could be made of the many Latin manuscripts of the *Speculum* which are still preserved. We have limited our work to the few which follow, in order to describe and illustrate some of the varieties of treatment. The miniatures may be compared with the woodcuts of the blockbooks by reference to our Chapter VI.

17. Emile Mâle, *L'Art religieux de la fin du moyen âge en France* (Paris, 1949), p. 236.

II–3.
c. The Marriage of Adam and Eve. d. The Temptation.
Speculum humanæ salvationis, Chapter I.
Bibliothèque Nationale, Paris, Ms. lat. 9584, fol. 5 recto.

Bibliothèque Nationale, Ms. lat. 9584

This copy is on parchment in small folio, 29.4 x 22 cm., and contains twenty leaves bound up in the wrong order. It was made sometime in the last quarter of the fourteenth century, from the same model as that of the Bibliothèque de l'Arsenal, Ms. 593, a model which lacked the text and pictures from Chapter XVI c and d, to XXIV a and b. Both copies are of Italian origin and contain the interrupted text and the date of 1324 in the Prohemium, which must be the date of the model, not of the copies.

At an unknown date Ms. lat. 9584 was divided in two, and the other portion is at Oxford. In the latter the text has been cut off and only the miniatures, in line and wash, remain. The two parts were reproduced together in a facsimile in 1926, and the presence of a miniature for Chapter XLV, from the Oxford portion, shows that the inscription of the complete manuscript was intended.[18]

18. James and Berenson, *op. cit.*

II–4.
a. The Fall. b. The Expulsion.
Speculum humanæ salvationis, Chapter II.
Bibliothèque Nationale, Paris, Ms. lat. 9584, fol. 5 verso.

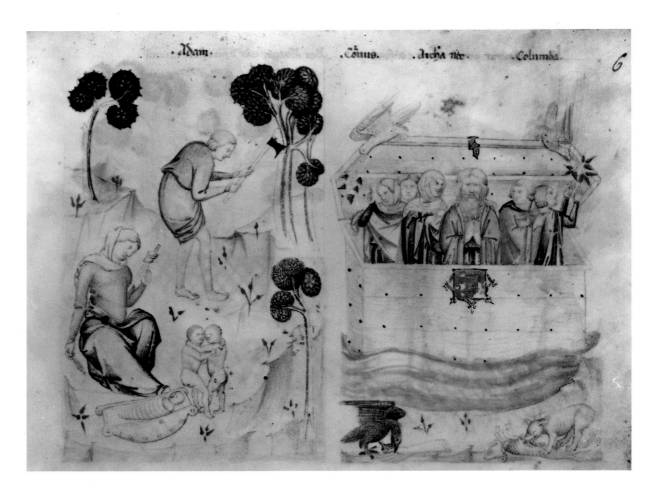

II-5.
c. Adam Tills, Eve Spins. d. Noah's Ark.
Speculum humanæ salvationis, Chapter II.
Bibliothèque Nationale, Paris, Ms. lat. 9584, fol. 6 recto.

The script is an Italian Gothic of the middle of the fourteenth century, and according to Bernard Berenson, the miniatures in pen and wash are Florentine from the last quarter of the century (figs. II–2, 3). He finds them the work of a miniaturist who had travelled widely and included, in his images, architecture with a Byzantine influence and armor in the French style. The clothing of persons in the mode of the day does not seem to appear in Tuscan art earlier than 1370, but it can clearly be seen in this manuscript (e.g. the angel in fig. II–4).

It is curious that in the miniature of Adam digging while Eve spins, a new baby is lying in a cradle beside Cain and Abel. Presumably the artist did not know that Seth was born long after the murder of Abel by Cain (fig. II–5).

Bibliothèque de l'Arsenal, Ms. lat. 593

Written in an Italian Gothic hand similar to B.N. Ms. fr. 9584 but not by the same scribe, this manuscript is on parchment in small folio size, 32.2 x 21.5 cm. It is a "sister" book to the Paris manuscript above and was produced in the same scriptorium, for the missing chapters are lacking in both, and it appears they were copied from the same model, dated 1324. The errors in

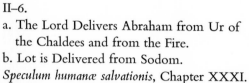

II–6.
a. The Lord Delivers Abraham from Ur of
   the Chaldees and from the Fire.
b. Lot is Delivered from Sodom.
Speculum humanæ salvationis, Chapter XXXI.
Bibliothèque de l'Arsenal, Paris, Ms. lat. 593.

II–7.
a. Christ Wept over the City of Jerusalem.
b. Jeremiah Lamented over Jerusalem.
Speculum humanæ salvationis, Chapter XV.
Bibliothèque de l'Arsenal, Paris, Ms. lat. 593.

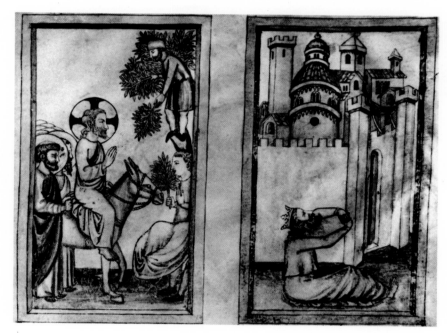

the miniature titles are also the same in the two manuscripts. Berenson thought that the miniatures in the Arsenal copy were done by an Umbrian artist, and he contrasts the "bald landscapes" and stiff rustic figures with the elegant flowing lines of the Florentine manuscript. Judging by the architecture in the miniatures, particularly in Chapter XV b, the view of the dome in Jerusalem (fig. II–7), he proposes that the illustrations were made after 1400, but the notice in the Samaran and Marichal catalogue attributes the illumination to Taddeo Gaddi (1300–1366), a Florentine.[19]

19. *Ibid.*, pp. 59, 71; Charles Samaran and Robert Marichal, *Catalogue des manuscrits en écriture Latine*, Vol. I, Musée Condé et Bibliothèques Parisiennes (Paris, 1959), p. 399.

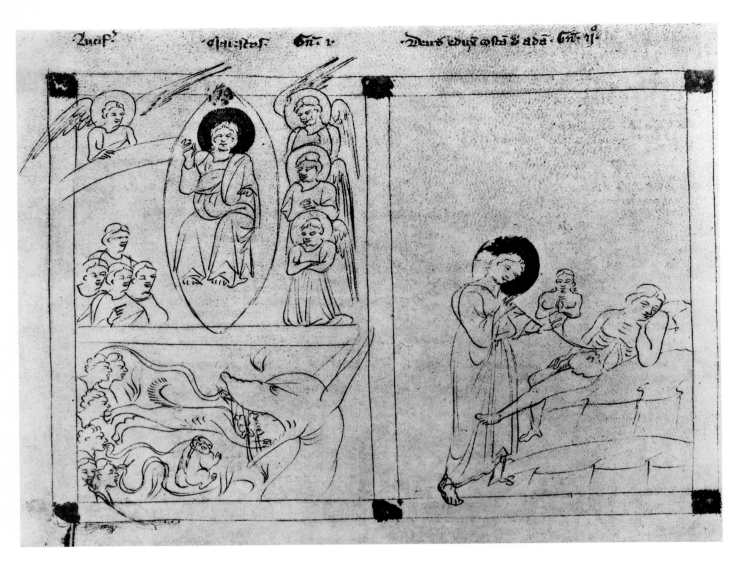

II–8.
a. The Fall of Lucifer. b. The Creation of Eve.
Speculum humanæ salvationis, Chapter I.
Bayerische Staatsbibliothek, Munich, Clm 146, fol. 3 verso.

Bayerische Staatsbibliothek, Clm 146

For their extensive study of the *Speculum humanæ salvationis*, Lutz and Perdrizet chose to reproduce, with commentary, the Munich copy Clm 146.[20] It is in folio, on fifty-one parchment
leaves, and contains the Prohemium, the Prologue, and forty-five chapters. There are 192 pen
drawings, and initials painted in red and blue (figs. II–8, 9, 10, 11). While this copy is not dated,
it was presumably written about the middle of the fourteenth century and it contains a sort of
colophon statement that it was done in the Johannite monastery at Selestat (near Strasbourg).
It was chosen as an authoritative text because of its origin near to the Dominican Monastery
where it was assumed that the *Speculum* was first written, and because of the obvious care of the
copyist. However it has since been proposed that this manuscript was copied from one which

20. Lutz and Perdrizet, *op.cit.*

II–9.
c. The Marriage of Adam and Eve. d. The Temptation.
Speculum humanæ salvationis, Chapter I.
Bayerische Staatsbibliothek, Munich, Clm 146, fol. 4 recto.

originated in Bologna about 1330, traveled to Toledo where it was destroyed in the Spanish civil war of the nineteen-thirties, but whose existence has been revealed by pictures of certain pages made by a Barcelona photographer.[21]

The miniatures of the Munich copy are framed in pen lines and in some of them the corners and the halos are painted in a terra cotta color, possibly to prepare them for the addition of gold. The only finished painted miniature, of God with a gold halo uniting Adam and Eve (fig. II–9), indicates that it was intended that all the miniatures be colored. The devil of the Temptation, who takes many forms in the *Speculum* illustrations, appears here as a basilisk with an enormous looped tail.

21. Evelyn Silber, "The Reconstructed Toledo *Speculum humanæ salvationis:* The Italian Connection in the Early Fourteenth Century," in Journal of the Warburg and Courtauld Institutes, XLIII (1980), pp. 32–51, pls. 2–10.

II–10.

a. Christ on the Cross.

b. Nebuchadnezzar's Dream of the Tree Cut Down.

Speculum humanæ salvationis, Chapter XXIV.

Bayerische Staatsbibliothek, Munich, Clm 146, fol. 26 verso.

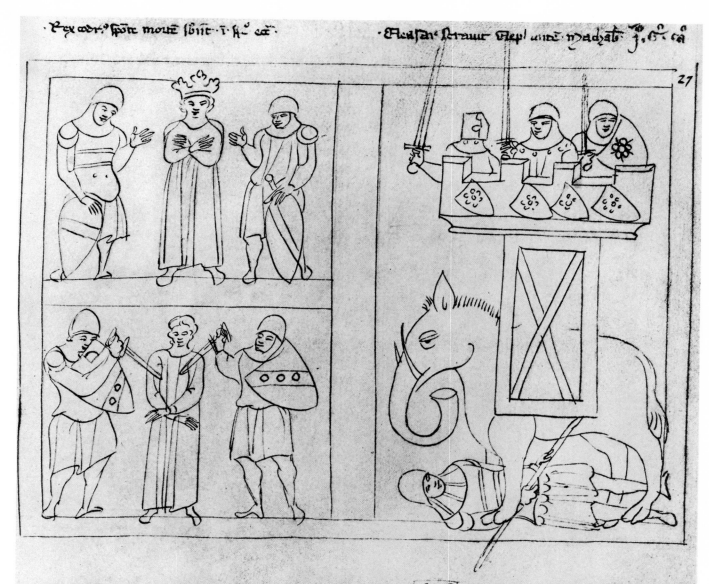

II–11.

c. King Codrus Dedicates Himself in Death.

d. Eleazar Kills the Elephant and is Crushed.

Speculum humanæ salvationis, Chapter XXIV.

Bayerische Staatsbibliothek, Munich, Clm 146, fol. 27 recto.

II–12.
a. The Resurrection.
Speculum humanæ salvationis, Chapter XXXII.
Yale University, The Beinecke Rare Book
and Manuscript Library, Ms. 27, fol. 36 verso.

Yale University, The Beinecke Rare Book and Manuscript Library, Ms. 27

This late fourteenth-century manuscript of the *Speculum humanæ salvationis* is bound with the Pseudo-Bonaventura *Meditationes de passione christi*. It was copied in England and was given to the Collegiate School in Connecticut by Elihu Yale in 1714. (The college was re-named for the philanthropist in 1718.) It is said to be the first illuminated manuscript to come to a North American institutional library. It contains 104 leaves of vellum which measure 28 x 19 cm. The *Speculum* part contains the Prologue, the Prohemium, forty-five chapters and an undated Explicit. Originally there were 180 drawings of which eighteen have been removed. The miniatures are drawn with a very fine pen, in ink of the same color as the text, but paler, and they were probably not made by a professional miniaturist (figs. II–12, 13). It is in its original binding, of a type known as a "girdle book." These were made by covering the volume, already bound in sheepskin on wooden boards, with an envelope of sheepskin which culminates in a knot formed at the end of the skin, and clasps. This *Speculum*, weighing three pounds eight ounces, would have been quite uncomfortable hanging from a girdle and was probably designed to hang from the saddle of a traveller on horseback.[22]

22. Thomas E. Marston, "The Speculum Humanæ Salvationis," in The Yale University
   Library Gazette, XLII, no. 3 (1968). See also, Cahn and Marrow, "Medieval and
   Renaissance Manuscripts at Yale: A Selection," in *ibid.*, LII, no. 4 (1978).

II–13.
The Creation of Eve, Chapter I b, fol. 7 recto.
Balaam's Ass and the Angel, Chapter III d, fol. 9 recto.
Jacob's Ladder, Chapter XXXIII b, fol. 37 verso.
Speculum humanæ salvationis.
Yale University, The Beinecke Rare Book
and Manuscript Library, Ms. 27.

This delightful manuscript on parchment was written ca. 1360. It contains seventy-one leaves, 35 x 20 cm., and thirty-four chapters with pictures painted in vivid washes. The archives of Dortmund reveal that it belonged to L. Kleppingk from 1372 to 1388/89 and hence it is known as the Cleppinck *Speculum*. According to an entry at the end of the text it was in the Cloister of Clarissa in Clarenberg, Westphalia, in about 1400. The manuscript is incomplete, lacking many leaves but ending with Chapter XL, so that it was probably copied as the abbreviated version. The miniatures are placed in an unusual way, with the four illustrations for each chapter on facing pages without text (Plates II–1 and II–2). The images are in two compartments in vertical sequence and are of formal dramatic design. The typological pattern of the *Speculum* is followed, but with extremely unusual interpretations in the miniatures. The rhymed text is inscribed in single columns on the tall narrow pages following the openings containing the miniatures.[23]

Hessische Landes- und Hochschulbibliothek Darmstadt, Hs 720

Written in a careful Bastarda hand in two prose columns on paper, this manuscript has 200 pen and wash drawings, four for each chapter in the usual typological program, but is unusual in that the chapters begin always on a recto page and end on the verso. There are sixty-four leaves, 36.5 x 27.5 cm., made in southern Germany about 1440, but the provenance of the codex is not recorded.

Its opening miniature on folio 1 verso is unusual for a *Speculum* manuscript. The page is divided vertically: the left half depicts the Tree of Virtues rising from a mandorla of Christ enthroned; the right half shows the Tree of Vices coming out of a winged monster (Plate II–4).[24] Unlike the Darmstadt Hs 2505 of the *Speculum*, the entry into Egypt of Chapter XI does not show the falling of the idols at the passage of Christ (fig. II–15).

23. Reproductions of the miniatures of this manuscript, in color but reduced size, were published with a few pages of the text in *Heilsspiegel*, with an Afterword and Explanation by Horst Appuhn, in Die bibliophilen Taschenbücher series, no. 267 (Dortmund, 1981). In this work two similar *Speculum* manuscripts are pictured on pp. 124–127.

24. The only other *Speculum* manuscript known to us with a version of the Tree of Virtues and the Tree of Vices is in the Bibliothèque Royale, Brussels, Ms. 9332, where it appears on fol. 121 verso.

Plate II–1.
a. The Adoration of the Magi.
b. The Magi See the Star.
c. Three Soldiers Bring Water to David.
d. The Queen of Sheba Brings Gifts to Solomon.
Speculum humanæ salvationis, Chapter IX.
Hessische Landes- und Hochschulbibliothek Darmstadt,
Hs 2505, fols. 18 verso and 19 recto.

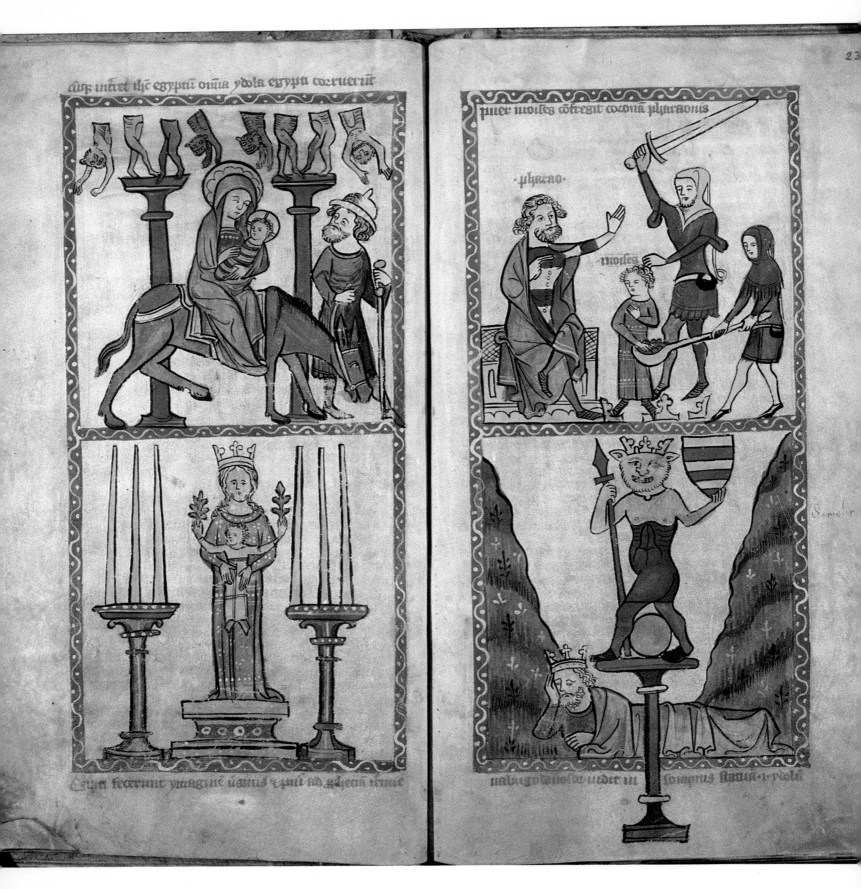

Plate II–2.

a. The Entry into Egypt and the Falling Idols.

b. The Egyptians Made an Image of the Virgin and Child.

c. The Boy Moses and the Burning Coals.

d. Nebuchadnezzar Dreams of a Great Statue.

Speculum humanæ salvationis, Chapter XI.

Hessische Landes- und Hochschulbibliothek Darmstadt,

Hs 2505, fols. 22 verso and 23 recto.

Plate II–3.
The Last Supper.
Speculum humanæ salvationis, Chapter XVI.
Hessische Landes- und Hochschulbibliothek Darmstadt,
Hs 2505, fol. 27 verso.

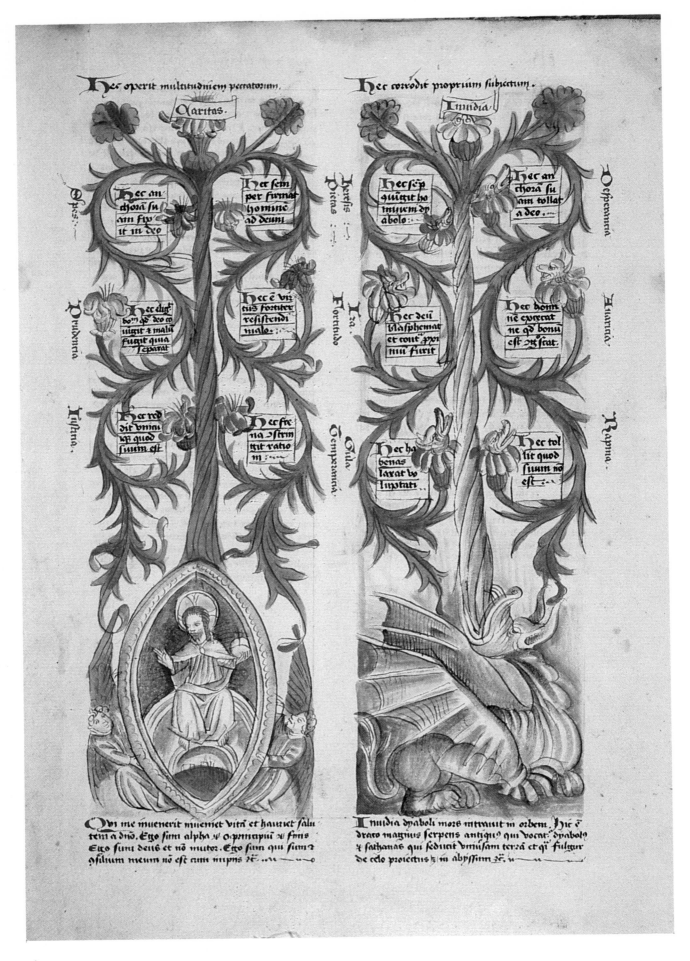

Plate II–4.
The Tree of Virtues and the Tree of Vices.
Speculum humanæ salvationis, Chapter XVI.
Hessische Landes- und Hochschulbibliothek Darmstadt, Hs 720, fol. 1 verso.

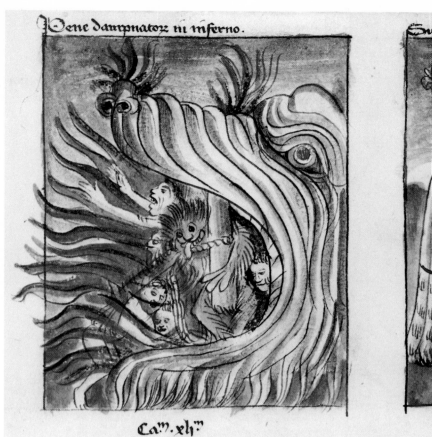

Vene dampnator in inferno.

Cam. xli.

Sic puniuit rex dauid hostes suos

Omnia ydola corruerunt nutu chu in egyptum

iosep

Egypten fecit ymagies Virgis cu puero
ppter iphos ieremie.

II–14.
The Pain of the Damned in Hell.
How David Punished His Enemies.
Speculum humanæ salvationis, Chapter XLI.
Hessische Landes- und Hochschulbibliothek Darmstadt,
Hs 720, fol. 47 recto.

II–15.
The Flight into Egypt.
The Egyptian Statue of the Virgin and Child.
Speculum humanæ salvationis, Chapter XI.
Hessische Landes- und Hochschulbibliothek Darmstadt,
Hs 720, fol. 17 recto.

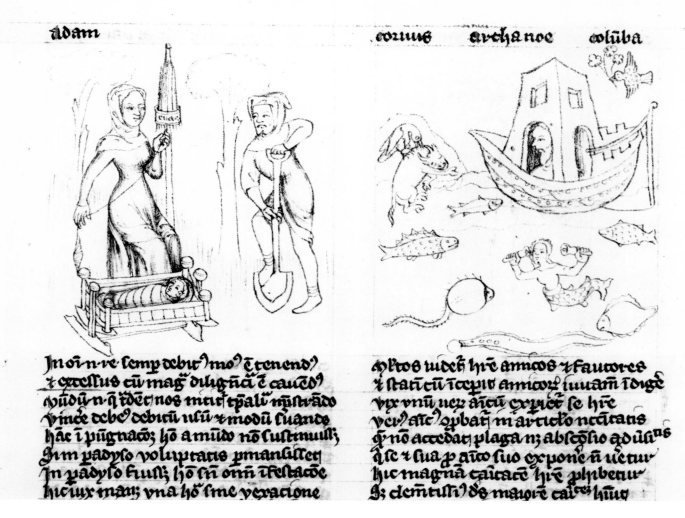

II–16.
c. Adam Tills and Eve Spins. d. Noah's Ark.
Speculum humanæ salvationis, Chapter II.
Harvard University, The Houghton Library, Ms. Lat. 121, fol. 5 verso.

Harvard University, The Houghton Library, Ms. Lat. 121

Written in a small rounded Gothic script in the typical two-column, twenty-five-line format on forty-eight vellum leaves, 23 x 16.5 cm., this manuscript includes forty-five chapters and seventy-five pen and ink drawings in a primitive but lively style (figs. II-16, 17, 18). There are single-line titles over the pictures, but no elaborate initials or illumination. After the first eighteen chapters, blank spaces are left for the miniatures, which were never completed. Those of the early chapters appear to be of Bohemian origin or influence and were done in the late fourteenth century. The manuscript was formerly in the Monastery of San Pedro de Roda in Catalonia and came to Harvard in 1943.[25]

25. *Illuminated and Calligraphic Manuscripts*, A Catalogue of an Exhibition, Harvard
College Library (Cambridge, 1955), p. 19.

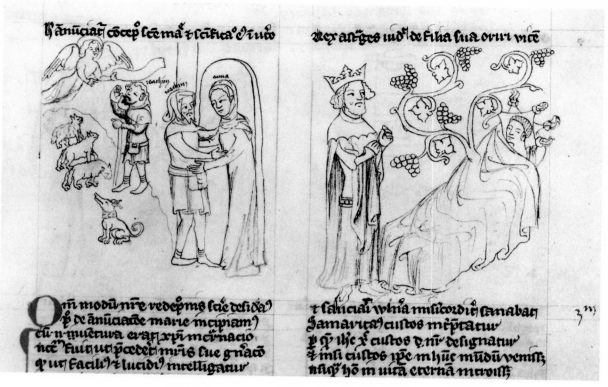

II–17.

a. The Annunciation of the Birth of Mary.   b. King Astyages Sees a Marvel in a Dream.
Speculum humanæ salvationis, Chapter III.
Harvard University, The Houghton Library, Ms. Lat. 121, fol. 6 recto.

II–18.

a. The Annunciation to the Virgin.   b. God Appears to Moses in the Burning Bush.
Speculum humanæ salvationis, Chapter VII.
Harvard University, The Houghton Library, Ms. Lat. 121, fol. 10 recto.

II–19.
a. The Gifts of the Magi.
Speculum humanæ salvationis, Chapter IX.
The Pierpont Morgan Library, M. 385, fol. 11 verso.

II–20.
c. David Kills Goliath.
Speculum humanæ salvationis, Chapter XIII.
The Pierpont Morgan Library, M. 385, fol. 16 recto.

The Pierpont Morgan Library, M. 385

This mid-fifteenth-century *Speculum* manuscript on vellum, 29 x 24 cm., was written in Flanders and contains, on folio 51 verso, a long prayer in Flemish verse. There are miniatures at the head of each column of twenty-five lines, with titles above them and the source reference beneath. All forty-five chapters are included. The illustrations, in pen and wash, are very spirited and well drawn, containing banderoles identifying the persons, and other inscriptions (figs. II–19, 20, 21). There are a few decorated chapter-heading initials.

The illustration in Chapter IX-a shows three magi, bearing their gifts; one points at a very large star while another grasps his arm in confirmation and joy. The third has removed his crown and holds the lid of his offering bowl while the Christ child seems to dip in his hand. The same scene is shown in Chapter XLV-e, but in that one a flimsy manger appears with a woven fence. The child is again putting his left hand into the bowl and holds the lid (or is it a wine goblet?) in his right.

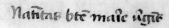

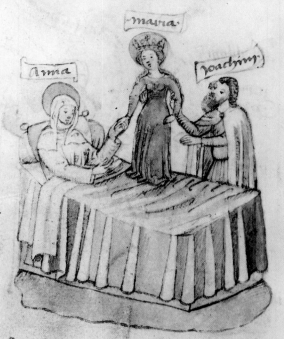

II–21.
a. The Nativity of the Virgin.
b. The Tree of Jesse.
Speculum humanæ salvationis, Chapter IV.
The Pierpont Morgan Library, M. 385, fol. 6 verso.

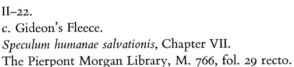

II–22.
c. Gideon's Fleece.
Speculum humanae salvationis, Chapter VII.
The Pierpont Morgan Library, M. 766, fol. 29 recto.

II–23.
a. The Nativity of Christ,
Chapter VIII, fol. 29 verso.

The Pierpont Morgan Library, M. 766

This English manuscript of the early fifteenth century has seventy-one leaves on vellum, 32.5 x 24 cm., of which two are blank. There are 192 pen drawings of very primitive character, without shading and with very little rendering of the ground or landscape. The costumes are partly imagined and partly those of the period, with elaborate attention to such details as buttons and nail-heads and the joints of armor (figs. II–22, 23, 24, 25, 26). Some of the scenes differ strongly in their iconography from other *Speculum* manuscripts, and as a result of the lack of perspective, the Christ child's cradle is floating in the air. There is no suggestion of a manger or shelter of any kind (fig. II–23). The drawings are in the same ink as the text which suggests that they were sketched by the scribe himself.

On folio 1 verso is written "Officium de Sancto Johanne de Bridlyntona" in a script very like that of the text. This Johannes was a regular prior of Bridlington in the County of York; he had studied at Oxford and was canonized in 1401. He was worshipped as a saint in Bridlington and its environs within a few years after his death in 1379.[26]

26. Karl W. Hiersemann, Prospectus for a *Speculum Humanæ Salvationis* manuscript
    (Leipzig, 1933), now Morgan Library M. 766.

II–24.

b. Daniel Destroys Bel and Kills the Lion,
Chapter XIII, fol. 34 verso.

II–25.

d. King Ammon Deals Dishonestly with David's Messengers.
Chapter XXI, fol. 43 recto.

II–26.

a. Christ Bearing his Cross.
Chapter XXII, fol. 43 verso.

b. Isaac Carrying the Wood for his Immolation.
Chapter XXII , fol. 43 verso.

Sensieut le prologue du trans
lateur pour le second volume
des annales historees des nobles
princes de hayun.
En pour sieulvant la
matere premise de
ceste pute oeure qui
ta est promis ou commenchemet
et premier prologue de la pre
miere partie ce volume. de chief
su commandement de mon dit tr
redoubte seigneur mons philippe

par la grace de dieu duc de bour
goigne de lotrinche de brabāt
et de sembourg conte de flande
dartois z de bourgoingue palatin
de hayun de hollande de zelāde
et de natiir come dit est selont
la possibilite de mon petiot et
foible engien me sui determinez
et enhardis dicelle pute oeure
translater et mettre en nre lan
guage maternelle quant a la sede
partie si auant que ie lay sceu

Ce volume entré de la Bibliotheque royale de Bourgog
apres la prise de Bruxelles en 1746, et qui depuis etoit a
placé dans la Bibliotheque du Roi à Paris a été renda
par la France, et replacé à Bruxelles dans la Bibliothe
de Bourgogne le 7 Juin 1770.

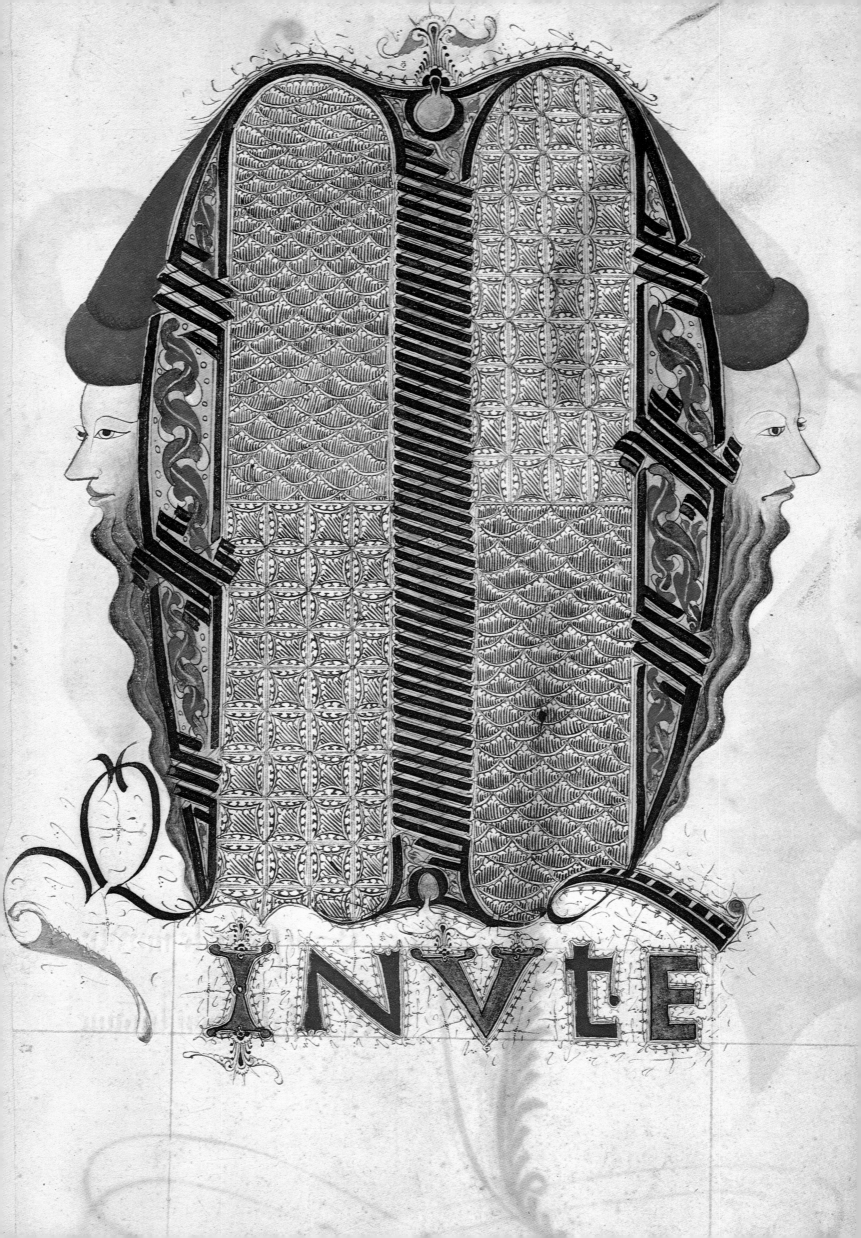

Ensieut le miroir
de la saluation humaine

III

Speculum Manuscripts in Translation

Sometime in 1448, Philip the Good, Duke of Burgundy, a passionate lover of beautiful books like his great-uncles, Jean, Duke of Berry, and Charles V of France, commissioned Jean Miélot to translate the _Speculum humanæ salvationis_ from Latin into French. During his reign (1419–1467) the library of the ducal court increased to the extent that its collection of manuscripts rivalled those of Pope Nicholas V at Rome, of Cosimo de ' Medici at Florence, and of Cardinal Bessarion at Venice.[1] He had inherited about two hundred and fifty manuscripts from his father, Jean the Fearless, according to an inventory dated 1420.[2] At the time of his own death, in 1467, he left to his son, Charles the Bold, some nine hundred manuscripts, as documented in another inventory.[3]

At his court he maintained scholars to compile books, scribes to copy them, translators, illuminators, and miniaturists. Among the scribes and translators the most prolific was Jean Miélot. To fulfill the order for translating the _Speculum_, Miélot prepared a dummy, or model book, on paper in folio size, written in his fine Gothic or Burgundian Bâtarde hand, and with sketches for most of the miniatures. He included fantastic decorated letters almost full-page size at the beginning and end of the manuscript, and illuminated capitals throughout the text.

This type of draft on paper, prepared to be presented and read aloud at court for the Duke's approval,[4] was called a _minute_, or model for a _de luxe_ manuscript. If it was accepted, it would then be inscribed on vellum or parchment and illuminated with miniatures by professional artists. A number of _minutes_ for fifteenth-century codices have survived and in the Bibliothèque Royale Albert I, in Brussels, is found Miélot's _minute_, entitled _Le Miroir de la salvation humaine_.

1. _La Librairie de Philippe le Bon_, catalogue edited by Georges Dogaer and Marguerite Debae (Brussels, 1967), p. 3.
2. Georges Doutrepont, _Inventaire de la "Librairie" de Philippe le Bon, 1420_ (Brussels, 1906).
3. Joseph Barrois, _Bibliothèque Prototypographique_ (Paris, 1830), p. 129.
4. Anthony Hobson, _Great Libraries_ (London and New York, 1970), p. 95.

Opposite:

Plate III–4. Second page with decorated initial S.
Minute for _Le Miroir de la Salvation humaine_.
Bibliothèque Royale, Brussels, Ms. 9249–50, fol. 1 verso.

The *minute* contains 112 leaves, 41 x 28.5 cm., with a text block of 29 x 19 cm., of twenty-two lines, on a fine sturdy paper.[5] It is handsomely encased in a modern binding of burgundy red leather, quarter-bound, with oak boards, and clasps in heavy brass.

The first page displays a giant decorated M with a face on both sides, suggesting a mirror, over the letters I N U T E, each in a different style of capital (Plate III-3). The title page, on the verso (Plate III-4), is a full-page illuminated letter with a winged dragon forming an initial S above the calligraphed "Ensieut le miroir de la saluation humaine" (Here follows the mirror of human salvation). On the next recto Miélot describes the commission (fig. III-1). A large D encloses a modest self-portrait of the pot-bellied translator in a bejewelled robe. Miélot holds a banderole inscribed with the motto "Savoir Vault mieulx que Avoir" (To know is worth more than to have). Beneath is his text, translated as follows:

> At the command and order of the very high, very powerful, very excellent prince, my most honorable lord Philip, Duke of Burgundy, of Brabant and of Limburg, Count of Flanders, of Artois, of Burgundy, of Hainaut and of Namur, I have to the best of my ability translated from rhymed Latin into clear French *The Mirror of Human Salvation*, then pictured, ornamented, decorated and written it in my hand. The year 1448.

The text of the *Speculum* translation begins on folio 2 verso, below a miniature, and is written across the page in a single column (fig. III-2). The caption above the miniature explains the subject, the fall of Lucifer and his accomplices from Paradise into Hell because of their pride. The picture appears to be finished. Lucifer's accomplices are not depicted, God is seated in a mandorla in the heavens, and Lucifer is shown as a winged bull being prodded into the mouth of Hell by an armored angel. This miniature was probably not made by Miélot although he might have copied it from the Latin manuscript he was translating. The illustrations near the beginning have the base coat of paint (figs. III-3-a, b, c, and 4-a) but are unfinished. Later in the *minute* they are line drawings (figs. III-4-b and c). Beneath the first two are written the chapter and verse of the Bible to which the text and illustration refer, but this is not continued beyond Chapter I. Miélot was a good decorator, translator, and scribe, but he was not a miniaturist and if these sketches are his, they were intended to show the subjects to the artist.

5. C. M. Briquet, *Les Filigranes*, edited by Allan Stevenson (Amsterdam, 1968), watermark 3544.

III–1.
Illuminated D with commission and date, 1448.
Minute for *Le Miroir de la Salvation humaine.*
Bibliothèque Royale, Brussels, Ms. 9249–50, fol. 2 recto.

III–2.
The Fall of Lucifer.
Minute for *Le Miroir de la Salvation humaine*, Chapter I.
Bibliothèque Royale, Brussels, Ms. 9249–50, fol. 2 verso.

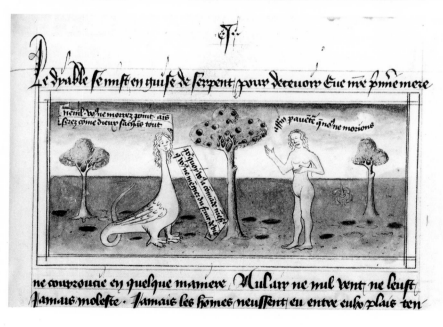

III–3.
a. The Creation of Eve, fol. 3 recto.
b. The Admonition, fol. 3 verso.
c. The Temptation, fol. 4 recto.
Minute for *Le Miroir de la Salvation humaine,* Chapter I.
Bibliothèque Royale, Brussels, Ms. 9249–50.

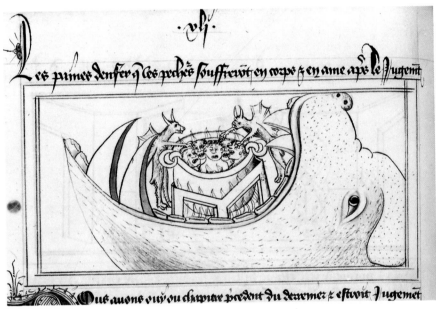

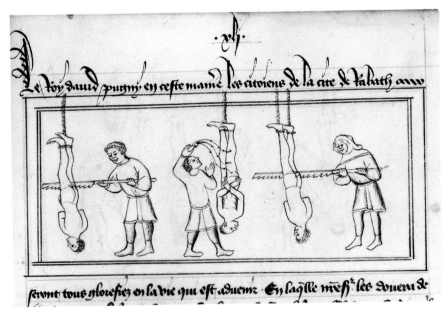

III–4.
a. Samson Rends the Lion Asunder, Chapter XXIX, fol. 59 verso.
b. The Sufferings of the Damned in Hell, Chapter XLI, fol. 82 verso.
c. How King David Punished his Enemies, Chapter XLI, fol. 83 recto.
Minute for *Le Miroir de la Salvation humaine.*
Bibliothèque Royale, Brussels, Ms. 9249–50.

The end of the text of the translation is followed by three full-page decorated, colored and gilded initials, like those at the beginning. Folio 98 verso is a large decorated C enclosing another self-portrait of Miélot above the lettering "y fine le Miroir de la salvation humaine" (fig. III–5). In Middle French the word for "here" was "cy," not "ici." Facing the initial is a letter E in the form of a toothed dragon or sea monster, similar to the one shown as the mouth of Hell (figs. III–2 and 6) above the letters "script & translate de Latin Ryme en francois" on 99 recto.

On the verso is an A (for "at") with a crossbar and two hanging links of decorative chain over the words "Lille à Brouxelle et à Bruges" (fig. III–7). The Duke of Burgundy had courts in the three cities, and Miélot must have worked on his translation in the three places. Seated in the letter A, on a coffer, is a robed and turbaned man; possibly the chains refer to the capture of Christians by Moslems in the Holy Land, as Philip's father, Jean the Fearless, had been in the crusade of 1396. Philip is known to have planned a crusade and, in fact, it is recorded that, as a boy, he dressed in Turkish costume and wandered in the grounds of the ducal palace, perhaps plotting the future campaign.[6]

The manuscript ends with a Prohemium (fig. III–8) in which each of the forty-five chapters is summarized, followed by an Explicit entitled *Epilogation des choses dessus* (Epilogue of the matters above) which states, translated from the French:

> I made and compiled the prohemium here above, explaining the things which are contained in this little booklet (ce petit livret). I have wished to do it for the contemplation of poor preachers who by chance do not have the means to buy the complete book. Because the stories are well-presented they will be able to preach with the aid of this little index which proceeds according to the chapters of the book.

Miélot finished his *minute* for *Le Miroir de la Salvation humaine* in 1449 and it was in April of that year, probably as a result of the Duke of Burgundy's approval of it, that Miélot was attached to the Ducal court with regular wages. The archives show that the Duke reimbursed him rectroactively for the eighteen months he had worked on Ducal commissions before this, presumably including the preparation of the *minute*.[7]

In his manuscript of the *Debat de noblesse*, Miélot refers to himself as "indigne chanoine de St. Pierre de Lille et le moindre des secretaires dicelluy seigneur et prince" (humble canon of St. Pierre of Lille and the least of the secretaries of this lord and prince), but, in fact, he was one of the most educated, talented, and accomplished men in the service of the court, at once copyist, illuminator, historiographer, and translator.[8]

6. Johanna Hintzen, *De Kruistochtplannen van Philip den Goede* (Rotterdam, 1918). See also Charles de Terlinden, "Les Origines religieuses et politiques de la Toison d'or," in Publications du Centre Européen d'Etudes Burgondo-Médianes, V (1963), pp. 35–46.
7. Alexandre de Laborde, *Histoire des Ducs de Bourgogne*, I (Paris, 1849), p. 400.
8. J. W. Bradley, *A Dictionary of Miniaturists, Illuminators, Calligraphers and Copyists* (New York, 1958), p. 324.

y fine le Miroir de la saluation humaine

III-5.
The first page of Miélot's three-page colophon.
Minute for *Le Miroir de la Salvation humaine.*
Bibliothèque Royale, Brussels, Ms. 9249–50, fol. 98 verso.

III–6.
The second page of Miélot's colophon.
Minute for *Le Miroir de la Salvation humaine.*
Bibliothèque Royale, Brussels, Ms. 9249–50, fol. 99 recto.

III–7.
The final page of Miélot's illuminated colophon.
Minute for *Le Miroir de la Salvation humaine.*
Bibliothèque Royale, Brussels, Ms. 9249–50, fol. 99 verso.

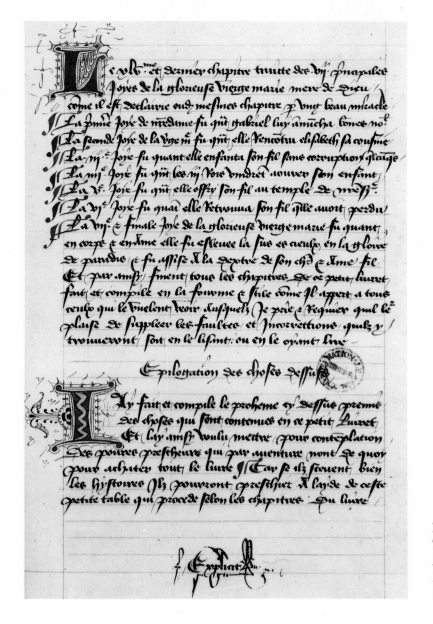

III–8.
The Explicit of the Prohemium.
Minute for *Le Miroir de la Salvation humaine.*
Bibliothèque Royale, Brussels,
Ms. 9249–50, fol. 112 recto.

    We find from the Explicit of the *Traité de vieillesse et de jeunesse* which he wrote at Lille in
1468, dedicated to Louis of Luxembourg, that he was born in a village in the bishopric of
Amiens.[9] Nothing is known of his early life, but his education, both secular and religious, must
have been thorough, for, in the archives of the church of St. Pierre at Lille, Miélot was entered
as a Canon from 1453 to 1472. He was probably not required to remain in residence, but he
exercised his canonical functions properly.[10] He was concurrently in the service of Philip the
Good until the latter's death in 1467. Records show that he worked afterward for Louis of
Luxembourg, Count of St. Pol, as well as for Charles the Bold, Philip's son and successor.[11]

9. Lutz and Perdrizet, *Speculum Humanæ Salvationis* (Leipzig, 1907) Vol. I, p. 107.
10. *Ibid.*, p. 108.
11. Bradley, *op.cit.*, p. 325.

According to the 1967 exhibition catalogue, *La Librairie de Philippe le Bon*, the *de luxe* copy for which the *minute* was prepared has not been preserved, as noted above.[12] But in the Bibliothèque Nationale, Ms. fr. 6275, a codex essentially ignored by scholars of Flemish illumination, there is an exact copy of the *minute* text. It is on vellum, 41 x 28.5 cm., (the same dimensions as the *minute*), richly illuminated and with fine miniatures. The text, not in Miélot's hand, is inscribed in the format of the Latin manuscripts, two columns on each page with a miniature at the head of each, the facing pages containing a full chapter. On folio 2 recto appears "translate en prose par jo Miélot, l'an de grace mil CCCCXLIX," the same year that the *minute* was completed, which may indicate only that it was copied verbatim and possibly this copy was made much later, although it is also dedicated to Philip the Good.

Strangely, it is not one of the three French *Speculum* translations listed in the 1467 inventory, nor is the *minute*.[13] However, the 1967 exhibition catalogue states in the Introduction ". . . l'inventaire dressé après la mort de Philippe le Bon est imparfait: plusieurs manuscrits sont cités deux fois, d'autres ne le sont pas du tout"(. . . the inventory drawn up after the death of Philip the Good is imperfect: several manuscripts are cited twice, others are not listed at all).[14]

On folio 2 verso (Plate III–5) the text begins "Cy comence le prologue du Miroir de la saluation humaine translate de latin en cler francois." After a Latin sentence, a preface in French follows, but without a dedication to the patron. Above the text is a splendid miniature, the left half showing a Dominican friar seated at a lectern writing on a large sheet,[15] in a typical Flemish study within an architectural arch. Miélot mistakenly attributed the original manuscript to Vincent of Beauvais (1190–1264) and this is presumably meant to be a portrait of him. On the right side is a landscape with distant castles, a river, and trees, above which, in a great cloud, is a representation of God the Father holding in one hand three arrows and in the other a letter or contract with three seals appended.[16] Below at the left is a dark male figure representing Death. This miniature is presumably by a follower of Jean Le Tavernier in whose atelier the rest of the illustrations appear to have been made some years after the date in the text.

---

12. *La Librairie de Philippe le Bon, op. cit.*, p. 14, Item 8.
13. Barrois, *op. cit.*, p. 129.
14. *La Librairie de Philippe le Bon, op. cit.*, p. 3.
15. See Pieter F. J. Obbema, "Writing on Uncut Sheets," in Quaerendo, VIII, 4 (1978), pp. 337 ff.
16. Perdrizet in his *Etude* describes this figure as the "Ancient of Days," crowned like the Vicar of Christ holding the very sharp arrows of the three scourges: war, pestilence, and famine. The parchment is a proper legal form by which God permits Death to decimate mankind by using the three arrows. There is a paragraph and a seal for each one.

Opposite:

Plate III–5. Opening page of the *de luxe* copy of Miélot's translation. *Le Miroir de la Salvation humaine*, Prologue. Bibliothèque Nationale, Paris, Ms. fr. 6275, fol. 1 recto.

comence le prologue du Miroir
de la salvation humaine translate
de latin en cler Francois
Briar justicie
eruduit multor
homies fulgebur qua
si stelle in perpetual
eternitate Cest a dire.
Culy qui enseignet
plusieur homes a Justice liuront come es
toutes en perpetuelles eternites et dist da
niel le prophete. Pour tant a leruditioy
z enseignement de plusieur Jay voulu fai
re ce liuret ou quel les liseurs pourront
prendre et donner bonne doctrine. Car
tes Je cuid que en ceste presente mortele
vie riens nest plus prouffitable a lome
que congnoistre dieu son createur z la
propre condition de soy mesmes. Ceste

congnoissance puent avoir les clers par
les escriptures Mais les rude ignorans
le ont pars les liuree des lays Cestassa pur
paintures Et pour ce a la gloire et lo
enge de dieu z pour lenseignemet des ru
des Jay delibere a larde de nres Sr faurez
compiler vingt liuret pour les lays. Et af
fin que Je puisse donner doctrine tant aux
clers come aux lays Je mefforcereray de le de
clairer aucunement en stile le plus cler z
le plus facile que faure Je pourray. Jen
tens doncques premierement demoustrer la
ruine z tres buscheement de lucifer z de ses
faulx complices. Et apres le defaullemet
de adam z de eue noz premiers purens z de
leurs successeurs aussi Et puis coment
nre saulueur ihesucrist nous a rachate pur
sa benoite incarnation z par quelles figu
res aussi il a premoustre ses Jadis sadite

Certes on doit tousiours tenir bonne maniere
en toutes choses/ et se doit on escheuer tous ey
ces en tresgrande diligence. Nous deuons donc
en gardant vsaige et maniere come il appteint
vaincre le monde qui se esforce de nous tirer
a soy en nous donnant les biens temporeulx. Et
se lomme eust demoure ou paradis de voluptez
il neust pas soubstenu du monde ceste bataille
le. Et eust este adens les paradis sans gleu
que infestation et ey apmes demeure il vne
heure sans aucune reparation Car sune fois
le aguaitte son enemi couuert lautffois son
amy familier se esforce de le buxeter et trom̃per
Et souuentesfois le trauaille vne petite mou
chette ou le blesche vng petit ver ou le mort
vne puche. Lome est trauaillie et moleste
a bon droit des creatures ou des elemens pour
ce quil sest esdrechie cont dieu son createur
La tire laquillome de ponchees et despines
et les bestes de la terre le deschirent de leurs
dens et de leurs cornes. Leaue le murdrie
de vaguues et de tempestes. Les larrons de
mer lenuaissent deglaiues et de rapines.
Lair lenfecte par pestilence et corruption.
et les oyseaulx du ciel le derompent de leurs
becz et de leurs vngsees. Le su ramanie la
char et les os enscendre. Et la fumere du
feu luy obscurcist les yeulx Nul homme neust
este en paradis enemi de laut. Et cy entre
plusieurs hommes se treuue agrant paine vng
vray amy. Tandre doncques quhome agrant
des richesses et honneurs en ce monde.
Lors samble il quil ait plusieurs amis

et bieueuillans. Mais tantost quil comen
cil auoir besoincg de ses amis. A paines pour
ra il trouuer quil en ait vng seul vray. Le
vray amy sespreuue en temps de necessite le
quel ne se enuye point pour quelanque for
tune ou aduersite. Cellu qui ne resoigne
point de exposer soy et ses choses pour son
amy. Il se demonstre auoir grant charite
en soy. Mais nix le tressebonnaire a eu
plusgrande charite. Car il a expose soy
mesmes et ses choses pour ses enemis.
cest pour nous. Nous estions enemis de
dieu et iugiez en chartre perpetuele.
Mais nous somes deliures par sa mise
ricorde. Certes il falloit que nous
enuefissions en la prison denfer dont ne
poyons estre tires hors par nul aidequelan
ques. Daufsele ne dame. Figure de lolue
En la parfin le pere de misericorde et le
dieu de toute consolation a donlaimet
regarde lestat de nre damnation. Et decre de nous
deliurer par soy mesm. Dur quil lui a plen nous
donner vng signe par lolue que le coulon appor
ta a ceulx qestoiẽt enclos en larche de noe
Ceste chose ptendoit la misericorde de dieu ad
uenir a ceulx q estoiẽt enclos ou buxe. Por loi
ne estoit donc et pmis le signe de salut non
mie seulemẽt a ceulx q estoient en larche noe
Mais a tout le monde. Et ceci moustra dieu
en maniere suffire come il appt a cellui q vielt
soigneusemẽt lire ce diuius ef septiẽ. O bon ihu
istruis nous affin q nous apndons les saites escptu
cz nous puissoe apnd ta charite et ton amour

On folio 1 verso and 2 recto there are two miniatures, one showing a group of men felling a tree (Christianity) from which each takes the part that fulfills his need: the swineherd takes the acorns, the carpenter the straight trunk, the fisher the curved branches for boat building, the writer gathers galls to make ink, etc. The other illustration shows five men with three documents with red seals appended. The Prologue states that Holy Scripture is like soft wax which takes the impress of any device, be it lion or eagle, and so one occurrence, in one connection, may prefigure Christ, and in another, the Devil.[17]

The final paragraph of the Prologue, on 2 recto, states:

> Ci fine le prologue du miroir de beauvais de l'ordre des precheurs et maitre en theologie, jadis confesseur du roy de France monseigneur saint loys, fait et compila en latin rime par doublettes, leques a este depuis translate en prose par Jo Mielot, l'an de grace mil CCCCXLIX, en la fourme et stile qui s'ensui.

> Here ends the prologue of the Mirror of Beauvais of the order of preachers and master in theology, formerly confessor to the King of France our sovereign Saint Louis, made and compiled in Latin rhymed couplets, which has since been translated into prose by Jo Miélot, the year of grace 1449, in the form and style which follows.

This Prologue is not to be confused with the Prohemium which, as in the *minute*, follows Chapter XLV. On folio 90 verso, preceding the Prohemium, is a miniature showing Miélot in his study copying the translation in two columns with the Latin two-column model held in his left hand. On a lectern and its bench are opened single-column books, perhaps his *minute* (fig. I–1). Below this is the statement erroneously crediting Vincent of Beauvais with the authorship of the original manuscript.

The miniatures throughout the manuscript, while not as exquisitely finished as those of the Prologue, are well composed, with strongly drawn figures, expressive faces, and fine landscape and architectural details. On the basis of the costumes and the relationship between the miniature of the Adoration of the Magi on folio 16v with the Adoration of Hugo van der Goes in Berlin, the miniatures were made sometime between 1485 and 1495.[18] The text corresponds throughout with that of the *minute*. See, for example, fig. III–2 compared with fig. III–9.

17. M. R. James and Bernard Berenson, *Speculum humanæ salvationis*, p. 7, translation of the Prologue.
18. These dates were suggested by Anne H. van Buren, Fine Arts Department, Tufts University, Boston.

Opposite:

Plate III–6. c. Adam Toils and Eve Spins. d. The Ark of Noah.
Le Miroir de la Salvation humaine, Chapter II.
Bibliothèque Nationale, Paris, Ms. fr. 6275, fol. 4 recto.

III–9.
a. The Fall of Lucifer. b. The Creation of Eve.
Le Miroir de la Salvation humaine, Chapter I.
Bibliothèque Nationale, Paris, Ms. fr. 6275, fol. 2 verso.

Opposite:

III–10.
c. The Admonition. d. The Temptation.
Le Miroir de la Salvation humaine, Chapter I.
Bibliothèque Nationale, Paris, Ms. fr. 6275, fol. 3 recto.

Dieu comande a Adam ⁊ a eue q̈ ilz ne mengeaf
sent poit du fruit de vie · Eu genesio le iijᵉ chap.

Le diable se mist en guise de sipẽt pᵒ̕ deceuoir
eue nře pᵛ̃ie mere · Eu genesis le iijᵉ chapit.

3

grant pechie pᵒ̕ tant quelle attrahy doulcemēt
home a faire pechie · Et ia soit ce q̈ cecy ne soit
pas trouue manifestement ou texte de la bible
touteffoies il est cuidẽ qlle le flatoit de doulces
parolles ❧ O tu home pense ⁊ considere q̈le
combien grande est la fraude de feme pᵒ̕ ce q̈ar
de toy de feme ⁊ la dextresse affin q̈ tu ne soies
trompe · Regarde adam q̈ estoit loruuque de mais
de dieu et le tresfort sanson · De lart · et malice
de feme a deceu telz ⁊ si grans homes · Coment
doie tu estre seur q̈t tu ne es tel ne si grant · Le
diable ne osa tempter le noble ⁊ sage hoe Adam
mais la feme plus hardie q̈ le diable le osa bē
deceuoir · Et ainsi le diable deceut ⁊ desfrauda
la feme ⁊ la feme condempna lome ⁊ toy ses
successez ensement · Mais se lome eust perse
uere ou comandemēt de dieu · Il neust iamais
souffert paine ne anguisse ne gouste mort q̈e
cōq̈s · Il neust soustenu foiblesse ne aucune
lassiure · Il neust senti iamais nulle enfer
mete ne maladie · Sa mere leust poʳte sans
pleur sans tristresse ⁊ sans doleur ce fust ne
sans chemy et sans labeur · Il neust iamais
conceu quelq̈ tribulation ne soustenu detson
ame ne quelq̈ confusion · Ses oreilles ne fussent
iamais assourdies ⁊ neust eu mal ne doleur
eu ses dens · Ses yeulx neussent iamais este
couuers ne obscurcie et ses piez neussent ia
mais clochie · Les fontaines et les riuieres
ne leussent iamais noye le feu ne la chaleʳ
du soleil ne leussent point bruste · Il neust
este beste ne oysel qui leust infestune conuou
cie eu quelque maniere · Nul air ne nul vet

ne leust iamais moleste · Iamais les homes
neussent eu cū eulx plait tenchone ne ri
ottes · Ains ilz se eussent entamez luy parmi
lautre come freres · Toute creature terriene
eust este subiette a lome leql eust tousiours
vescu en ioie et liesse sans cure ⁊ sans soit.
❧ Et quant il eust pleu a dieu son createur
lors illeust pris ⁊ mene la sus ou ciel en corpz
⁊ en ame · Nul home quel quil soit ne presume
encerchir pourquoy dieu a voulu creer lome
leql il scauoit quil deuoit trebuchier par
pechie · Pourquoy aussi il voult creer cre a
telez desquelz il congnoissoit par auant et
certemement la ruine ⁊ le grief trebuche
ment ❧ Et pourquoy il voult endurcir le
cuer du Roy pharaon · Et voult amollir a
penitence le cuer de marie magdalaine · ❧
Pourquoy il enuoia contricion A saint pi
erre qui lauoit renie iij fois · Et pour
quoy il permist q̈ iudas se desesperast poʳ
son enorme pechie · Pourquoy il inspira la
grace de soy conuertir a vng des larrons · et
pourquoy il ne luy chalut donner samblable gra
ce a son compaignon · Pourquoy aussi il eslu
tre a soy vng pecheur et lautre non · Il
ne soit home tant soit il sage ⁊ prudent q̈
presume encerchier ces choses Desssus dre
Toutes ces euures de dieu ⁊ lez samblables
ne sont point a enquerir ne encerchier par
les engins humaine · Monsʳ saint pol la
postre samble soubz ee toutes ces questue ey et
dist ainsi · Dieu endurcist cellui q̈l vult
et a pitie et mercy de cellui qui luy plaist.

Adam z euc tfpaiffoit le comandemt de dieu
quit ils mecoreit la pome · en genesis le iije ch.

Adam et euc furet boutez hors de padis triste
p lagrele de dieu / en genesis le vje chapitre.

Ous auons ouy ci deuant coment
Dieu honnoura lome · Or oyons aa
pres coment lome fist soy mesmes
vil z ozt · Quant lome fu en hault honneur il
ne lentendi poit Ame en fu deiette pour ce quil
se esdrecha cont Dieu son createur Come fu
iette hors du paradis de voluptte en ceste vallee de
miseve z de pouvete · Il tint pou de compte de lon
nez q lui auoit este donee dont il trouua depuis
mainte tribulation z doleur · Il yssi hore de pa
radis q estoit vng lieu ioieux z souef et entra

la delectation du monde samble est belle mais
son fruit est dampnation etnele Le monde
aussi est raisonnablemt compare au trahistre
Iudas q par son faulx et doleveux baisier li
vra ihucst auy suifs Le monde baille auy dia
ble vng tel signe q iudas bailla auy enemie
de nresz Et dist le monde Cellui q ie baise
vuy en lui donat richesses z honez cestli te
nez le bi et le tourmentes sans fin etnelemt
Toutesfois les richesses ne sont point tous
iotz a dampnation Ains prouffitent a plu

III–11.
a. The Fall of Adam and Eve. b. The Expulsion from the Garden.
Le Miroir de la Salvation humaine, Chapter II.
Bibliothèque Nationale, Paris, Ms. fr. 6275, fol. 3 verso.

III–12.
a. The Adoration of the Magi. b. The Magi See the Star.
Le Miroir de la Salvation humaine, Chapter IX.
Bibliothèque Nationale, Paris, Ms. fr. 6275, fol. 16 verso.

Miélot left a number of *minutes* for other translated texts, trial pages of his large illuminated initials, and verses and texts of his own composition which are bound together in Ms. fr. 17001. It is a folio volume of 116 pages on paper, 41 x 28.5 cm., a section of which has the same watermark as the *minute* of the *Speculum*.[19] Entirely in Miélot's hand, the drafts are from various dates up to 1470. Three major translations are included: *L'Epistre de Cicéron à son frère Quintus; Briève compilation des histoires de toute la Bible;* and *Histoire du mors de la pomme.*[20]

The manuscript opens with a table of contents added by a later owner which omits many of the texts included in the volume. Folio 2 recto relates the legend, widely accepted in the Middle Ages, concerning the naming of Adam, which had an oriental origin as indicated by the Greek names of the four stars involved. Miélot relates that God sent the four archangels to the four corners of the earth, and they returned in succession with the initial letters of the stars they found there: Anatole, Disis, Arthos, Messembrios. Folio 2 verso is devoted to a large labyrinth or maze in which the letters M I E L O T may be found. A labyrinth of this sort appears in the pavement of the cathedral of Amiens, in which bishopric Miélot was born, and evidently provided inspiration for him. These elaborate paving mazes exist in the floors of many medieval churches and sometimes contain the name of the master designer.

Folio 3 recto carries a large illuminated C (fig. III–13) enclosing a drawing of a lavishly robed king and a lady, in a vaulted room. Below are the letters O P Y E composed of strapwork bands, to spell "COPYE." On the verso (fig. III–14) is an equally elaborate large D framing a portrait of a bishop, inscribed at the base "Saint Foursy Confes." Below the illuminated D are the strapwork bands of the letters U N E, to spell "D'UNE" beside a plain moon face in the position of a following letter, the significance of which is mysterious.

There is a large illuminated M on 4 verso (fig. III–15) like that in the *minute* for the *Miroir*, decorated with spiral acanthus leaves. "Saint Foillain m(ar)tir, Frère a St. Foursy," appears in the left arch of the letter and "Saint Ultain, Confes., Frère a St. Foursy," in the right. Below are the illuminated letters I N U T E. The three pages together, with their fantastic graphic elaboration, simply spell "Copye d'une Minute." The last word ends with another illuminated E and a P, separated with fish motifs, which may have been done only to fill out the line.

19. Briquet, *op.cit.*, watermark 3544; also found in B.N. Ms. fr. 17001 are watermarks 1739 and 1740.
20. Robert Bossuat, "Jean Miélot, traducteur de Cicéron," in Bibliothèque de l'Ecole des Chartes, XCIX (1938).

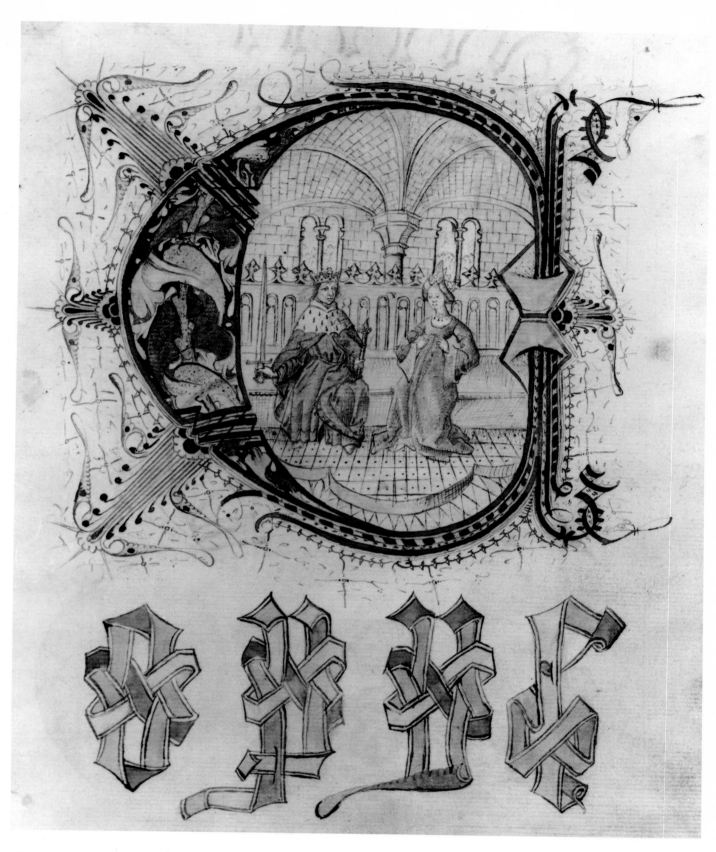

III–13.
Historiated initial and strapwork letters for "COPYE."
Jean Miélot workbook.
Bibliothèque Nationale, Paris, Ms. fr. 17001, fol. 3 recto.

III–14.
Historiated initial for "D'UNE."
Jean Miélot workbook.
Bibliothèque Nationale, Paris, Ms. fr. 17001, fol. 3 verso.

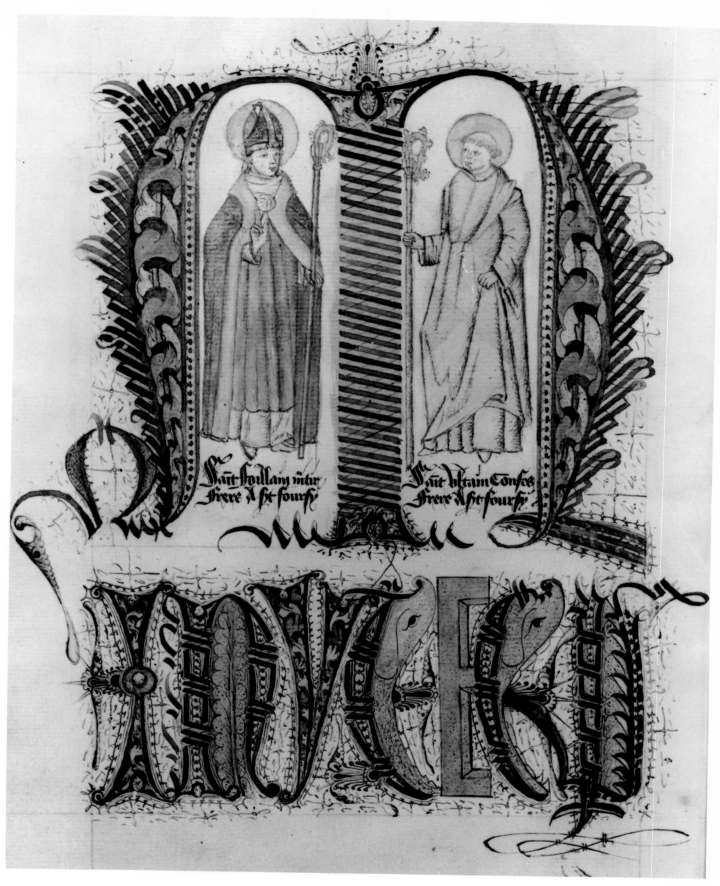

III-15.
Historiated initial for "MINUTE."
Jean Miélot workbook.
Bibliothèque Nationale, Paris, Ms. fr. 17001, fol. 4 recto.

The sketch for an illustration on 5 verso (fig. III–16) shows an interior scene captioned "(C)oment Maistre Jehan mielot prestre Indigne chano(i)ne de lille: presente sa translation." The giant P at the left leads into the text which explains the functions of a prologue, a prohemium, and a preface, possibly a trial page for a *de luxe* manuscript.

The translation of the letter of Cicero to his brother Quintus follows on folios 8 to 25 and ends with "dans l'an mil CCCC, soixante huyt" (1468). A copy of this translation is preserved also in the Royal Library at Copenhagen.[21] On folio 26 recto is inscribed "Fait a Lille," on 26 verso "Par Moy" in illuminated capitals and letters, and on 27 recto appears another maze in a different form but again with the letters of Miélot's name inserted.

The workbook also contains a draft for the translation of the *Brève compilation des histoires de toute la Bible* from the Latin text of Jean d'Udine, which appears, as another *minute* on paper, in the Brussels Library, Ms. II 239 (fig. III–17). In both cases the text and the drawings are inscribed side-turned. The preliminary sketch for a schematic map follows, showing the division of the earth after the Deluge into the three continental sections for the sons of Noah. A more finished form is found in the same Brussels Ms. II 239, which also contains a Miélot drawing of a presentation, showing the Duke receiving the book in his bedchamber with clerics and courtiers in attendance and, on 54 verso, a genealogy of the Miélot family.

The last text in Ms. fr. 17001 is the *Histoire du mors de la pomme*, a sequence of dialogues in verse, possibly one of Miélot's rare attempts at authorship, with each page illustrated with crude line drawings. His listed works are almost entirely devoted to translations, edited versions, and transcriptions of the works of others.[22]

Two miniatures of a much later date appear on the last two pages of the volume. The first shows St. Luke at an easel, with his symbol, the ox, lying beside it and an angel behind him mixing ink or paint on a stone. At the left the Virgin Mary is posing for her portrait with book in hand. The pictures of the Virgin that St. Luke was said to have painted in the first century are all works of a much later date.[23] The second image is of St. Matthew writing in an open, bound book, while a kneeling angel, his symbol, holds out the pot of ink. Miélot may have copied these from admired models (fig. III–18).

A very revealing study could be made of the relationship of this manuscript to Brussels Ms. II 239 and the Copenhagen copy of the Cicero letter. In any case, Ms. fr. 17001 is of great interest in the study of the preparation and production of codices. It is a remarkable example of the workbook of a scribe, illuminator, and translator of the prolific Burgundian court.

21. N. C. L. Abrahams, *Description des manuscrits français du moyen âge de la Bibliothèque Royale de Copenhague* (Copenhagen, 1844), p. 33.
22. Lutz and Perdrizet, *op.cit.*, pp. 108–111; F. A. F. T. Reiffenberg, *Bulletin du Bibliophile Belge*, II (Brussels, 1867), p. 381.
23. Donald Attwater, *The Penguin Dictionary of Saints* (Harmondsworth, 1965), p. 223.

III–16.
Jean Miélot presents his translation to Philip the Good. Trial page.
Jean Miélot workbook.
Bibliothèque Nationale, Paris, Ms. fr. 17001, fol. 5 verso.

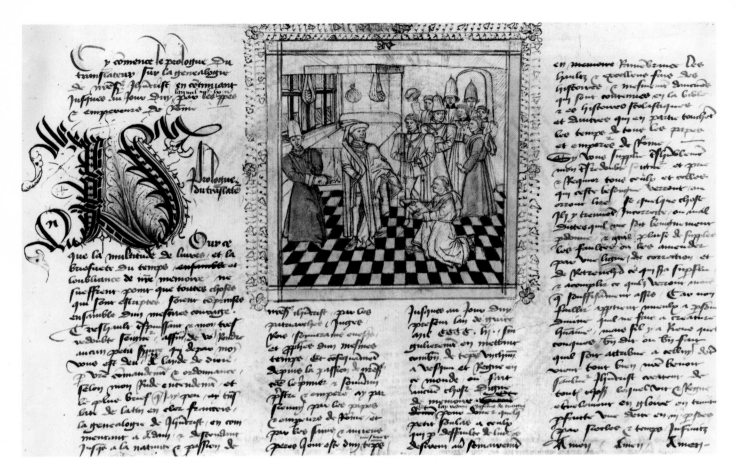

III–17.
Brième compilation des histoires de toute la Bible.
Bibliothèque Royale, Brussels, Ms. II 239, fol. 1 recto.

III–18.
The last two sketches in Miélot's workbook.
a. St. Luke painting a portrait of the Virgin Mary.
b. St. Matthew writing the Gospel.
Bibliothèque Nationale, Paris, Ms. fr. 17001, fols. 115 verso and 116 recto.

This *de luxe* manuscript is a French translation of the *Speculum*, entitled *Le Miroir de l'humaine Salvation*. It was acquired by William Hunter's agent at the Gaignat sale held in Paris in 1769.[24] The Explicit states that it was written at Bruges in 1455. There are sixty-three folios of an original sixty-four, written on vellum, 30.3 x 21.6 cm. in two columns of thirty-seven lines, in a Burgundian Bâtarde. The text is continuous, but at the beginning of each of the forty-two chapters, wherever they fall on the page, there are four narrow adjoining miniatures, the one at the left in color and the other three in grisaille with touches of gold. The skies are deep blue, often with gold stars. All of the four images together are the width of the two columns but occasionally, although they have the same base line, the individual miniatures are made taller to fill in the blank space of the previous chapter ending. The chapter ending text is often carried from the left to the right column to provide a rectilinear area for the miniatures. These do not have captions or titles as do those of the Latin manuscripts and the other French translations. Each chapter text begins with a decorated initial.

On folio 1 (Plate III–1) is a page-width miniature of the scribe kneeling to present the volume to his patron, possibly Philip the Good. Beneath this is a Prologue with decorated margins above and below. Curiously, this text does not contain a dedication to the patron nor does it identify the translator as is so carefully done in the books of Miélot. In the miniature, the Duke is seated on a marble throne within a vaulted and columned structure open on all four sides. The proffered volume is richly bound in blue with gold clasps and bosses. At the left are two standing female figures. The nearest, representing the Synagogue, in accord with medieval symbolism, is blindfolded and has a crown toppling from her head. In her left hand she holds a broken standard with a pennant, and in her right, the Tables of the Law. Beside her a white-coifed nun representing the Church holds a standard bearing a cross, and in her other hand a golden Chalice and Host.[25] This miniature has been attributed to Willem Vrelant, and the remaining forty-two panels to his atelier.[26] We know from the list of guild members in Bruges[27] that in 1454 Vrelant was working there; according to some scholars he and his assistants produced more than all the other miniaturists of Bruges put together,[28] but currently there is some doubt about the very large oeuvre attributed to his atelier.

24. *Catalogue of the Manuscripts in the Library of the Hunterian Museum in the University of Glasgow*, edited by John Young and P. H. Aitken (Glasgow, 1908), p. 68.
25. *Ibid.*, p. 69.
26. For this information we are indebted to Jack Baldwin, Keeper of Special Collections, The Library, University of Glasgow.
27. W. H. James Weale, "Documents inédits sur les enlumineurs de Bruges" in *Le Beffroi*, IV (1872–73), pp. 238 ff.
28. L. M. J. Delaissé, *A Century of Dutch Manuscript Illumination* (Berkeley and Los Angeles, 1968), pp. 74, 77.

In the Hunterian Catalogue the translation is attributed to Jean Miélot, but it does not correspond to the wording of either Miélot's *minute* or to B.N. Ms. fr. 6275. Following the Prologue the text begins on folio 1 verso "Ad ce donques que nous ne resamblons pas Lucifer." This copy omits the last three chapters and the Prohemium of the Latin manuscripts. Chapter 42 ends on folio 61 verso with "le pere et le fils et le saint esperit amen," immediately followed by the Explicit (fig. III–19).

Et ainsi fine ce present proces du myroir de lumaine saluation fait & translate de latin en franchois a bruges lan de grace mil iiij & cinquante cincq.

And thus ends this present account of the mirror of human salvation, made and translated from Latin into French at Bruges, the year of grace 1455.

III–19.
The Explicit with the place and date.
Le Miroir de l'humaine Salvation.
The Hunterian Museum Library, Glasgow, Ms. 60, fol. 61 verso.

O œ doncques. que nous ne re fambloue pas luafer. quant nous fommes refluifans en feotennite ʒ habondanœs Des Richeſſes tranſitoures Baines ʒ cozruptibles de œ moztel monde . Et que noʒ enuironnez des mobiles biés de foztune ne nous efleuons en œ treſhoʒrible pechie doʒ guel . ¶ Premierement nous beudzons a raœmpter le cas de luafer . angele de treſexœlleute beauſte Voir et reluiſant entre ſes aultres . qui foit Boyant aouzne et adoube des œuures de dieu . ʒ monte ou hault troſne entre ſes gerarchies ʒ mo narchies des aultres angelʒ ¶ Il qui tant eſtoit Bel ʒ ad meſure que nulʒ plus ſourmonte doʒgueil cöme

migrat ſuboʒna ʒ attray a ſoy pluſeurs angelʒ deſquelʒ il ſe fiſt adourer cöme dieu non reœgnoiſſant les biens Diœſliu qui tant lauoit ex auchie . Mais non obſtant œ cöme œ pechie fuſt trop cruel ʒ deteſtable a liu qui Boulout preſider ou ſiege Imperial . Langel faint michiel ſadzeſta a liu . Et cöme œſtoit raiſon apres ſa malediction il le fiſt tre Buſchier du treſhault au treſBas auec tous ſes cöpliœs en lieu tenebzeup . ou quel il regne ʒ reʒnera pardurablement . ſans Ia mais auoir Bne ſeule dzaɡ me de Ioie œleſtiele . Et amſy il fu deboute du Roy aulme des cieulx par œ mef fait . ¶ Comme fu adam de paradis terreſtre . Du ɡl adam fait ʒ procree ou champ

III–20.

a. The Fall of Lucifer. b. The Creation of Eve.
c. The Admonition. d. The Temptation.
Le Miroir de l'humaine Salvation, Chapter I.
The Hunterian Museum Library, Glasgow, Ms. 60, fol. 1 verso.

III–21.
a. Christ Conquers the Devil. b. Bananias Kills the Lion.
c. Samson Rends Asunder the Lion. d. Ehud Pierces Eglon.
Le Miroir de l'humaine Salvation, Chapter XXIX.
The Hunterian Museum Library, Glasgow, Ms. 60, fol. 42 recto.

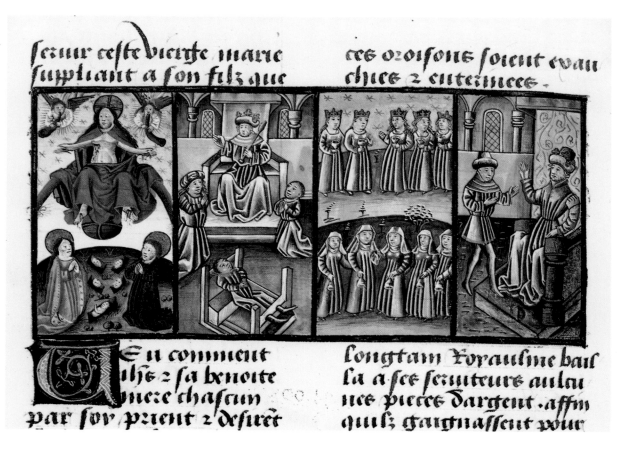

III–22.
a. The Last Judgment. b. The Parable of the Ten Talents.
c. The Parable of the Wise and Foolish Virgins. d. Mene, Mene, Tekel Upharsin.
Le Miroir de l'humaine Salvation, Chapter XLII.
The Hunterian Museum Library, Glasgow, Ms. 60, fol. 57 verso.

Plate III–7.
Opening page miniature of the translator's presentation.
Le Miroir de l'humaine Salvation.
The Hunterian Museum Library, Glasgow, Ms. 60, fol. 1 recto.

Plate III–8.
a. The Pain of the Damned in Hell. b. King David Punishing His Enemies.
c. Gideon Punishing His Enemies. d. Pharaoh and His Army Drowning in
the Red Sea.
Le Miroir de l'humaine Salvation, Chapter XXXVI.
The Hunterian Museum Library, Glasgow, Ms. 60, fol. 59 recto.

A ce donques que nous ne resam
blons pas lucifer quant nous
sommes reluisans en lextremite
et habondance des richesses tran
sitoires vaines et corruptibles de ce mortel mõ
de · et que nous enuironnes des mobiles biens
de fortune ne nous esleuons en ce treshorrible
pechie dorgueil · Premierement nous verrons
a raconter le cas de lucifer angele de tresexcel
lente beaute voire et reluisant entre les aut̃ s
qui soy voirent aorne et adoule des euures de
dieu · et monte ou hault troisie entre les hier
chies et monarchies des aultres angeles · Il
qui tant estoit bel et admesure que nul plus
surmonte dorgueil comme meschant suborna
et attray a soy plusieurs angeles desquelz il
se fist aorer comme dieu, non recongnoissant
les biens dicellui qui tant lauoit exaulcie
mais non obstant ce cõme ce pechie fust trop
cruel et detestable a lui qui vouloit presider ou
siege imperial langele saint michel sidressa
Et cõme cestoit raison apres la malediction
il le fist tresbuchier du treshault ou tresbas
auec tous ses complices en lieu tenebreux ou
quel il est et sera pardurablement sans ja
mais auoir vne seule drachme de ioye celesti
elle · et ainsy il fu debouté du roiaume des

ceulx par ce meffait · Et comme fu adam
de paradis terrestre duquel adam fait et procree
ou champ de damas a la samblance du roy e
ternel du lymon de la terre la homme de caste
parfait estant en son premier somme · et ayat
este aucune espace de temps ou doulz et plai
sant paradis de delices cõme seigne[ur] et maistr
lors de sa coste fu aree eue la preste a marie[r]
laquelle p[ar] lordonnance de dieu lui fu donnee
a mariaige, non pas ad ce quelle fust cause de
la malheurete quil lui aduint, mais affin
quelle lui fist secours ayde et loyale cõpaignie
Lors se prindrent ilz a aruir: la terre et a mar
cher sur le gracieux herbaige dicelle place aor
nee et paree dieu scet cõment Et de tous les
biens dicelle leur donna dieu puissance et
liberte duser excepte dun arbre seulement
nõme larbre de vie · duquel le fruit leur fu ex
pressement deffendu · Parquoy iceulx esta
blis en celle grande maieste et bienheurete
ilz deuoient bien regratier ce dieu qui tant
de biens leur vouloit quil les auoit collaquei
en lieu incorruptible, net cler doulz seurin
soef air · et arrouse dune plaisant fontaine
sourdant habondamment et soy estandant p[ar]
diuers ruisseaux desquelz les paisibles vndes
descouuans sembloient argentees · Lequel

This French translation of the *Speculum humanæ salvationis* was written in a Bâtarde on forty-three parchment leaves, 38.2 x 28.3 cm., with text in two columns. It contains forty-two chapters and 168 miniatures. The Prologue, the Prohemium, and the last three chapters of the complete Latin manuscripts are not included.[29] It is entitled *Miroir de l'humaine salvation* and is not listed in Seymour de Ricci's census,[30] nor in the French translations described by Lutz and Perdrizet,[31] but it appeared in later supplements and catalogues, and its provenance is described in detail by Kessler.[32]

The text is not the translation of the Miélot *minute*, but it is identical in wording with the Glasgow copy, after the Prologue of the latter. The text begins on folio 1 verso "Ad ce donques que nous ne resamblons pas Lucifer" as in the Glasgow manuscript and ends on folio 43 recto "le pere et le fils et le saint esperit amen." There is no Explicit to furnish us with a date or place of its execution, but a comparison of the two texts through photographs and diapositives (fig. III–20, Plate III–9) shows them to be the same translation.

The miniatures are arranged on facing pages as in the Latin manuscripts, one at the head of each column of text, four to each chapter, and with their Latin captions or titles. The New Testament picture is in color but the three prefigurations which follow are mostly in pastel tints with grisaille figures rendered in a pale sculptural manner. The skies are a strong blue with gold stars, giving a sense of an eerie nocturnal world to the Old Testament scenes. In the Chapter I-c scene, God is admonishing a rather elderly Adam against eating the fruit of the tree, and in the background Adam is relating the message to Eve. In Chapter II-d, the Ark of Noah, with its domed super-structure, appears to be the prefiguration of a space capsule, with the animals peering out of arched windows and a circular aperture at the top for sending forth the raven and the dove (fig. III–23).

There were apparently at least three miniaturists in the Newberry manuscript.[33] According to Kessler the first 144 miniatures recall the style of a Dutch artist who contributed miniatures to the Queen Mary Hours (an English commission), to the Hours of Mary van Vronensteyn, and to the Dutch Bible of Evert van Soudenbalch. But it is now thought that all of the miniatures are by Flemish masters, not Dutch.[34]

29. Herbert L. Kessler, "The Chantilly *Miroir de l'humaine salvation* and Its Models," in *Studies in Honor of Millard Meiss*, edited by Irving Lavin and John Plummer (New York, 1977), I, p. 276.

30. Seymour de Ricci, *Census of Medieval and Renaissance Manuscripts in the United States and Canada*, 3 Vols. (1935–40; reprint New York, 1961).

31. Lutz and Perdrizet, *op. cit.*, pp. 104–105.

32. Kessler, *op. cit.*, pp. 276–277, fn. 14.

33. *Ibid.*, p. 277.

34. Correspondence with James Marrow, Department of Art History, University of California, Berkeley, and with Anne H. van Buren, Fine Arts Department, Tufts University, Boston, supports the assumption that no Dutch artist is involved in Newberry Ms. 40.

Plate III–9.
a. Good Angels Confirmed and Bad Thrown Down.
b. Eve Formed from the Rib of Sleeping Adam.
Le Miroir de l'humaine Salvation, Chapter I.
Newberry Library, Chicago, Ms. 40, fol. 1 verso.

III–23.
c. Adam Toils and Eve Spins. d. The Ark of Noah.
Le Miroir de l'humaine Salvation, Chapter II.
Newberry Library, Chicago, Ms. 40, fol. 3 recto.

Three French translations of the *Speculum* are listed in the inventory of the library of Philip the Good at the time of his death in 1467, as follows:[35]

757. Ung autre livre en papier couvert de parchemin blanc, intitulé au dehors: Le Miroir de humaine Salvacion; comançant au second feuillet *Par ordonnance de Dieu*, et au dernier, *par tout leur desir.*

759. Ung autre livre en pappier covert d'ais noirs, intitulé Le Miroir de la Salvacion humaine, comançant au second feuillet, *Notre Seigneur forma Adam*, et au dernier, *le XLVème.*

760. Ung autre livre en parchemin couvert d'ais rouges intitulé au dehors: Le Miroir de humaine Salvacion; comançant au second feuillet, *Preceptum datur*, et au dernier, *commun regis Assueri.*

Another inventory of the Burgundian ducal library was made in Ghent in 1485, some years after the death of Philip and of his son, Charles the Bold. The following French translation of the *Speculum* is listed:

1620. Item, ung livre en parchement de lettre bastarde couvert de cuyr rouge et de clous et de cloans de léton, intitule: Le Miroir de l'umaine salvacion, ou il y a en chacun feuillet trois hystoires de viel testament et un du novel; commenchement au second feuillet, *lieu n'estoit pas garni d'un arbre ne de deux*, et finissant, *le Pere et le filz et le Saint-Esperit. Amen.*

A third inventory was drawn up in Brussels in 1487 which included the following entry:

1760. Ung grant volume en papier couvert de cuir noir, à tout deux cloans de léton et cinq boutons sur chacun coté, historié et intitulé, Le Miroir de la salvacion humaine; en commanchant ou second feuillet, *Nostre Seigneur forma Adam*, et finissant au dernier, *qui procède selon les chapitres du livre.*

35. Barrois, *op. cit.*, p. 129.

This last manuscript, on paper, is clearly the same volume as item 759 of the 1467 inventory, and it ends with the Prohemium which indicates that it contained all forty-five chapters.

The manuscript listed in 1467 as item 760 and in 1485 as item 1620 must be the one now at the Newberry Library, for, although the text quotations are the same in the Glasgow copy, the opening phrase, *Preceptum datur*, is the caption of the third miniature. There are no titles or captions in the Glasgow manuscript. The text beneath, in both copies, is "lieu n'estoit pas garni d'un arbre ne de deux" as in the inventory, and at the end of the forty-second chapter, each has "le Pere et le fils et le saint-esperit. Amen." The phrase in the inventory item 760 "commun regis Assueri" appears as the caption over the last miniature of the Newberry manuscript. In the Glasgow copy this phrase is lacking.

The two manuscripts were probably copied from an anterior translation, for the difference in format would preclude the assumption that either was copied from the other. Many of the volumes in the Burgundian library were acquired by purchase or gift, and the lack of a dedication to an illustrious patron, which was very much in the tradition of the Valois house and the court of Burgundy, might indicate that these manuscripts were produced by independent ateliers. In the presentation miniature of the Glasgow copy, the costume of the scribe or translator who offers the book is apparently not that of a canon or monastic. He is wearing a blue-sleeved robe lined with brown fur and a fold of red and gold thrown over his left shoulder and falling down in back.

The Newberry manuscript follows a traditional Latin one in its format and miniature captions. As indicated by the inventories it remained in the Burgundian library until after 1577, when it was still listed in the Viglius catalogue of the Royal Library.[36]

The preparation of the translation used in these two manuscripts presents some interesting questions. The Miélot *minute* and the *deluxe* copy, B.N. Ms. fr. 6275, were dated 1449, and even if the Paris manuscript was actually made later but copying the date of the *minute*, they must have been known to those connected with the court of Philip the Good. He had often commissioned more than one translation of the same text. Although there was already a translation into French of the *Historia destructionis Troiæ* of Guido delle Colonne in his library, he ordered two more versions made.

It is clear from the inventories that the Newberry translation was in the Duke's library, and it is clear from its Explicit that the Glasgow copy was made in Bruges in 1455. If we accept the inventories as evidence although they do not list the two dedicated and identified Miélot copies, it seems likely that the Glasgow copy was never part of the Burgundian library.

36. F. Frocheur, "Inventoire de·Viglius," in *Catalogue des manuscrits de la Bibliothèque Royale des Ducs de Bourgogne* (Brussels-Leipzig, 1842), cclx.

III–24.
a. Mary Conquers the Devil. b. Judith Decapitates Holofernes.
Le Miroir de l'humaine Salvation, Chapter XXX.
Newberry Library, Chicago, Ms. 40, fol. 30 verso.

Opposite:

Plate III–10.

c. A Sign Appears in the Sky.

d. Solomon Placed a Throne for His Mother at His Right Hand.

Le Miroir de l'humaine Salvation, Chapter XXXVI.

Newberry Library, Chicago, Ms. 40, fol. 37 recto.

Apocalipsis xii ca.

bouche divine du filz ia avant embrachie le corps
glorifie et sa mere baisoit la precieuse bouche
dicelle qui tant humblement savoit cent mille
fois baisie lors quil prist son humanite en icelle
laquelle tant estoit administree de beatitude a
leure de son assumption que les ancians angeles
ardans en lamour de dieu voiant si belle maistresse monter au ciel et estre honnouree du
hault roy disoient comme par admiration.
Que est ista que ascendit de deserto delicis
affluens innixa super dilectum tanquam sponsa
Cest adire. O entre nous voions qui est ceste
dame qui monte du desert effundant mer-
veilleusement tous delices et se siet sur nostre
roy comme son espouse. Ausquelz elle respon-
di doulcement. Inueni quem quesiui et
quem dilexit anima mea. Cest adire. Jay
trouue cellui que iay quis et cerchie et que
mon ame a curieusement ame. Je le tiens
comme mon filz mon espoux et mon pere.
et suis seure que ie demourray tousiours par
sa grace auecques lui. Pourquoy
il est a noter que celle assumption fu iadis
demonstree a Jehan en lisle de pathmos quant
il vit ou ciel apparoir vne merueilleuse for-
me de femme auant ou circuite dicelle le
soleil le enuironnant de ses rays et couronnee

Tercii Regum ii ca.

dune couronne aornee de douze cleres estoilles
signifians lonneur et la reuerence que
les douze apostres faisoient a icelle. lesquelz
furent tous comme dit est a son trespasse-
ment glorieusement le couronnans christam
de laintes gracieuses et reluisans
Item ceste venerec assumption nous de-
monstra iadis salomon qui seant et pre-
sidant ou siege de son glorieux throsne haul-
tement et merueilleusement aorne dor et
de pierres precieuses enrichy. il appella sa
mere. et par grant amour la fist seoir au
dessus de lui. et en monstrant la parfaite
amour quil auoit en icelle. il la couronna
comme dame et souueraine maistresse de
son royaume. Par lequel salomon nous
entendons ihesus nostre benoit saueur
qui selon la maniere recitee sumptu-
eusement en son throsne assist sa glorieuse mere a la dextre partie en la couronnant
et receuant tant richement et honorable-
ment que ce nest a raconter. Ouquel siege elle est honnouree des anteles qui in-
cessamment loent sa precieuse virginite
son missis maintien. sa douce faconde. son
beau regard. sa glorieuse assistence. et les
euures p[ar] lesquelles elle a deseru nostre ami

Plate III–11.
a. Mary Conquers the Devil. b. Judith Decapitates Holofernes.
Le Miroir de l'humaine Salvation, Chapter XXX.
Musée Condé, Chantilly, Ms. fr. 139.

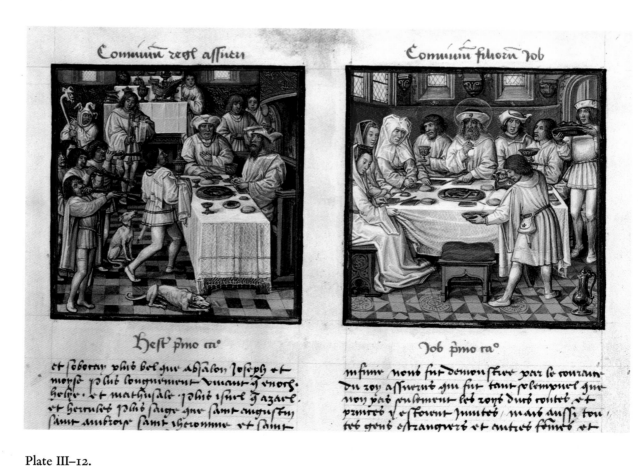

Plate III–12.
c. The Feast of King Ahasuerus. d. The Feast of Job's Sons.
Le Miroir de l'humaine Salvation, Chapter XLII.
Musée Condé, Chantilly, Ms. fr. 139.

Musée Condé, Chantilly, Ms. fr. 139

This splendid manuscript, entitled *Le Miroir de l'humaine Salvation*, came to the Musée Condé through the Bruyère-Chalabre sale of 1841. It has forty-three vellum leaves, 39.5 x 30 cm., written in two columns of twenty-eight lines with 168 miniatures and initials in gold and colors. Arms are painted on two detached leaves at the beginning and end of the text. It contains forty-two chapters.[37]

The Chantilly manuscript is based partially on the one now in the Newberry Library, Ms. 40, in its text and most of its illustrations, and for others, on the blockbooks. For many years this codex was considered to be the copy in the library of Philip the Good which is described in the inventory of 1467. That description fitted the book exactly. However, the inventory made of the Ducal library in Ghent in 1485, including the *Miroir*, listed the exact wording of the beginning of 2 recto, "Lieu n'estoit pas garni d'un arbre ne de deux," which appears on 2 recto of the Newberry and the Glasgow manuscripts. This text appears on folio 4 of the Chantilly *Miroir* which, therefore, cannot be the volume described in the inventory.

Further evidence is provided by the two inserted leaves of the Chantilly manuscript which bear the coats of arms of its early owners. The first is the arms of the Flemish family Le Fèvre. The second leaf shows an angel carrying, in one hand, the Le Fèvre arms and in the other those of the Dutch family Van Heemstede. Archives show that Roelant Le Fèvre married Hadewij van Heemstede in the second half of the fifteenth century.[38] Whether Le Fèvre commissioned the Chantilly manuscript is not known.

Even more significant is the style of the Chantilly miniatures, which are characteristic of Ghent-Bruges art about the year 1500 and are much more sophisticated than those of Newberry 40, although they often follow its subjects and compositions. The miniatures of the latter were used as models for 123 of the 168 pictures by the Chantilly illuminator, who refined the figures and clothed them in the costumes of the later period. There are significant compositional modifications in more than forty of these miniatures. The artist also copied twenty-five complete compositions and incorporated details from twenty-four others from the woodcuts of the blockbook *Speculum*.[39]

37. J. Merguey, *Les Principaux manuscrits à peinture du Musée Condé à Chantilly* (Paris, 1930), Notice 67.
38. S. van Leeuwen, *Batavia Illustrata* (The Hague, 1685), I, p. 980.
39. Kessler, *op.cit.*, pp. 277 ff.

III–25.
c. Lamech Harassed by His Two Wives.
d. Job Whipped by the Devil while His Wife Watches.
Le Miroir de l'humaine Salvation, Chapter XX.
Musée Condé, Chantilly, Ms. fr. 139.

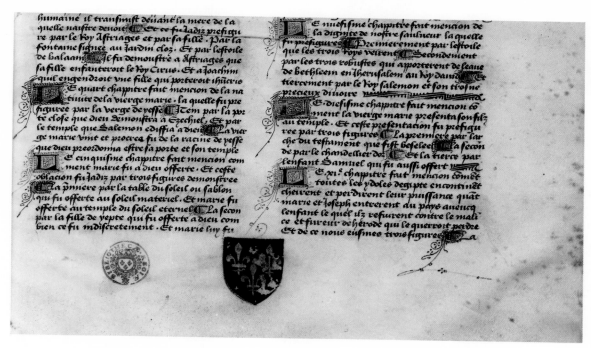

III–26.
Opening page. Detail.
Le miroir de lumaine sauluation.
Bibliothèque Nationale, Paris, Ms. fr. 188.

Bibliothèque Nationale, Ms. fr. 188

A French translation titled *Le miroir de lumaine sauluation*, written sometime after 1460, was commissioned by Louis of Bruges for his fine library at Gruthuyse. It included, according to a reconstruction of the library made in the nineteenth century, fifty-three vellum leaves in-folio, written in two columns of forty lines, with a fine miniature at the head of each, 192 miniatures in all. The Prohemium and forty-five chapters were included, the last three with eight miniatures each, and finally a genealogy of the kings of France.[40] It came into the collection of Louis XI and eventually into the Royal Library in Paris, but it had already been divided about 1500, for the section on the French kings is not bound in with the *Miroir*.

On folio 1 recto of the Gruthuyse manuscript there is a shield composed of a blue ground with three *fleurs de lis*. There are no captions or titles for the miniatures but they contain lettered banderoles, the first of which states, "coment es tombe du ciel Lucifer." The initials are elaborately colored and gilded throughout.

The catalogue by Van Praet of the Gruthuyse library credits Miélot with the translation, and even cites the *minute* conserved in Brussels, but the wording is given for the beginnings of the Prohemium and the text, which do not correspond to the Miélot translation or to that of the Newberry-Glasgow-Chantilly manuscript. It would seem that Philip the Good and Louis of Bruges were competing for French translations of the *Speculum* in splendid manuscripts to grace their great libraries.

40. J. B. B. Van Praet, "Bibliothèque de Louis de la Gruthuyse" in *Recherches sur Louis de Bruges*, VI (Paris, 1831), pp. 104–105. See also Claudine Lemaire, "De bibliotheek van Lodewijk van Gruuthuse," in *Vlaamse Kunst op Perkament* (Bruges, 1981), p. 224.

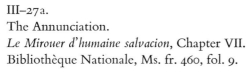

III–27a.
The Annunciation.
Le Mirouer d'humaine salvacion, Chapter VII.
Bibliothèque Nationale, Ms. fr. 460, fol. 9.

III–27b.
The Annunciation.
Le Miroir de humaine salvation.
The J. Paul Getty Museum, Malibu, Ludwig Ms. XI 9.

Bibliothèque Nationale, Ms. fr. 460 and J. Paul Getty Museum, Ludwig Ms. XI 9

These two closely related manuscripts in French were probably copied from a single model. Each is on 95 parchment leaves, with miniatures which are about the same width but the Latin captions around the arched gold frames are missing in Ms. fr. 460. In that codex also the scribe's lines are ruled throughout but many pages lack the text. However, on the second leaf, the wording commences, "Par ordonnance de Dieu," and on the last page ends, "par tout leur desir," which corresponds to the wording of Item 757 in the 1467 inventory of the Burgundian library.[41]

The handsome Getty copy, with one miniature on each page above the two text columns, was acquired in the spring of 1983 through the purchase of the Ludwig collection of manuscripts.

41. Paulin Paris, *Les manuscrits français de la Bibliothèque Royale de Paris* (Paris, 1836–1848), IV, p. 200. See also Anton von Euw, *Die Handschriften der Sammlung Ludwig*, Vol. III (Cologne, 1982), pp. 89–94.

III–28.
The Kingdom of Heaven.
Speculum Humanæ Salvationis, Chapter XLII.
Bibliothèque Municipale, Saint-Omer, Ms. 184, fol. 25.

Bibliothèque Municipale, Saint-Omer, Ms. 184

Originally in the Abbey of Saint-Bertin in Saint-Omer, this manuscript, 29 x 21 cm., on paper, contains drawings and verses in French octosyllables inspired by a set of tapestries with scenes from the *Speculum*, which were commissioned by the Abbot sometime before 1461. The most extraordinary of the illustrations is on folio 25, a full-page drawing of The Kingdom of Heaven with archaic Parisian and later Flemish elements which place it artistically in the second half of the fifteenth century. No similar representation of Heaven exists in any other *Speculum* manuscript. In the same volume are found descriptions of other treasures of the Abbey.[42] There are three other *Speculum* manuscripts in the Bibliothèque Municipale: one which is also from Saint-Bertin, Ms. 182, is in Latin on vellum without miniatures; Ms. 183, which came from the Abbey of Clairmarais near Saint-Omer, has the best miniatures, with a Latin text and the French octosyllabic verses; and Ms. 236, copied from the Clairmarais one, which came from the Chapter library of Notre Dame at Saint-Omer and has very mediocre miniatures.

42. Bert Cardon, "Een uitzonderlijke hemelvoorstelling in een Speculum Humanae
    Salvationis-handschrift uit de voormalige abdij van Saint-Bertin te Saint-Omer,"
    in *Archivum Artis Lovaniense. Bijdragen tot de Geschiedenis van de Kunst der Nederlanden
    opgedragen aan Prof. Dr. J. K. Steppe*, edited by M. Smeyers (Louvain, 1981), pp. 53–66.

III–29.
a. The Kingdom of Heaven. b. The Queen of Sheba and King Solomon.
Miroir du salut humain, Chapter XLII.
Staatsbibliothek Preussischer Kulturbesitz, Berlin, Ms. 403.

Staatsbibliothek Preussischer Kulturbesitz, Ms. 403

A unique translation of the *Speculum* into French verse is entitled *Miroir du salut humain*. It is on 54 leaves, 34.5 x 29 cm. with 192 colorful miniatures with red titles, each one at the head of a column of 26 lines which contain alternate blue and red initials. It was written on parchment in a French hand but not the Burgundian Bâtarde of Jean Miélot. Delaissé dates its execution as about 1455 and attributes it to Miélot but that clearly identified translation in the *minute* is in prose.[43]

The margin beside the miniature at the opening of each chapter has a leafy panel of decoration which Delaissé related to the atelier of Jean Mansel. Friedrich Winkler saw the influence of Simon Marmion in the miniatures. In German catalogue descriptions of the manuscript its date varies from 1465 to 1480.[44]

43. L. M. J. Delaissé, *La Miniature Flamande* (Brussels, 1959), Item 239.
44. Friedrich Winkler, *Die Flämische Buchmalerei des XV u. XVI Jahrhunderts* (Leipzig, 1925), p. 160; U. Finke, *Katalog der mittelalterlichen Handschriften und Einzelblätter in der Kunstbibliothek* (Berlin, 1966), p. 116; *Zimelien, Abendländische Handschriften des Mittelalters aus den Sammlungen der Stiftung Preussischer Kulturbesitz Berlin* (Wiesbaden, 1975), p. 193.

III–30.
a. The Descent from the Cross.
b. Jacob Laments the Death of Joseph.
De spieghel der menscheliker behoudenisse, Chapter XXV.
British Library, Add. Ms. 11.575, lxviiii.

British Library, Add. Ms. 11.575

A translation of the *Speculum* into Flemish verse, *De spieghel der menscheliker behoudenisse*, was made in the beginning of the fourteenth century. This copy of that translation, dating from the early fifteenth century, is on parchment, 26.6 x 19.3 cm., in two columns of forty-four lines on each page, and was written in a single hand in a *Littera Cursiva Formata*. The manuscript contains only 97 leaves of the original 122, and 155 pen and wash drawings of which 100 are erased or badly damaged. It was in the library of G. Kloss, a Frankfurt historian and collector, until it was acquired by the British Museum in 1840.[45]

45. L. M. Fr. Daniels, *De Spieghel der menscheliker behoudenesse* , Studien en tekstuitgaven van Ons Geestelijk erf, IX (1949). See also J. Deschamps, *Catalogus, Middelnederlandse handschriften uit Europese en Amerikaanse bibliotheeken* (Leiden, 1972), pp. 120–121.

III-31.
a. Opening page with illuminated initial.
b. Text page.
Spieghel onser behoudenisse.
Haarlem Stadsbibliotheek, Ms. II 17, fol. 1 recto.

Haarlem Stadsbibliotheek Ms. II 17

A manuscript entitled *Spieghel onser behoudenisse* is on deposit at the Frans Hals Museum in Haarlem. It is the only translation of the *Speculum* into Dutch prose, or the North Netherlandish language, and the text, abbreviated, is printed in the two Dutch blockbook editions. The manuscript is complete, 15.4 x 10.5 cm., on vellum in 231 leaves, forty-five chapters, in an excellent, clean condition, written as a private prayerbook without drawings or miniatures, except for a decorated initial at the beginning of the text, after the Prohemium. It shows no signs of having been used as printer's copy for the blockbooks so there was probably an antecedent manuscript, now lost, from which both were copied.

At the end there are two inscriptions as follows (in translation):
I. This book belongs to Cayman Janss van Zierichzee, living with the Carthusians outside Utrecht. The Lord be praised now and forever. Amen.
II. This book is finished anno domini 1464 on the 16 of July. An Ave Maria for the scribe.

It would appear to have been written for the important Karthuizenklooster Nieuwlicht which had a script that influenced the typefaces of the earliest Utrecht printers.[46]

46. *Supplementum Codices Manuscripti Membranei* (Haarlem, 1852): see also
Fr. B. Kruitwagen, O.F.M., *Laat-Middeleeuwse Paleografica, Paleotypica, Liturgica, Kalendalia, Grammaticalia* (The Hague, 1942).

IV

Blockbooks of the Low Countries

The blockbook editions of the *Speculum humanæ salvationis* cannot be analyzed without investigating, at least briefly, the blockbooks which preceded them or were being made concurrently. There were some thirty-three xylographic books of different origins, of which about one hundred examples are known. Among these a significant number were produced in the Netherlands in the fifteenth century.[1] Very few of these are dated, but in a general chronological order those which were the most widely distributed in chiro-xylographic and xylographic editions were as follows: the *Apocalypse*, the *Exercitium super Pater Noster*, the *Spirituale pomerium*, the *Ars moriendi*, the *Biblia pauperum*, the *Canticum canticorum*, and the *Speculum humanæ salvationis*. All are printed on one side of the paper only, or anapistographically. But with the *Speculum humanæ salvationis* a new phenomenon appears in the history of the blockbook and the history of printing. In the *Speculum* the woodcuts were printed as in other blockbooks, by rubbing the paper placed on the block which was coated with water-based ink. But the *Speculum* text was printed from movable metal characters in varnish-based ink, on a printing press. Its production will be discussed in Chapter V.

The blockbooks described in this Chapter are related to the *Speculum* in various ways: in purpose, in content, or in artistic style. They were all devoted to the propagation of the faith through pictures and text. They all interpreted events drawn from the Bible or other sources in medieval religious thought. The woodcut pictures in all were meaningful even to the illiterate and semi-literate, and they aided clerics and preaching monks to dramatise their sermons.

1. A. J. J. Delen, *Histoire du Livre et de l'Imprimerie en Belgique des origines à nos jours*. Deuxième partie (Brussels, 1930), p. 42.

IV–1.
The Angel with the Censer.
The Angels with Trumpets.
Apocalypse blockbook, Schreiber III.
Det Kongelige Bibliotek, Copenhagen.

The artists arranged the scenes in ways which were faithful to tradition but which show a variety of models and sources. Whether the cutters of the pictures were also the designers cannot be determined, but in the simplicity of composition and the strength of line, they created styles strikingly appropriate to the discipline of cutting in wood.

The editions of the blockbooks described here have been tabulated with reference to the localization of examples and other detailed information by W. L. Schreiber and Arthur M. Hind, to whose works the reader is referred for more documentation.[2]

Apocalypse

The *Apocalypse* is a xylographic book printed from full-page blocks carrying two horizontal pictures, and with the texts usually cut in framed rectangles within the picture borders. The images are done in outline with no shading or cross-hatching and there is no background landscape. There were six editions of the blockbook, the last three probably German. All have forty-eight leaves, except the third which has fifty and a revised text. It was copied from the earlier editions by an equally skilled cutter who probably is responsible for cutting both the text and the images (fig. IV–1). The second edition is printed from the same blocks as the first but with signature marks added (the same letter appears within facing pages on a sheet).

It is generally agreed among scholars that the *Apocalypse* is the most ancient of the blockbooks although there is wide divergence of opinion on the date of the first edition, ranging from about 1400[3] to as late as 1450–52.[4] Manuscripts of the *Apocalypse* seem to have originated in northern France and in England and were very popular. From manuscripts, of which a typical example is in the Bodleian Library at Oxford (Auct. D4.17), the fantastic and bizarre subjects, texts, and the format of the blockbooks were derived.[5] The style, the composition, and the iconography of the pictures were inspired by models in both manuscripts and tapestries, such as the numerous versions listed in the inventories of the collections of the Dukes of Burgundy. In fact the woodcuts are closely related to the famous *Apocalypse* tapestries at Angers, made about 1380 by Nicolas Bataille, after the miniatures or drawings of an artist working for the Burgundian Court, Jean Bandol, called Hennequin de Bruges.[6]

2. W. L. Schreiber, *Manuel de l'amateur de la gravure sur bois et sur métal au XVe siècle* (Berlin, 1891–1910), Vol. IV; Arthur M. Hind, *An Introduction to a History of Woodcut* (1935; reprint New York, 1963) Chapter IV.

3. Delen, *op. cit.*, p. 46, dates the first edition at 1400; H. T. Musper, "Xylographic Books," in *The Book through 5000 Years*, edited by H. D. L. Vervliet (London and New York, 1972), p. 345, places it at 1420; Schreiber, *op. cit.*, p. 3, and Hind, *op. cit.*, p. 218, both give the date as about 1430.

4. Allan H. Stevenson, "The Problem of the Blockbooks," IV, p. 4, unpublished notes of lectures given at the University of Amsterdam, 1965, now in the Haarlem Stadsbibliotheek.

5. Gertrud Bing, "The Apocalypse Block-Books and their Manuscript Models," in Journal of the Warburg and Courtauld Institutes, V (1942), pp. 143–158.

6. Delen, *op.cit.*, p. 43.

IV–2.
Apocalypse blockbook,
Schreiber III (details).
Det Kongelige Bibliotek,
Copenhagen.

St. John in the Presence of the Prefect.

The Distribution of Trumpets.

Antichrist with the Executioner.

Antichrist Causes a Bishop to be Killed.

Two editions of this blockbook are preserved. They each contain a series of ten woodcuts interpreting the Lord's Prayer, with explanatory texts. The first edition is chiro-xylographic with Flemish text written beneath the woodcuts, but the banderoles in the pictures are in Latin. The unique copy, lacking, however, leaves 1 and 9, is in the Bibliothèque Nationale in Paris (fig. IV–3). The style of the miniatures has been related to that of Robert Campin of Tournai (the Master of Flémalle). According to Delen, the costumes are typical of the early years of the fifteenth century.

Of the second edition, two copies exist, one at the Bibliothèque, Université de l'Etat à Mons, which has the Latin text above the image and the Flemish translation below (fig. IV–4). In the other copy, that of the Bibliothèque Nationale in Paris, the text beneath the image has been cut off, presumably by someone with a strong prejudice against the vernacular. In this edition, evidently produced some years after the first, the woodcut pictures are much more elaborate.[7] While the compositions are based on the first set of blocks, the costumes and the diagonal parallel lines of shading indicate a later date. The text is cut in the wood within rectangles and banderoles.

Between these blocks and those of the *Spirituale pomerium* there is a strong similarity of artistic style which suggests that both books may have been produced by one artist or atelier chosen by the author, who was presumably responsible for both texts (see figs. IV–3, 4, 5, and the text on the *Spirituale pomerium*).[8] Evidence points to the origin of the two *Exercitium* editions in the communities of the *Devotio moderna* at either Sept-Fontaines or Groenendael (near Brussels), or both. This is adduced from the Flemish text, the character of the work that indicates its usage by preaching clerics, and the attribution of its authorship to Hendrik van den Bogaerde (1382–1469). After ten years as Prior of Sept-Fontaines, Bogaerde was named Prior of Groenendael in 1431. A catalogue listing his writings, which has been preserved, includes both an *Exercitium super Pater Noster* and the *Spirituale pomerium*.[9] Possibly under his direction, the first edition may have been produced at Sept-Fontaines and the second at Groenendael. The first set of blocks may have been lost or considered unsuitable for the new text in both Latin and Flemish. Each of these communities was a center of book production, with an impressive library of manuscripts.

7. Louis Lebeer, "Le Dessin, la gravure, le livre xylographique et typographique," in
    Bruxelles au XVe siècle (Brussels, 1953), pp. 203–205, states that the woodcuts of this
    edition were executed from drawings by Vrancke van der Stockt. See also
    Flanders in the Fifteenth Century: Art and Civilization, catalogue edited by
    E. P. Richardson (Detroit Institute of Arts, 1960), pp. 222–223.
8. Lebeer, *Spirituale Pomerium* (Brussels, 1938), p. 15.
9. For a discussion of the relationship of these two blockbooks see Delen,
    op. cit., pp. 52–56.

IV–3.
Chiro-xylographic first edition.
Exercitium super Pater Noster.
Bibliothèque Nationale, Paris, Xyl. 31.

IV–4.
Xylographic second edition.
Exercitium super Pater Noster.
Université de l'Etat à Mons,
Bibliothèque, Fonds anciens 1797-B*.

IV-5.
The Nativity.
Spirituale pomerium blockbook.
Bibliothèque Royale, Brussels, Ms. 12070.

Strictly classified, the *Spirituale pomerium* is not a chiro-xylographic book but a manuscript of twenty-five leaves in which twelve block prints are variously mounted, at the head, the middle, or the foot of the pages. This would indicate that the scribe planned the layout of the text to include the pictures. The images are printed on the same kind of paper as the text. The only copy is at the Bibliothèque Royale in Brussels.

In an inscription on the verso of the first page is the name "Henricus ex Pomerio" by which Van den Bogaerde was also known. As already noted, the text of the *Exercitium super Pater Noster* has also been ascribed to him. At the end of the *Spirituale pomerium* is the following statement in Latin without the proper contraction marks: *explicit sp(irit)uale pomeriu(m) editu(m) anno d(omi)ni m ccccxl.* Many authorities agree that the woodblocks may be dated from about the same time as the manuscript, 1440.

The subject of this mystical tract is the divine blessings. The xylographic text at the base of each block states the three blessings which are symbolized by three apples, and are intended to inspire spiritual meditation for the twelve hours of the day. The blocks show four scenes drawn from the Old Testament and eight from the New. Each one contains a tree beneath which a pious soul, represented by a young girl, gathers the three apples of the divine benefactions. On successive pages are pictured twelve biblical events from the Creation to the Coronation of the Virgin, each explained by texts in banderoles cut in the block.

As in the case of the woodcuts of the *Exercitium* second edition, the artistic style has been related to the work of Roger van der Weyden, who had a known connection with the monastery of Groenendael where one of his paintings was preserved. It is recorded that after his death in 1464, masses were said there for his soul.[10] The style has also been associated with the work of the Master of the Redemption, named for an altarpiece in the Prado, who, in turn, has been thought to be Vrancke van der Stockt.[11] He was a student of Van der Weyden and succeeded him as the master painter of Brussels.[12] If the designs for the *Spirituale* were made about 1440, either Van der Weyden or Van der Stockt could have been the artist.

10. Lebeer, *Spirituale, op.cit.*, p. 30.
11. *Ibid.*, pp. 38–39.
12. G. Hulin de Loo, "Vrancke van der Stockt," in *Biographie Nationale de Belgique*, XXIV (Brussels, 1926–1929), cols. 66–76.

The first edition of the xylographic *Ars moriendi* is acknowledged by some art historians as the great masterpiece of the Netherlandish blockbooks. It was extremely popular (some twenty editions are known), no doubt because of the pervasive fear of death from the plagues and pestilences which ravaged Europe from 1347 until the seventeenth century. The book appeared later in many editions with typographically printed text, some using copies of the original woodcuts. Priests, called constantly to the bedsides of the moribund, used the pictures and texts to help prepare the pious for the hereafter.

The Weigel copy of the blockbook in the British Library is probably the oldest, produced about 1450 (fig. IV–6). It is in Latin, but subsequent editions are known in French, Dutch, and German. Thirteen groups of blocks with text banderoles were used in the twenty blockbook editions.[13] They were printed on one side of the paper facing a page of xylographic text. In the first ten scenes the pictures show the devil and his demons trying to seize the soul of the dying man through temptations, and the attendants giving good counsel at the deathbed. The eleventh picture is of the triumph over all temptations in the hour of death. The text, thought to have been inspired by the writings of Jean Gerson (1363–1429),[14] was intended to serve as a manual for clerics.

The *Ars moriendi* occupies a special place in the history of woodcuts and of the blockbooks. Unlike most of the others it is not concerned with typology or Old Testament prophecy, or with the Gospels. The artist drew the subjects and compositions from a series of eleven small engravings of about 1440 by the Master E.S., the only complete set of which is in the Ashmolean Museum at Oxford (fig. IV–7). The vigor and refinement of the blockbook pictures surpass the level of the engravings of the Master E. S.; faulty perspective is corrected and text banderoles are added.[15] It has been suggested that these fine blocks should be attributed to the immediate entourage of Roger van der Weyden, although, among the thirteen groups of illustrations, several different styles may be found.

13. Schreiber, *op.cit.*, IV, p. 257.
14. Delen, *op.cit.*, p. 61.
15. Lionel Cust, *The Master E. S. and the 'Ars Moriendi'* (Oxford, 1898).

IV–6.
Xylographic first edition.
Impatience.
Ars moriendi blockbook, Schreiber Ia.

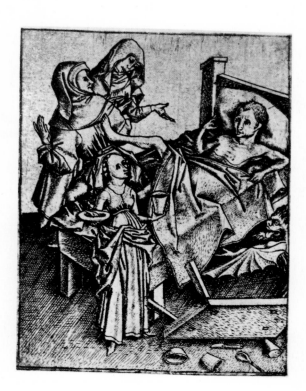

IV–7.
Line-engraving by the Master E.S.
Impatience.
Ars moriendi.

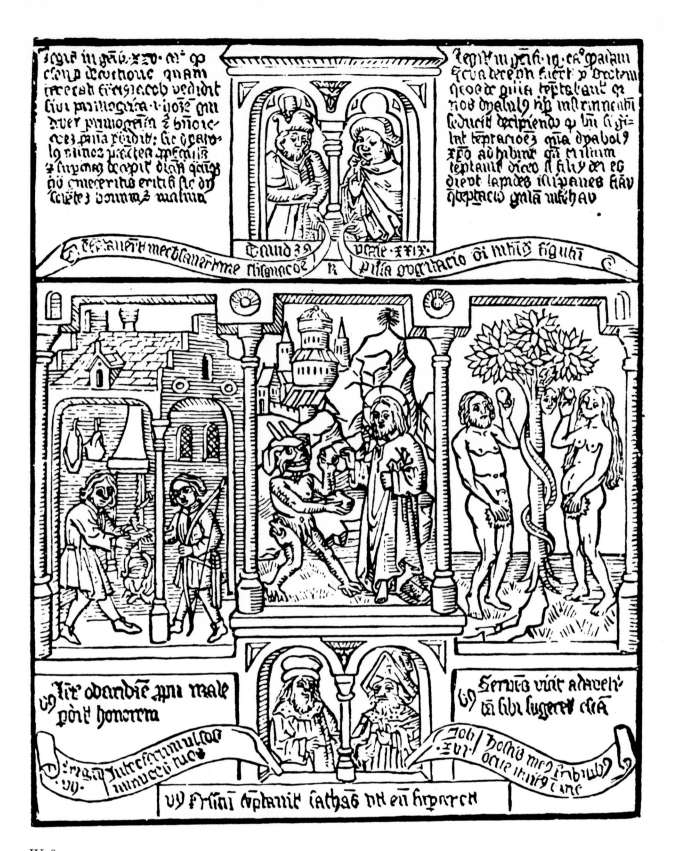

IV–8.
The Temptation of Esau.
The Temptation of Christ.
The Temptation of Adam and Eve.
Biblia pauperum blockbook, Schreiber III.

Plate IV–1.
a. Isaac Bearing the Wood for his Sacrifice.
b. Christ Bearing the Cross.
c. Elijah and the Widow of Zarephath.
Biblia pauperum manuscript.
British Library, Kings Ms. 5, fol. 16.

Plate IV–2.
Christ and the Van Amerongen patrons.
The Hours of Mary van Vronensteyn.
Bibliothèque Royale, Brussels, Ms. II 7619, fol. 97 verso.

The name *Biblia pauperum* was used as early as the thirteenth century for various typological summaries of the Bible which might perhaps have been more accurately called *Biblia picta*, a title which appears in the manuscript of this work in Munich.[16] It was by no means as popular in its manuscript form as the *Speculum humanæ salvationis*. Some sixty-eight surviving manuscripts were documented in 1925,[17] but the blockbook editions appear to have been even more widely distributed than the *Ars moriendi*. The ten xylographic editions depend upon a single prototype and have forty anapistographic pages. Most of these are of a small square folio size, and within the framed architectural arrangement of the pictures, the text is carved in banderoles and rectangular units (fig. IV–8). They recount the story of the Fall and Redemption through the life of Christ, the central New Testament subject being flanked by scenes of Old Testament prefigurations, with portraits and predictions of four prophets, usually two above and two below.

Another edition of the *Biblia pauperum* consists of fifty pages, in which the ten extra subjects are partly borrowed from the *Speculum* and which survives in a unique copy at the Bibliothèque Nationale. A chiro-xylographic edition, of German origin, in thirty-four leaves is found in a single copy in Heidelberg, which is dated as early as 1420 by Musper, but which is thought to have been made in the late 1460's by Hind and Koch.[18] For the Netherlandish editions, scholars' dates vary from 1440 to 1480.

Research by art historians has brought to light some interesting relationships between dated illuminated manuscripts and the blockbook woodcuts. One of these is the richly decorated manuscript usually referred to as the Hours of Mary van Vronensteyn. It was originally owned by Jan van Amerongen, sheriff of Utrecht from 1468 to 1470, and his shears device can be seen on his cloak (Plate IV–2).[19] The date of the manuscript, 1460, is taken from its Sunday calendar in which a pointing hand is directed to the year 60 in the part dealing with the fifteenth century. Van Amerongen married Mechtelt Hendricksdr of Ghent, but they had no children and she left the Book of Hours to her niece Maria van Raephorst, who in 1520 married Lubbert de Wael van Vronensteyn. Thereby the manuscript acquired its name.[20]

16. Bayerische Staatsbibliothek, Clm 22098.
17. Henrik Cornell, *Biblia Pauperum* (Stockholm, 1925).
18. Musper, *op.cit.*, p. 340; Hind, *op.cit.*, p. 242; Robert A. Koch, "New Criteria for Dating the Netherlandish Biblia Pauperum Blockbook," in *Studies in Honor of Millard Meiss*, edited by Irving Lavin and John Plummer (New York, 1977), I, p. 285.
19. L. M. J. Delaissé, *A Century of Dutch Manuscript Illumination*, p. 45.
20. K. G. Boon, "Een Utrechtse Schilder uit de 15de Eeuw, de Meester van de Boom van Jesse in de Buurkerk," in *Oud Holland* LXXVII (1961), p. 51, note 2.

Among the historiated initials there are some in which the pictures appear to be copied from certain scenes in the forty-leaf edition of the blockbook *Biblia pauperum* (fig. IV–9).[21]

The artist of the twelve full-page illustrations of the Hours has been credited with certain miniatures in the Dutch Bible of Evert van Soudenbalch, now in Vienna, and with the painting of the Calvary, now in the Museum of the Rhode Island School of Design at Providence (fig. IV–10). To this artist is attributed the Christ Nailed to the Cross now in the Walker Art Gallery at Liverpool, and a mural painting, after 1453, of the Tree of Jesse in the Buurkerk in Utrecht (fig. IV–11). This group of paintings is related to a triptych of the Crucifixion, at Utrecht, which shows a view of the town and must be dated 1460–1465. Between 1455 and 1470 the only painter known to have received commissions from the Buurkerk was Hillebrant van Rewijk and he therefore might be considered the creator of the works above. His son may have been the better-known Erhard van Rewijk or Reuwich who made the famous woodcuts for Breydenbach's *Peregrinationes in Terram Sanctam,* which were printed under his name at the press of Peter Schöffer in Mainz in 1486. It has been suggested that the miniatures, mentioned above, of the Evert van Soudenbalch Bible and the full-page pictures of the Vronensteyn Hours might be his juvenile work.[22]

21. Maurits Smeyers, "De invloed der blokboekeditie van de Biblia Pauperum op het getijdenboek van Maria van Vronensteyn," in *Bijdragen tot de geschiedenis van de grafische kunst opgedragen aan Prof. Dr. Louis Lebeer* (Antwerp, 1975), p. 378; see also Koch, *op.cit.*, I, p. 285.
22. Boon, *op.cit.*, pp. 59–60.

IV–9.
Comparison of details of the *Biblia pauperum* with initials in
the Hours of Mary van Vronensteyn.
Bibliothèque Royale, Brussels, Ms. II 7619.
a. Ham Mocking Noah. b. Joseph Cast into the Well.
c. Jonah Thrown to the Whale.

IV–10.
The Master of the Tree of Jesse in the Buurkerk.
The Crucifixion with Two Thieves, ca.1450–60.
Museum of Art, Rhode Island School of Design, No. 61.080.

IV–11.
Master of the Tree of Jesse in the Buurkerk.
Fresco, The Tree of Jesse.
Rijksdienst voor de Monumentenzorg, Zeist.

The two editions of the *Canticum canticorum* are printed in a brownish ink, from two sets of sixteen blocks of Netherlandish origin. The thirty-two scenes are placed as two horizontal panels on each page. In the banderoles are text verses drawn directly from the Song of Songs. There is no typology in the concepts, but rather the Old and New Testaments seem to be merged in the symbolism of Mary as the Bride and Jesus as the Church.

The medieval interpretation of the Song of Songs as prefiguration of the New Testament was the subject of many religious treatises. The passionate metaphors of devotion in the verses were interpreted as expressing God's love for his people, or Christ's love for his Church, and Mary is elsewhere seen as a symbol of the Church. The cult of the Virgin, which appeared in the twelfth century and developed throughout the thirteenth, was extensively drawn from the writings of St. Bernard (1090–1153) on the Song of Songs, in which he applied many of its references to the Virgin Mary as the Bride.[23]

In the woodcuts Mary wears a nimbus and a crown and is accompanied by tall maidens (Song of Songs I, 3). Jesus is identified by the nimbus with a cross which always symbolized one of the Trinity: Father, Son, or Holy Ghost. Since his robes are like those of the maidens, only this nimbus distinguishes Christ from the other figures in the scenes. The blocks were probably made in a religious community, for in the first picture, at the right, appear Brothers occupied with the work of the harvest (fig. IV–12).

The first edition of the *Canticum* is much superior to the second in simplicity of composition and the grace and elegance of the figures. It has been considered an artistic masterpiece, with all the poetry of the Song of Songs captured in these blocks.[24] The artist can be associated with the first artist of the *Speculum* woodcuts, or at least with the atelier where he worked (fig. IV–13).

In style of design and cutting there are striking likenesses to the *Biblia pauperum* and to the *Speculum humanæ salvationis*. The background trees as little pyramids of horizontal strokes, the tufts of small straight lines indicating grasses, the lines of drapery, the rectangular slabs of earth or stone in the landscape, the shading of walls and figures with short horizontal lines, the leaded windows and tiled floors of the interiors, all show some consistent techniques which unite these three blockbooks and suggest that they should be assigned to the same circle of artists and/or engravers. The addition of several varieties of plants in the *Canticum* that do not occur in the *Biblia pauperum* seems to place it later. The *Speculum* editions, with text printed in a press, may have been later still, but the blocks may have been made long before that took place, since they show a less sophisticated style than those of the *Canticum*.

23. Emile Mâle, *The Gothic Image* (1913; reprint New York, 1958), p. 233, translated from *L'Art religieux du XIIIᵉ siècle en France* (Paris, 1898), as *Religious Art in France of the Thirteenth Century*.

24. Delen, *op.cit.*, p. 73.

IV-12.
Canticum canticorum blockbook, Schreiber I.

IV–13.
Canticum canticorum blockbook, Schreiber I.

Scholars in several fields have made studies attempting to date the blockbooks by various methods but a survey has demonstrated how vague and arbitrary are the criteria on which the dating has been done in the past.[25] In the cases of the *Spirituale pomerium* and the *Exercitium super Pater Noster* the inscriptions of Henry van den Bogaerde established a date. But where there is no information from provenance, church celebrations, or archives, art historians have often based their conclusions on such evidence as drapery folds with hooks or loops, horizontal or vertical shading with hatching, correctness of perspective, or linear style, all of which assume a sort of steady and predictable "evolution" or development of woodcut art. But it is unreasonable to assume that these elements evolved in identical stages in the various ateliers of the time, particularly during any single decade. On the contrary, we may assume that there were concurrently artists and ateliers where there was innovation, and others which clung to earlier traditions. To this must be added the consideration of whether the work was done by copying a miniature or model, or conceived originally.

The watermarks of papers, when their date is established by comparison with a dated sheet in which an identical mark appears, show only the date before which the printing of a particular leaf could not have been done. The blocks may have been designed and cut a few years or decades before the paper was made, and the printing could have been done long afterwards.

In recent years several art historians have studied intensively the relationship of blockbooks to miniatures in manuscripts of which the completion date is known, or can be logically assumed, as well as to Dutch and Flemish painting of the period.[26] In the case of the *Speculum* there has also been extensive research into its relationship with the earliest printing in the Netherlands.[27] The *Speculum* editions are explored in the following chapter through study of the types, the text printing, the papers, and the woodcuts.

25. Hélène Verougstraete-Marcq and Roger Van Schoute, "Le Speculum humanæ salvationis considéré dans ses rapports avec la Biblia pauperum et le Canticum canticorum," in De Gulden Passer, LIII (1975), pp. 363 ff.
26. See works listed in the Selected Bibliography by Bing, Koch, Smeyers, Marrow, Calkins, and others.
27. Wytze and Lotte Hellinga, *The Fifteenth-Century Printing Types of the Low Countries*, 2 vols. (Amsterdam, 1966).

V–1.
The Coster family pedigree (detail). Haarlem Stadsbibliotheek,
deposited in the Frans Hals Museum, Haarlem.

V

Blockbook Editions of the Speculum

For centuries the *Speculum humanæ salvationis* blockbooks have been a source of speculation and controversy.[1] Until the late nineteenth century they were usually considered to be the work of Laurens Janszoon Coster (1405–84) in Haarlem, where a statue on the market place still honors him with the invention of printing. The editions have been thought, by some, to be the earliest books printed with movable type in a press. But the fact that they were not dated and that the printer and location of the press were not identified have made their position in the history of Western bookmaking hotly contested.[2] It is, however, generally agreed that the *Speculum* blockbooks originated in the Low Countries.

The Speculum and the Coster Question

The name of Laurens Janszoon Coster first appeared as the inventor of printing in a pedigree of the Coster family which was drawn up in 1559 but supposedly copied from an earlier document. It stated, "Sijn tweede wijff was Louris Ianssoens Costers dochter die deerste print in die werlt brocht Anno 1446" (his second wife was Louris Janssoens Coster's daughter who brought the first print into the world in the year 1446). It appears to imply that it was the daughter who invented printing, but probably the word "die" refers to the father and should be translated as "the one who." The document is preserved by the Haarlem Stadsbibliotheek (fig. V–1).

1. Lotte and Wytze Hellinga, "Die Coster-Frage," in *Der gegenwärtige Stand der Gutenbergforschung*, edited by H. Widmann (Stuttgart, 1972), pp. 232–42.
2. Gottfried Zedler, *Der älteste Buchdruck und das frühholländische Doktrinale des Alexander de Villa Dei* (Leiden, 1936). See also Zedler's *Von Coster zu Gutenberg* (Leipzig, 1921), and *Die neuere Gutenberg-Forschung und die Lösung der Coster-Frage* (Frankfurt, 1923); H. Th. Musper, *Die Haarlemer Blockbücher und die Costerfrage* (Mainz, 1939).

The humanist poet, engraver, and print-dealer, Dirck Volkertsz Coornhert, writing in 1561, mentions a "very rough" kind of printing being done in Haarlem according to local tradition. He does not name Coster, nor does his contemporary, the Haarlem printer, Jan van Zuren, whose writing on the invention of printing (now lost) was later versified by the learned Petrus Scriverius in an homage to Coster in 1628.

In a treatise by Hadrianus Junius entitled *Batavia* (an old name for Holland), written in 1568 and published at Leiden in 1588, Coster is credited with the invention of movable characters and with printing a *Speculum* in Haarlem about 1440. The Hadrianus account of Coster's invention stated that on Christmas Eve, when everyone was at church, an apprentice of Coster's stole his type and equipment and took it to Mainz, where he printed a *Doctrinale* with the same characters. As for the invention of the method, Hadrianus relates that Coster first cut single letters in the bark of a beech tree (perhaps in the immemorial custom of cutting initials on trees), but had the inspiration to lift them out and print words from their reverse sides. Through some method of casting he was supposed to have created metal types with which he printed whole pages on paper or vellum. Supporters of the story have cited the statement of the veteran printer Ulrich Zell on the invention of printing in 1440 to the author of the Cologne Chronicle (Johann Koelhoff II, Cologne, 1499), which appears in that volume as "die eyrste vurbyldung vonden in Hollant vyss den Donaten" (the first prefigurations were found in Holland in the Donatuses). The study of the earliest Dutch printing shows that there were, indeed, Donatuses printed, but there is no clear proof to connect them with Haarlem or Coster.

Dating, Localization, and Attribution

Many writers, published as long ago as Gerard Meerman in 1765[3] and as recently as Wytze and Lotte Hellinga in 1972 and 1973,[4] have explored the problems of the printer, place, date, and sequence of the *Speculum* editions. In 1863, William Young Ottley summarized the major earlier studies and added his own extensive research, but the questions continued to remain unresolved.[5] In 1871 Henry Bradshaw of the Cambridge University Library proposed a date by citing the only one in a first edition of the *Speculum* blockbook, 1471, written in red in a fifteenth-century hand in a Munich copy (Universitätsbibliothek München, Cim. 52, Xyl. 10). Since then the first edition is usually listed as "not after 1471."[6] He also located the printer in Utrecht, based on the use there of two of the blocks by Jan Veldener in his edition of the *Epistelen en evangelien* in 1481. How and when Veldener obtained the blocks is not known, but their use

3. Gerard Meerman, *Origines Typographicæ* (The Hague, 1765).
4. Lotte and Wytze Hellinga, "Die Coster-Frage," in *Der gegenwärtige Stand der Gutenbergforschung*, edited by H. Widmann (Stuttgart, 1972). See also Lotte Hellinga, "Prototypographie," in *Le cinquième centenaire de l'imprimerie dans les anciens Pays-Bas*, exhibition catalogue of Bibliothèque Royale Albert Ier (Brussels, 1973), pp. 66–67.
5. William Young Ottley, *An Inquiry Concerning the Invention of Printing* (London, 1863).
6. Henry Bradshaw, "List of the Founts of Type and Woodcut Devices used by Printers of Holland in the Fifteenth Century," in *Collected Papers* (London, 1889), pp. 258–280.

V–2.
Doctrinale of Alexander de Villa Dei, in the Saliceto type of
the Printer of the Text of the *Speculum*, Hellinga 5: 123 G.
The final page of the only surviving complete copy.
Cambridge University Library, Inc. 3300.

does not locate the printing of the text in Utrecht, and, indeed, the blocks may never have belonged to the text printer.[7] In the *British Museum Catalogue of Books Printed in the XV Century*, Vol. IX (BMC IX), the products of the press are assigned to the "Printer of the Text of the Speculum." Perhaps the anonymous printer wished to follow the example of the author of the manuscript, and out of humility, to remain unknown. In any case, this identification has come to be used to designate the producer of the early Netherlandish printed works formerly referred to as "Costeriana."

The same types as those in the *Speculum* were used extensively, as well as related type faces, in Doctrinals (fig. V–2), Donatuses, and Distichs, of which fragments continue to be found (fig. V–3), but none, as yet, with a date, printer's name, or location.[8] Editions in these types (with certain other features), which are generally accepted as the most ancient to be printed in the Low Countries, are called Netherlandish prototypography. The only date on any other example is an owner's inscription of 1472 on the Darmstadt copy of *De salute corporis*. This book is set in a Dutch blackletter, named for the author as the Saliceto type. It is similar to the *Speculum* type, but larger. The printer of the *Speculum* had two other types, the Valla, for printing Laurentius Valla's translation of Aesop, and the larger Pontanus type, used in that writer's *Singularia in causis criminalibus*. These types are grouped together because of their use in similar texts and their likeness of forms.

The only documentary evidence of a press in the Low Countries near the middle of the fifteenth century is in the inventory made at the death of a nun of the Bethany convent at Malines (Mechelen), Jacoba van Loos-Hensberghe, in 1465. This states that she had inherited from her brother "*unum instrumentum ad imprimendas scripturas et ymagines*" (an instrument to print writing and pictures). The inventory also included "*novem printe lignee ad imprimendas ymagines cum quatuordecim aliis lapideis printis*" (nine wood blocks for printing images, with fourteen other stone blocks).[9] Could Jacoba's late brother have been our mysterious, anonymous printer? No. He was the Bishop of Liège.

Several scholars have made studies of the possibility of a printing workshop in Malines in the 1460's. Three prints, and one leaf combining xylographic and typographic printing, which have been attributed to the Convent of Bethany, have been preserved. The leaf is headed by a woodcut carrying the title *Ecce panis angelorum* and it is in the Brussels Royal Library. However, based on a study of the characters, it has been concluded that the original could not have been printed before 1530.[10] It is generally accepted that the press which printed the text of the *Speculum* editions and the schoolbooks in *Speculum* types was located in the northern Low Countries, but it is not known in what city it operated.

---

7. L. A. Sheppard, "Introduction to the Presses, Holland," in BMC IX, p. xxiv.
8. Lotte Hellinga, "Further Fragments of Dutch Prototypography," in Quaerendo II, 3 (1972), pp. 197 ff.
9. Edward van Even, *L'Ancienne Ecole de Peinture de Louvain* (Brussels and Louvain, 1870), p. 104.
10. Kamiel Heireman, S.J., "Le prétendu atelier Malinois," in *Le Cinquième Centenaire*, *op.cit.*, pp. 538 ff., pl. 147.

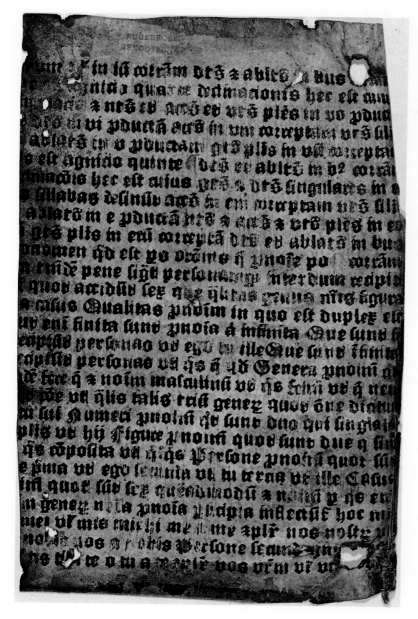

V–3a.
Donatus fragment in Hellinga Type 2*, with some sorts from Type 3, printed by the Printer of the Text of the *Speculum*. Presumably because of the shrinkage of the parchment, it measures 98 mm. for 20 lines instead of 103 mm. as in two leaves of the *Speculum*.
Edition II. Ruusbroecgenootschap, Antwerp (633a)B.

V–3b.
Block for a xylographic Donatus.
Rijksmuseum Meermanno-Westreenianum,
The Hague.

V–3c.
Satan and the Scribe.
Woodcut on verso of Donatus block above.
Rijksmuseum Meermanno-Westreenianum,
The Hague.

The types used in the editions of the *Speculum* have been described in BMC IX and in the work of the Dutch scholars Wytze and Lotte Hellinga.[11] The measurement of the characters is based on millimeters required for twenty lines of text from the base of the first to the base of the twenty-first line. The letter G, in the following descriptions, refers to Gothic, a blackletter form of type.

Four editions were produced, two in Latin with verses in rhymed couplets, and two in Dutch prose translations. The order of their production was debated for several centuries, but the accepted sequence today is as follows. The dates given for the editions are those deduced by Allan H. Stevenson from his study of the watermarks of the various papers used.[12]

I. First Latin edition (c.1468), with blocks in good state and Hellinga Type 1 : 110 G (figs. V–4, 6, 7, 8).

II. First Dutch edition (c.1471), with block borders occasionally broken, in Hellinga Type 1: 110 G, but with two pages printed in another type, Hellinga Type 2 : 103 G (figs. V–5 and 10). The Latin captions in the woodcuts are translated into Dutch at the head of each column.

III. Second Latin edition (c.1474), with the blocks showing further deterioration, in Hellinga Type 1, still in good state. Twenty pages of this edition have text in xylographic imitation of the first Latin edition (fig. V–9).

IV. Second Dutch edition (c.1479), with the blocks even more damaged, and the text in Hellinga Type 1, but cast on a smaller body. The characters are badly worn, poorly printed in a sooty black ink, and unevenly aligned (fig. V–11). This led some writers to think that this was the first edition.

Unlike the complete manuscripts, the blockbook editions do not contain a Prologue, and the Prohemium precedes the illustrated section. The Prohemium occupies four or six leaves (the latter including a blank leaf), according to the edition. The rest of the book is made up in three gatherings of fourteen leaves and one of sixteen.

11. Wytze and Lotte Hellinga, *The Fifteenth-century Printing Types of the Low Countries,* (Amsterdam, 1966), I, pp. 4 ff.
12. C. M. Briquet, *Les Filigranes,* edited by Allan H. Stevenson (Amsterdam, 1968), p. 95.

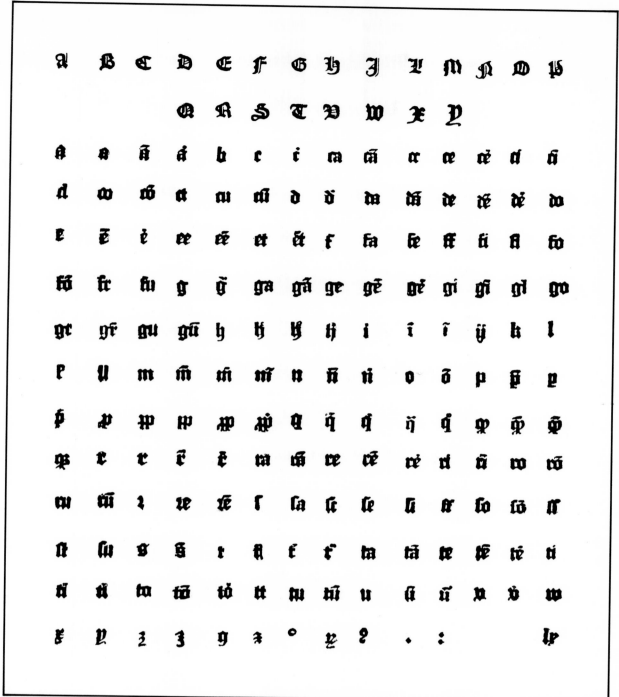

V-4.
Characters in Speculum Type I,
Hellinga 1: 110 G.
From Gottfried Zedler, *Von Coster zu Gutenberg* (Leipzig, 1921).

V–5.
Characters in Speculum Type II,
Hellinga 2: 103 G.
From Gottfried Zedler, *Von Coster zu Gutenberg* (Leipzig, 1921).

Only twenty-nine of the forty-five manuscript chapters are printed in the blockbooks although the blocks were made for many more. The text follows the sequence of the manuscripts for the first twenty-four chapters. Then only five are added, possibly to sell the shorter editions more rapidly at a lower price, or perhaps because of the limits of available paper. Some idiosyncracies in each of the four editions shed light on early printing, and these are examined below.[13]

13. The blockbooks studied were as follows:
   Edition I: Munich, Bayerische Staatsbibliothek, Xyl. 37 and Universitätsbibliothek, Cim. 52 (Xyl. 10); Brussels, Bibliothèque Royale, B 1596 L.P.; Haarlem Stadsbibliotheek, Inv. II, No. 16; The Hague, Museum Meermanno-Westreenianum, 36A-1; New York Public Library, *KB + 1471.
   Edition II: The Hague, Museum Meermanno-Westreenianum, 36A-2; British Library, IB. 47000.
   Edition III: British Library, IB. 47001; Bibliothèque Nationale, Xyl. 44 and Xyl. 45; The Hague, Museum Meermanno-Westreenianum, 35A-4; Library of Congress, Inc. X. S 72; The Pierpont Morgan Library, Ch.L. f 1614; E 11 B.
   Edition IV: Haarlem Stadsbibliotheek, Inv. II, No. 14 and No. 15; The Henry E. Huntington Library, Xyl. H-C 14924.

Prohemiū cui?dam incipit noue cōpilaciōis
Cui? nome et titul? ē speculū huāne saluacōis
Expediens vider et vtile qp pmo i hñ phemio exponat
De qb? materijs et histoȓijs i qlibz capło dicatur
Et qui diligenter hoc prohemiū prstiduerit
De titali totū libru quasi p se intelligere poterit
In pmo capło igitur de casu luciferi et sociorū suoȓ
De formacione ade et eue et de dignitate ipsorū
In pdcis capło duob? patet nra recēpcio dāpnacio
Et in alijs cap'os sequētib? patet nostra reconciliato
Sed notādū qp i singuł capło mod? iste seruatur
Qd de nouo testamēto ponitur vna veritas recitatur
Postea de veteri testamēto trēs histoȓie ampliatur
Que ipsā noui testamēti veritatē figurasse ostēdbāt
In tercio capło incipit hūi nuciū nre saluacōnis
Vbi agitur de cōcepciōe et sātificacōe bte marie virginis
Cū eni deus humanā naturā assumere decreuisset
Congruū fuit ut matrē de qñ nasceretur prenutteret
Illud prefigurata fuit p regē astragē et eius filiā
Per fontē signatū in oȓto cōcluso et p stellā balaam
Astragi regi mōstratū ē qp filia sua regē tytū generaret
Joachi dictū ē qp ana vxoȓ sua gnaret qñ xpm portaret
Et hāc cōclusā in vtero matris spūs sōis sanctificaret
Per quā hō exul tāqp p stellā maris repatriaret
In qrto capło agitur de beate marie vginis natiuitate
Que figurata fuit p virgā egressā de radice yesse
Et p poȓtā clausā qñ dñs ezechiel premonstrauit
Et p tēplū salomois qd ipse dño suo edificauit
Marie enim oȓtum habuit de radice yesse
Quā dñs preordinauit poȓtā suā et templum esse
In qnto capło agit quo maria dño i tēplo fuit oblata
Et hec oblacio fuit olim trib? figuris pmonstrata
Per mēsā solis i tabulo qñ fuit oblata i tēplo soł malis
Sic maria fuit oblata in tēplo veri solis eternalis .
Itē p filiā yepte qñ fuit oblata dño licet indirecte
Sed maria fuit oblata dño rite et pfecte
p oȓtū suspetibilē de qñ regia ysarū patriā suā videbat
Ita maria oblata dño i tēplo sēp gtēplaciōe instebat
In sexto capło agit quo maria vio fuit desponsata
Et hec despōsacio fuit in tribus figuris prefigurata

V–6.

Edition I: In this edition the first five pages are devoted to a Prohemium or summary, in rhymed prose, of the contents of each chapter (fig. V–6). This ends with a statement about the usefulness of the Prohemium for poor preachers who cannot afford the entire book. Presumably the Prohemium was distributed separately (it is a single gathering of the book), but no examples of it have been preserved as an entity. At the end there are two lines about the Second Joy of the Virgin Mary, the Visitation from her cousin Elisabeth, the queen of Assyria, which, since it occurs in Chapter XLV of the manuscripts, does not appear anywhere in the blockbook editions (fig. V–7). Perhaps the manuscript from which the printer worked, which would have had all forty-five chapters, accidentally lacked these lines, and the scribe wrote the necessary insertion at the bottom of the page. The compositor may not have noticed the place which had been marked for insertion in the manuscript and simply added the lines to the last column. This error appears also in the second Latin edition but was rectified in the Dutch prose translations.

Another curious printer's error appears in the first Latin edition as compared to Latin manuscript Clm 146 in Munich. It is the addition in Chapter II, at the head of the third column, of a line which should be line 51 of Chapter VI: *Maria autem viro in desponsatione jungeretur.* The correct line 51, Chapter II, is: *In omni enim re semper debitus modus est tenendus*, which appears as line 52. How could such a mistake happen unless the printer were tipsy, or, starting work before dawn on a winter morning by the light of a single flickering candle, he accidentally opened his manuscript to the wrong page, and was too drunk with sleep to notice his error? He has also omitted the word *autem* and made arbitrary contractions of the Latin words. Furthermore, in order to make up for the extra line and still retain the standard twenty-five line column, he took the liberty of condensing two lines into one, using most of line 61 with the last two words of line 62, the rest of which is omitted, thereby breaking the rhyme scheme. In Chapter VI, where line 51 is missing, in order to fill the twenty-five-line column, the typesetter ended it with the line which should begin the next column. Then to bring that one up to proper length, he introduced an unrhymed line, which does not appear in the manuscript at all, after the first couplet. In fact the width of the column is too narrow for the type, which causes excessive contractions and lines broken over to the ends of succeeding lines. A "poor preacher" would have had trouble deciphering the text but might have relied more on the pictures to inspire his sermons.

The woodblock titles cut beneath the pictures are transposed in Chapter XXII c and d. The caption for the Spies Carrying the Grapes appears beneath the scene of the Killing of the Heir to the Vineyard, and *vice versa*. This seems to show that the letter-cutter was not the cutter of the pictures.

Item dolorem marie prefigurauerūt adam et eua
Qui centū āns luxerūt p morte abel filij sui seta
Item neomi q̃ orbata filijs noluit pulchra vocari
S; maria id est amara dixit se velle appellari
In xxvi° capl̄o agitur quo corpus dn̄i est sepultū
Et de dolore marie mr̄s domini iuxta sepulchrū
Et hoc p regem dauid olim p̄figurabatur
Qui feretrū abner cū luctu et dolore sequebatur
Et per ioseph qui in cisternā i deserto est missus
Et per ionam qui in mari a ceto est deglūtitus
In xxvij° cā° agit q̃o xp̄s de īferni lῑbo scōs libāuit
Et h̄ oli exitus filiou isr̄l de egipto p̄refigurauit
Item abrahā quē dn̄s liberauit de hur caldeorum
Et loth quē dn̄s liberauit de submercione sodomor
In xxviij° capl̄o agitur quomō xp̄us resurrexit
Et hoc patz p sampsonē qui portam gase destruxit
Et p ionā qui post triduū vm̄? exiuit de ventre cet
Et p lapidem repbatū q̃ fact? ē in capud anguli
In xxix° capl̄o agitur de districto mdicij extremo
Quod p̄figurauit pabolice quidam nobilis homo
Qui tradēs seruis suis bona abijt in regionē lōgiquā
Et accepto regno redijt potēs exiēs cōputacōnē reū
Itē p prudētes virgines que fatuis oleum negauerūt
Quia tūc nec deus nec scī oleū mie rῑpnatis p̄buerūt
Itē patet per mane thetel phares excitacionem
Quod signat numerū appensionem et diuisionem
Iudiciū enim istud tractabitur p numerū & appēsiōē
Et cōsūmabit p bonoz et maloz p̄petuā diuisione
Predictū p̄henuū huius libri de contentis compilaui
Et p̄ter pauper predicatores hoc apponere curaui
Qui se forte nequierīt totum librum sibi ꝑpare
Possūt ex ipso p̄henno li sūmē historias p̄dicare
Scd̄m signū gaudij eterni pt quiniū regis assueti fuisse
Quia nullū legim? tā longū & tā solēpne quiniū hr̄e

V–7.
Speculum humanæ salvationis blockbook, Edition I, Latin unmixed.
End of the Prohemium, Hellinga Type 1: 110 G.
The last two lines were added in error.

Hic ūgo maria desponsatur ioseph   Hic zara desponsatur thobie uuon

P prædtū cūplo audiui? qūo mala kuit oblata   Tū it se differēdā magnā habē vident
Cōseptē audiat? quo ā ōre viro kuit despōsata   Matrimoniū sūm et bonū ē approbatur
Quare dūs voluit matrē viro despōsari   Si tū tēp? itēdo mod? debite teneatur
De hijs possūtū octo radones assignari   Melior autē ē mūonio castitas vidualis
pūmo ne xpē fornicadoē gcæpisse putaret   Sz optiā ē ā sop excelliū mūdicia ūginalis
Et tāgā fornicatē i iudicio cōdempnaretur   Mūmonia debetur fructus tricesimus
Scūdo ut viro viri adiutolo ā mistelo frueret   Viduis sexagesimus ūginibus cētesimus
Et gātā pgētē nō solivaga ā vana putaret   Predosū phibetur esse auricalcum
Terdo ne dyabol? iarnacōetā xpi iuestigaet   Predosius argentū. sz priosissimū aurū
Et virginē sine viro cōcæpisse cōlidcāret   Lucifer autē mane gsurgēs videt ē lucidū?
ōcto ut maria testē sūū castitatis hrē pbaret   Luna āt ē lucidior. sz sol lucidissimus
Quia plē maito miūā alte i crederetur   Dulds videt ē letida ā delctado hūi? seculi
Quito ut series genealogie p viz tegētur   Dulddior bo ē ameitas padili sz dulcissiā celi
Et genealogia xpi a ioseph vio maie pducēt   Quāvis āt ā sop excellat ā optiā sit ūgitas
Mos scūptuē kuit genealogiā ducē nō ad ūgo   Tū nō valet nisi servet sū mētis itegritas
Sed tūūmō ad sponsos et mares   res   Qui eni ūgitatē servātē carne et nō mēte
Sexto ut mē oisū sūōtā ēstā approbaretū   Non hūtū aureolā virgineā in eternitate
Et a nullo spnendū ā i iusandū demōstraet   Que autē mētē ūgo ē ā sū violentē corrūpat
Septiō ut ūgitatē mūonia servaī licē docet   Non pditū aureolā sz dupliciā remuneratē
Si vtergā giumā ratū et placitū teneret   Habebitū āt aureolā p mētis ūginitate
Octauo ne giugati de sua salute despareutū   In sup pūmū p passione violēt sibi illata
Et ūgis tū se elcūs ā se despectos cogitaretū   Aureola āt pdita p mentis corrupdone
Dēm eni statū ā bsī servatū dūs apūbaē veie   Recupari potest i hac vita p cōtridonē
et ideo mē sua ūgo despōsata ā vidua eāt   bat   Que autē carne volūtarie violatur
Quauis hij tres statis sū ē pbarentur   Illius aureola nulla ūtridē recuparur
     Mathi ā luē pō ralis ā ōcto samāā distiē iūo   Thobie xiēo cal?

V–8.
Speculum humanæ salvationis blockbook, Edition I, Latin unmixed.
Chapter VI a and b. Hellinga Type 1: 110 G.

Hic vero maria desponsatur ioseph   Hic sara desponsatur thobie minori

V–9.

Speculum humanæ salvationis blockbook, Edition III, Latin mixed.
Text traced from Edition I and cut in wood.

Edition II: The second edition was produced by rubbing the same blocks, but with the printed text translated into Dutch prose. This edition contains a different oddity. The text is printed in the same characters as the preceding Latin edition, Hellinga Type 1 : 110 G, except for the two conjugate leaves, Chapter XXIII columns a and b (fig. V–11), and Chapter XXVIII columns c and d. This leaf is printed in a smaller, battered type known as Hellinga Type 2 : 103 G. Did Type 1 become unavailable, or tied up in another book, thus forcing the printer to use a worn-out face to complete the edition? Or did he accidentally start setting from a wrong case, and continue when, or if, he discovered his mistake, because the types were similar?

Edition III: This is a reprint of the Latin text of the first edition, but the type has been re-set. It is certainly the most baffling of all four. It contains twenty pages of text cut in wood from tracings of the printed pages of the earlier edition (fig. V–9). These are printed by rubbing on the back of the paper, with the text blocks coated by the same watery ink and rubbed at the same time as the illustration blocks. To us, the most logical explanation for the twenty xylographic text pages is that the making and rubbing of the illustration blocks was done first, and in another location than the printing of the text.[14]

14. Zedler, in *Von Coster zu Gutenberg* (Leipzig, 1921), p. 81, assumes that the text was
   printed first. If this had been the case there would have been no reason for the printer
   to use one side of the paper only, and thereby double the cost.

V–10.
Text of the nailing of Jesus to the Cross.
From the fourth line on, the translation
corresponds to the blockbook.
Spieghel onser behoudenisse manuscript, 1464.
Haarlem Stadsbibliotheek, Ms. II 17,
Chapter XXIII.

Cristus badt voor sijn crucers

N den voergaende capittel hebbē wi gheweert
hoe cristus syn cruys droech veruolghende
laet ons hoe hi badt voerde ghenē die
hem crucede Die ridderē leydē dat cruys op
ter aerdē en cristum ontcledde so reckedē si
hem daer op wt Die eerste hant nagheldē si
wiß enē nagel daer an En die ander hant
naghelden si daer na wt treckende mit linen
toten anderē gaet En doen si dien an ghesla-
ghē hadde toghē si die voeten wt mit linen
en mit enē nagel sloghē si beide die voetē an
Dese wtreckinghe seit die heer inden salm
ende werd daer van Si hebben werbort
mijn handē en voetē en hebbē al mijn gebē-
te ghetelt En doe xps dese wreethā ghele-
den hadde bewees hy hem sijn alre goedertie-
renste minne wāt hy sinē hemelscē vader
voer hem badt En gaf ons een exempel
onse vianden te minnē wanneer wi onse viā-
dē minnē en voer hē bidden so bewisē wi ons
te wesen sonen gods ende broederen cristi
Cristus heeft ons gheleert onse vianden te
minnē op dat wi moghē wesē sonē sijns va-
ders die indē hemel is Ten is niet groot
te minnē die ons wel doen en onse vriendē
Matheꝰ xxv lucas xxiij iohēs xiij

Dit sijn die vinders der constē

Mar tis alre meest te minnen die ons warde
liken veruolghen ende onse vianden die tot
derē cruytstē xpm opter aerden en daer na
buerden si hem leuendich op indē hoghen
Dit ghelt dat vā Xpo ghesproken is indē cen-
re was wilen eer in tubal tubalcaym broeder
voer ghefigureert Jubal en tubalcaym waren
lamech kinderen en warē vinders der constē
en musike wāneer tubalcaym mit dē hameren
die tonē gheluyt makede so vā tubal wt der
gheliich dat wi dat ghelet Xpi wt dat hamer-
flach des cruces so wāneer die crucers Jhm
ande cruce sloghē en seide vader ōgheefter hē
wāt si niet en wete was si doen was si en
weten niet dat ic dit si cruus v joe bi wart
dat die kide en die ioye dē joē gods tekenē
badde nimermeer en badde si dē joē gods den
constc der gloriē gecruist vā so groe swetichē
was dese melodie dat inder seluer vren drie
duisēt mēschē bekeert wordē treēmelie so sijn
die ioeē ghesegureert biden vinderen der smeden
kostē wāt si eerst vōdē dese maniere des cruces Ten was ghee recht dat een mensch mit
nagelen angheht soude wordē mer dat u mit
reie gehange wordē rhent si fforwē wel so prest
weert   Genesis in sijn vierde capitel

V–11.
Spieghel der menscheliker behoudenisse, Edition II, Dutch mixed.
Chapter XXIII a and b. Hellinga Type 2: 103 G.

Our hypothesis is that the blocks were rubbed onto the blank sheets, which were then delivered to the text printer (who may never have seen the blocks themselves). When the printing of the text was completed, they were returned to the original workshop for gathering, binding, and distribution. In the case of the second Latin edition twenty of the sheets may have been damaged or lost in transit between the text printer and the house where the books were put together. Instead of preparing a new set of woodcut sheets of illustrations to be sent to the text printer to complete the edition, the missing texts were cut in wood and both the blocks and the texts were printed together by rubbing, an economical solution in time and expense. Since no black type-printing ink was available there, both woodcuts and text blocks were rubbed in the watery yellow-brown ink which had been used for the pictures. There must have been a copy of the Latin first edition on hand, for the text was traced on a transparent sheet, or the actual printed sheet was made transparent with oil, so that it could be flopped and fastened to an uncut block for cutting the characters in reverse. The cutting corresponds exactly in size and spacing to the printed pages.

Edition IV: The printer must still have had the matrices for the missing type for the twenty pages, for he evidently recast the characters on a different body size, and used the font heavily, possibly for the schoolbooks of which so many fragments have been found. It appears, much worn, in the second Dutch edition. The smaller body of Type 1 (fig. V–12), which we examined in the Huntington Library in California (formerly the Pembroke copy),[15] measured 106 mm. instead of 110 mm. for twenty lines. Could it simply be exposure to the dry Southern California climate which caused the paper to shrink? Alas, such an airy explanation is contradicted by the fact that most pages of one of the copies, Haarlem Inv. II, No. 14, which we measured in 1979, required only 104 mm. for twenty lines. This edition is usually referred to as the "unmixed" Dutch issue, but in Haarlem, Inv. II, No. 15, there are actually four pages in 110 mm. type. Pages sixteen through nineteen are missing. We assume that pages twenty through twenty-three were taken from the first Dutch edition and bound into this copy, but evidently pages sixteen through nineteen were not available. The other Haarlem copy, Inv. II, No. 14, had also been taken apart some time in the past, and the pages were mounted on larger sheets.[16]

There is another oddity in this fourth and last edition of the *Speculum* blockbook. In Chapter XIX, column two, the biblical reference line "Genesis IX capitel" is printed upside-down in all known copies (fig. V–12). This might indicate that the characters within the line were attached to the text by some method too difficult to correct. The question will be dealt with further in the section on the printing, below.

15. *Spieghel der menscheliker behoudenisse.* Henry E. Huntington Library and Art Gallery, San Marino, California. Xyl. H-C 14924.
16. Haarlem Stadsbibliotheek, Inv. II, No. 14 and Inv. II, No. 15, deposited in the Frans Hals Museum, Haarlem.

Cum derisit iesum suum noe et alu et g dolebant.   philisin samipsone excecatos deriserunt.

[Gothic blackletter text, left column]

Ham bespottede noe sinen vader
sijn aelicht mit spuwe te bedecken die l
len eer woerlic genoech bedeckede mit eente
wolcpne der wolke Die iode die dataelicht cpi
mit spuwe besmettede sijn voer gefigureert bi
Lasgodie des gegote calfs Doe die kinre van
istahel he drechte god maken wouten Aaron ende
hur marien man dit weststonde hem ende doe d
weerdich weesende op hem so overliepe si hur
eii op he spuwede foe hebbe si hem mit spuwe
besmoerct Die verowerdichte hur want hare
afgodie weststont Die pharifeen donweerdich
tegon want hi haere meet benspede Die iode d
ie egon bsinatede bspottede die hebbe wilen eer
gefigureert geweest bi kam noes soen kam d
mogelic sine vad geeert soude hebbe d leestm
t oft dz he staltelic bespot eii bsmet te hebben
Also soude die iode egom eer bewesen hebbe mi
si wot geproeft he dere eii bespottede Eii al ist
dz noe deerlic vii sine eigh zoe bespot was na
ctans was veel deer barliker die bespotige
epi Noe was bespotbine sine tabernatel dae
et iemant e sach erist wot bespot i des biffops
huus d die ongadesige was oft die menichte
Noe was bespot stapende ende niet wetende

Gheleck d capitel

[Gothic blackletter text, right column]

Die philistine bespotte sampson

Epistel wort bespot wake eii nz horende Noe
die wit bespot alle vii ene soen Epistel was be
spot vii alle eii vate beleu met Noe hadde twe
sonen medelide mit he Epistel en hadde niemet
mit he lidede Die vorseide iode die egom bespot
sij vulen eer gefigureert bidelphilistine saf
son widde Die philistinen vige fampso eii staken
he vuit sij oge eii hi bespotede bespotte si he
Sato d sij alre groste sterchz so heeft hi die si
gur epi bi eere gelikenisse Salo die liet hem
des willichlic blis Eii also vuoude epistel willich
lic vade iode gebore eii bespot wot Ende and
vuerf doet sampso behagede so vutac hi hi he
seer vuerlic tege sij viide Eii also int ende d
vuerrelt ist wecomede vade viide epi vuaneer
hi mit mache eii mogetheit sal comen te horael
hoe danige vutate hi dan doen sel te te
side en mach ges sense noch tonge vute
So vulte de sijn viide alle pu liden dau dat
lichtso mogete eii woornich rechters te sien
So sel hi dan seggen gaet ghij vutaledoe i da t
ewiige vier Eii sine vrienden seggede Coemt
ende belit dat ewiige rijck mijns vaters

Iudeum cu capi tel

V–12.
Spieghel der menscheliker behoudenisse, Edition IV, Dutch unmixed.
Chapter XIX c and d. Note upside-down reference at the foot of column.
Henry E. Huntington Library and Art Gallery, San Marino, California, 104685.

Whether early interchangeable type characters in Europe were cast as flat metal plates or on more easily held shanks of about the 2.5 cm. height of modern types has long been a source of speculation. The method of holding a page of type together is also uncertain. There is a possibility that letters were composed and held in place in a metal tray or galley coated with beeswax and placed on the bed of the press. Heating the back of the galley would facilitate the removal or replacement of the characters.

A similar method appears to have been used in Korea from the eighth century on. Ancient Korean wood types, about 1.25 cm. high, survive They taper slightly from top to bottom, which would have permitted wax to push up between the letters when they were set in a wax-coated tray. The surfaces of the letters could then have been levelled by tapping with a block and mallet. This would have held them securely and compensated for differences in their heights. Such type forms still exist in the National Library in Seoul.[17] But as yet no evidence of the beeswax "lock-up" method of the fifteenth century has appeared in Europe. In Korea and China lines of type were known to be held together with thread, string, wire, or bamboo strips through holes in the bodies of the characters. In 1868 some metal type characters which had holes in the shanks were fished out of the Saône near Lyon. For a time it was believed this showed that the same tying-up method was used in Europe, but it was subsequently demonstrated that the holes were due to faulty casting.[18]

An ancient practice in the early printing houses was to wind twine around the sides of the whole page, as is done today for quick proofing and for storage. This method, if it was used for prototypography, would explain the sometimes irregular alignment of characters. It might also account for the upside-down line at the foot of a column in the second Dutch edition of the *Speculum*. The printer could have decided it was too much trouble to untie the form when, or if, the error was discovered. If the text was printed from cast metal plates, the line would have had to be sawed off, turned around, and remounted, no small task. However there is no evidence preserved of such plate casting.

We believe that individual characters on rectangular shanks, cast in adjustable molds, were used for the *Speculum*. As for the invention, the anonymous printer could have been experimenting concurrently with Gutenberg. History is full of independent discoveries in different

17. T. F. Carter, *The Invention of Printing in China and its Spread Westward*, 2nd edition, revised by L. C. Goodrich (New York, 1955); see also Pow-key Sohn, *Early Korean Typography* (The Korean Library Science Research Institute, Seoul, 1971), p. 6.
    We are indebted to Muir Dawson of Los Angeles for the information about the type forms in Seoul.
18. Sem L. Hartz, "Notes on the 'Types Lyonnais Primitifs,'" in Quaerendo, IV, 4 (1974), pp. 285 ff.

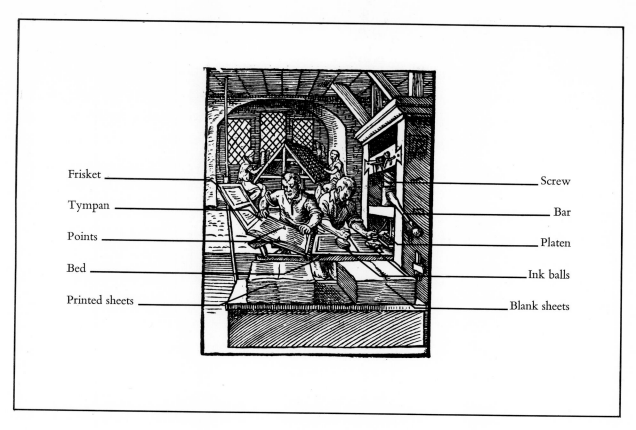

Frisket

Tympan

Points

Bed

Printed sheets

Screw

Bar

Platen

Ink balls

Blank sheets

V–13.
Wooodcut by Jost Amman, 1568, showing the use of ink balls, and the
tympan and frisket open.

places simultaneously, and movable type had reached its time.[19] The letters could have been
fixed in a frame by the simple pressure principle of opposing wedges. Straight strips of wood
and wider blocks placed between the wedges and the form would have filled out the frame.
We know such strips were used in printing the *Speculum*, between the text columns, because on
several pages they accidentally became inked and printed.

In the Jost Amman woodcut of an early press (fig. V–13) the major parts can be clearly seen.
At the right, the surface of the type, on the bed of the press, is being coated by means of ink
balls. In the center is the tympan, a frame stretched with paper or parchment. The printed sheet
was correctly stationed by being pierced through points in the tympan. This is hinged to the
press bed on one side and on the other to a frame called the frisket. Holes were to be cut into
the sheet stretched across it, to expose the printing areas and mask out the blank spaces. The
frisket was folded over the tympan and held the paper in place. Then both were folded onto the
type form and all were pushed halfway beneath the press for printing the first page, and all the
way for the conjugate page. One can see the bar at right which was pulled by hand and turned
the screw to press down the platen and print the page. Sometimes the frisket was miscut and
the characters used to fill out the type lines or column depths were also printed.

19. Curt F. Bühler, "A Note on Zedler's Coster Theory," in The Papers of the Bibliographical
    Society of America, XXXVII (1943), pp. 67–68.

The papers used for the *Speculum* blockbooks were small folio sheets about 30 x 44 cm., which barely permitted the rubbing of two adjacent woodcuts, 19.5 x 10.5 cm., across the top of the sheet. The same papers are found also in dated civic records of northern European cities, and they have been used as evidence for dating the printing of the various editions. They were generally of good quality and served well for printing the blocks by friction, though not well enough to prevent the water-based ink from coming through, and therefore the paper was printed on only one side.

Paper was made by dipping a rectangular wire screen mold, with its deckle frame, into a vat of rag pulp, shaking the mold to mesh the fibers, and depositing it on a pile with interleaved felts to absorb the water. Then the pile was squeezed in a screw press and the sheets were separated and dried.

Two molds with the same watermark design were used alternately by the workers, to keep the process continuous. They had a "laid" formation, with closely spaced wires (about six per centimeter) in the long direction and cross-wires, called "chain-lines," woven at wide intervals (about 4 cm. apart). The design of the watermark, shaped in wire, was sewn to this screen by loops of wire thread which often show as bright spots in the outline when a light is placed behind the sheet. The design can be traced (though this method is often unreliable), or it can be photographed at a one-to-one ratio. A better method is the beta-radiograph which uses an isotope plate with an X-ray film. This gives an accurate image of the variations in the thickness of the paper caused by the wires, chain-lines, watermarks, and sewing dots, but not of the printing on the paper. In 1970 Thomas Gravell developed a method which was quick, inexpensive and equally accurate.[20] It uses Dupont Dylux 503 photo-sensitive paper, and exposure through Diazo fluorescent lamps. Electron radiography is also being used in short exposure times to make very sharp images.[21] The precise images produced by these techniques can show the shape and position of the watermark and sewing dots which are caused by the repeated shaking of the mold. This may reveal the sequence in the production of the sheets and provide evidence for dating, when the mark is identical with one in a dated sheet.

We have no way of knowing how many copies of the first Latin edition, or any of the others, were produced. Considering its scarcity today, the number may have been small. Only nine complete copies of the first edition have survived, of which we were able to examine six (see note 13). Probably the house where the woodblocks for the proposed edition were made would have bought just enough paper for current use and sale. The printing of the text must have involved another expense. Only when the pages had been returned from the printer, gathered, glued back to back, and probably bound, could the books be sold and the investment made for more paper and printing another edition.

20. Thomas L. Gravell and George Miller, *A Catalogue of American Watermarks 1690–1835* (New York and London, 1979).
21. See *Gutenberg-Jahrbuch*, edited by Hans Joachim Koppitz (Mainz, 1981); Peter Amelung, "Die Abbildung von Wasserzeichen. Vorbemerkungen zur Beschreibung eines neuen Verfahrens," pp. 97, 98; Joachim Siener, "Ein neues Verfahren zur Abbildung von Wasserzeichen," pp. 99–102.

Edition I: Each edition of the *Speculum* had a different basic "running" paper in the illustrated part of the book, usually beginning with the first chapter. When that was exhausted similar sheets were purchased in small lots from a paper merchant, or sheets of the same size and quality which were left over from other books were used to complete the edition. The excellently preserved copy of this edition in the New York Public Library has five gatherings: one of three sheets, three of seven sheets, and one of eight sheets, or thirty-two sheets in all. It is collated a:6, b-d:14, e:16, the numbers referring to leaves. The portion with woodblocks, in gatherings two through four (b-d), is printed on a paper with an Anchor and Cross watermark. But the fourth gathering contains a single sheet with a Unicorn. The fifth gathering starts with an Anchor sheet, but the remaining seven inside sheets have Unicorns. Finally, the first gathering, containing the Prohemium, which was printed last (when the number of chapters was known), begins with a Unicorn, but the two interior sheets have Bull's Heads.

It would appear from the evidence of the watermarks that enough paper was bought with the Anchor and Cross device for the first twenty-one chapters, or three gatherings of seven sheets, or fourteen pages. After the rubbing was completed, only eight more chapters were added, instead of the usual twenty-four more found in the manuscripts. Perhaps the paper merchant had in stock just Unicorn watermarked sheets. There was enough to print the seven interior sheets of the last signature. The Anchor and Cross sheet was used as the first wrap-around sheet for the fifth gathering. The Unicorn paper was also used to print the first sheet of the Prohemium and another few sheets were used to make up a shortage in the second sheet of the fourth gathering. (In the Haarlem copy this sheet has the normal "running" paper Anchor mark.) But two more sheets were still needed to complete the Prohemium, and for this Bull's Head stock was found. The limited paper supplies at the time normally precluded having the same watermark throughout an edition, and extra quantities were purchased as needed.

V–14.
Watermarks in Edition I.
Bull's Head; Unicorn; Anchor and Cross.

Edition II: The next printing was the first Dutch edition, of which we examined two of the four surviving copies (p. 118, n. 13). It had as its "running" stock a different Unicorn; this time the beast is found vertically on the page. In the British Library copy, the text of the first gathering, a two-sheet, four-page Prohemium, is printed on the Unicorn stock, as are the next three gatherings of seven sheets each. One sheet of this copy, the fourth in the second gathering, is on paper with a large Gothic P. The fifth gathering begins with a Unicorn sheet, but then comes a mixture of three Bull's Heads and four more Gothic P's. One Bull's Head is different from the others. This is the sheet used for the printing of the text with Hellinga Type 2 : 103 G. It is in a battered condition, apparently because neither the previous Bull's Head stock nor the original type, Hellinga 1, were available.

Edition III: An analysis of the watermarks of the papers of the second Latin edition shows a great variety in both the pages combining woodcuts with type and those which are entirely xylographic (see note 13). The basic "running" stock has a large Y with a tail that curls into a heart. Briquet found it only in this edition of the *Speculum*, but it also exists in the account books for 1475 in the Gemeente Archief in Haarlem.[22] This mark was apparently made in honor of Yolande II when she became Duchess of Lorraine in 1473. Other marks are scattered with no apparent pattern through different copies. There is another Y with a trefoil tail, probably also intended to celebrate the Duchess. It is also found in the third edition of the *Apocalypse* block-book in Copenhagen.

The Anchor and Cross watermark makes a connection with the "Printer of the Text of the *Speculum*." The twin marks appear several times in his printing of the Pontanus *Singularia* (Hellinga Type 4 : 142 G). They are also found in a *Biblia pauperum* in the British Library and a third edition of the *Apocalypse* in the Musée Condé at Chantilly. The Y-trefoil mark appears in his Saliceto *Tractatus de salute corporis* (Hellinga Type 5 : 123 G), as well as the Pontanus.

Edition IV: We examined three copies of the second Dutch edition with the type re-set but very worn (see note 13). The "running" paper is a Bull's Head with a shield of Metz and a star above it. Several other marks make their appearance haphazardly. There is a Gothic monogram for Maria (mā) in a circle with a shield of Metz below. The same mark appears in Veldener's printing at Utrecht of the *Fasciculus temporum* dated 1480. There are also a Gothic P and two Hands of Blessing in the *Spieghel* edition.

Of the above watermarks which appear in Briquet's *Les Filigranes*, the dates given are earlier than those assigned by Allan Stevenson from his studies of the watermarks of the blockbook editions. Unfortunately it is not always possible to tell if Briquet's tracings are *identical* with our beta-radiographs. Precise dating by watermark is still questionable.

22. Allan H. Stevenson, "The Problem of the Blockbooks," VIII, pp. 6–12.

V–15.
Watermarks in Editions II, III, and IV.

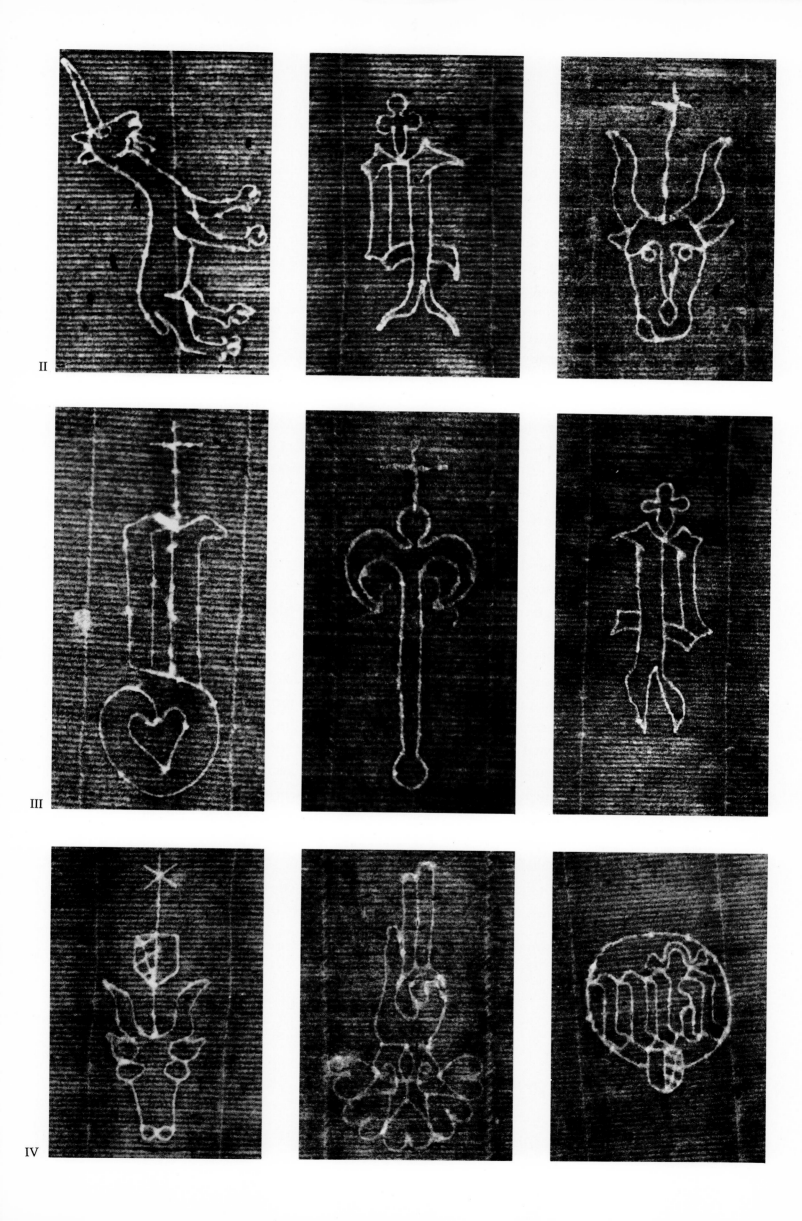

II

III

IV

The same illustration blocks are used throughout the four editions. Their shape and dimensions clearly indicate that they were intended to be part of the pages of a book, and each is captioned in Latin cut into the block. The drawing, cutting, and rubbing of the blocks could have been done much earlier than the printing of the text and could, in sequence, have been separated by periods of time.

As determined by differences in the vertical measurement of the blocks on conjugate pages, a separate double-image block was cut for each page. The smooth framing arch and round column bases of the first two pictures of each chapter were probably designed to indicate that they were to be printed on the versos, or left pages, and the broken arch and plane-based columns indicated the rectos, or last half of the chapter (see figs. V–11 and V–12).

The few banderoles which were cut away to the borders, Chapters XXV b (p. 190) and XXIX d (p. 199) must have been left blank to be inscribed by hand. Would this indicate that the blocks were designed for a proposed chiro-xylographic book? But the letter-cutter has incised the lettering in the earlier block of the Annunciation in blockbook Chapter VII a (p. 154). In the copy of the Latin first edition in the New York Public Library (formerly the Inglis copy), and the one in the National Library in Florence, the banderoles of the last woodcut, Chapter XXIX d, for "Mene, Mene, tekel upharsin," are not cleared out and print as solid bands.[23] This must have been corrected, after a few rubbings, by clearing away to the borders as is shown by other copies of this edition. It is most unlikely that a chiro-xylographic book was planned, for the labor of writing the extensive text, as well as lettering the banderoles, would have been excessive for an edition of even moderate quantity.

It is generally agreed that there were two artists or woodcutters at work on the series. The first designed the pictures for Chapters I through XXIV, the next manuscript chapter is omitted, and in Chapter XXV of the blockbooks, a new artist is seen, or possibly only a new cutter. The architectural framing of the scenes and the solidly centralized or diagonally balanced compositions are very like those of the earlier chapters, but the form of the trees is rounded and the bodies are stockier, with broader heads. The hatchings for shading are frequently diagonal rather than horizontal. Finally, the figures are often larger within the frame.

Drawings were made, and blocks cut, for more of the manuscript chapters (if not all forty-five) than were used in printing the twenty-nine chapters of the blockbooks. Jan Veldener sawed in half all of the woodcuts (58 for 116 pictures) which appear in the books and used them in his Culemborg edition of the *Speculum* in 1483, together with eleven more by the artist/ cutter of the later blocks (see our Chapter VII).

The first artist of the woodcuts either was a known Netherlandish master of the period or worked in his atelier. Mention has been made in Chapter I of the magnificent Book of Hours

23. C. Doudelet, *Le Speculum Humanæ Salvationis à la Bibliothèque Nationale de Florence* (Ghent and Antwerp, 1903), p. 39.

V–16.
The Hours of Catherine of Cleves.
The Pierpont Morgan Library, New York, M. 945, f. 78, compared with
Speculum humanæ salvationis blockbook, Chapter XIX c (detail).

of Catherine of Cleves, which most art historians agree was completed about 1440.[24] The
manuscript contains several miniatures which in their style and subjects show that the illuminator was aware of the woodcuts of the *Biblia pauperum* and the *Speculum humanæ salvationis* or
of lost models which may have been used for both the blockbooks and the miniatures in a
closely knit community of book producers. There is a version of the goat nibbling the grapes
in the *Speculum* woodcut of the Shame of Noah (Chapter XIX c) which in size and drawing is
very close to the illumination in the Cleves manuscript.

24. For discussions of the Book of Hours of Catherine of Cleves, see the following:
   L. M. J. Delaissé, *A Century of Dutch Manuscript Illumination* (Berkeley and Los
   Angeles, 1968); John Plummer, *The Hours of Catherine of Cleves* (New York, 1966);
   Friedrich Gorissen, *Das Stundenbuch der Katharina von Kleve* (Berlin, 1973).

The possibility must also be accepted that the artist of the blockbooks was influenced by the Cleves miniatures rather than the reverse. Since the workshop where the Hours was made is known to have continued production through the middle of the century, it may be that an artist from the circle of the Cleves Master was actually involved in designing the woodblocks of the *Speculum*.[25] We may hope that further explorations by art historians and bibliographers will reveal more about the connection between the contemporary manuscript illumination and the *Speculum* blockbooks.

A relationship has long been assumed between the Altarpiece of the Blessed Sacrament painted by Dirck Bouts (c.1415–1475) for the church of St. Pierre in Louvain and the blocks for Chapter XVI of the *Speculum*.[26] In 1464 a contract was executed by which the Confraternity of the Holy Sacrament of Louvain, a group of wealthy burghers organized for pious and charitable purposes, commissioned Dirck Bouts to paint a triptych for the larger of their two chapels in the choir of St. Pierre. It was to be dedicated to the Eucharistic rite, which had enormous popularity at the time, and the Brothers chose two theologians to inform Bouts on the subjects and arrangement of the panels. They based the iconography of the triptych on the *Speculum humanæ salvationis*, which had been widely accepted as an authoritative work for more than a century.

Bouts' triptych depends on the pictures of the blockbook not only in the selection of the subjects but also in the general compositions of the five scenes. They have been enriched by many details. Portraits of the theologians and possibly the artist himself are included in the central panel of the Last Supper.[27] In the Eating of the Paschal Lamb, on the table are the type of glasses made in the Meuse and Brabant regions.[28] The painting of the Gathering of the Manna draws its concept of the Heavenly Bread from the biblical description: the manna is "small as the hoar frost on the ground" (Exodus XVI:14). The pitchers used for gathering it are of the same shape as those in the *Speculum* blocks and are probably typical of that period and location. If the Bouts triptych did depend on the blocks (and we know of no manuscript miniatures with these same compositions), the dating of the first edition at 1468 on the evidence of watermarks is thus brought into question, for the blockbook must have existed before the 1464 contract.

25. Robert G. Calkins, "Parallels between Incunabula and Manuscripts from the Circle of the Master of Catherine of Cleves," in Oud Holland, XCII (1978), p. 147 and p. 160, fn. 33. See also James Marrow, "A Book of Hours from the Circle of the Master of the Berlin Passion: Notes on the Relationship between Fifteenth-Century Manuscript Illumination and Printmaking in the Rhenish Lowlands," in Art Bulletin, LX, 4 (1978), pp. 591–616.
26. Doudelet, *op.cit.*, p. 11.
27. Shirley Neilsen Blum, *Early Netherlandish Triptychs*. (Berkeley and Los Angeles, 1969), p. 66.
28. *Flanders in the Fifteenth Century: Art and Civilization*, Catalogue of Exhibition, edited by E. P. Richardson (Detroit, 1960), p. 107.

The triptych of the Blessed Sacrament is thought to be the first panel painting of this subject to be done in the Netherlands and its focus on the act of Communion, in the central panel, was unusual. Bouts appears to have worked with Roger van der Weyden on the angels for the vault of one of the chapels of the church of St. Pierre[29] before undertaking the commission for the altarpiece. Both Bouts and Van der Weyden are known to have had strong relationships to the Groenendael community of the *Devotio moderna*.

We have discussed in Chapter IV the production of blockbooks, specifically the *Spirituale pomerium* and the *Exercitium super Pater Noster*, at Groenendael, or possibly at Sept-Fontaines, or both. We have outlined the great importance of the many houses associated with the *Devotio moderna* in fifteenth-century book production in the Low Countries. We know that they contained woodcutters, illuminators, scribes, miniaturists, and binders. They were also, we assume, in somewhat the same position as a publishing house, i.e., they chose the texts, selected the artists or ateliers for the illustrations, commissioned the text printing, and distributed the editions. The production of two of the editions in Dutch, and the use for which they were intended, strongly suggests that the blockbook editions of the *Speculum* can be linked with the houses of the *Devotio moderna*. It also seems logical that the woodblocks remained in the possession of one of the communities (probably Groenendael or Brussels) where Veldener could have seen them when he set up his press nearby in Louvain, in 1475, or before he left for Utrecht in 1478 (see our Chapter VII).

While the name of the printer, the place, and the dates of the printing of the *Speculum* blocks or text cannot, as yet, be determined, the continued research of art historians, bibliographers, and typographers may combine to solve these mysteries.

29. G. Hulin de Loo, "Sur la biographie de Dieric Bouts avant 1457," in
    Mélanges d'histoire offerts à Henri Pirenne (Brussels, 1926), pp. 257–62.

Lastsis madnicat palstha aut disiaplis sins | manna datur filiis isrl in deserto

Sudei mandincatit agin palstale | Melchisedeth optulit abste panez vinu

V–17.
a. The Last Supper.
b. The Gathering of the Manna.
c. The Jews Ate the Paschal Lamb.
d. Melchizedek Offered Abraham Bread and Wine.
Speculum Humanæ salvationis blockbook, Chapter XVI.

V–18.
The Last Supper.
The Gathering of the Manna.
The Jews Ate the Paschal Lamb.
Melchizedek Offered Abraham Bread and Wine.
Retable of St. Pierre at Louvain.

VI–1.
Typical page from *Speculum* blockbook Edition IV.
Henry E. Huntington Library, San Marino, California, Xyl. H–C, 14924.

VI

Speculum Woodcuts and Miniatures

At the head of each page of the *Speculum* is a woodcut containing two scenes with captions below, in Latin, often heavily contracted. In the following descriptions these have been spelled out and a translation given. The biblical or other source reference for the text appears usually at the foot of the column and is occasionally erroneous or sometimes missing altogether. In a few cases a reference is made to the *Legenda aurea*, the *Historia scholastica*, or some other medieval text. Parenthetical references are to the Douay-Rheims version of the Vulgate.

The text of the *Speculum* is not always concerned with the explanation of the illustration but is often devoted to the significance of the prefiguration. Certain events are thus distorted at the expense of the biblical or legendary accounts to serve the typological concept.

From Chapters I through XXIV the subjects follow the manuscripts of the *Speculum*. After this, only manuscript chapters XXVI, XXVII, XXXI, XXXII, and XL are included in the twenty-nine chapter blockbook editions.

carus luaferi   dis creauit homies ad ymagine t similitudine sua

CHAPTER I

a. *Casus Luciferi*
   (The Fall of Lucifer)

God, shown throughout this chapter as Jesus Christ, is surrounded by the blessed angels in Heaven. Below is the
scene of the Fall of Lucifer and his followers into the gaping
mouth of the Leviathan, of the book of Job XLI, which is
commonly identified with the inferno. The fallen angels
are represented with wings, horns and cocks' feet. The Fall
of the Angels is first found in Judeo-Greek literature of
Alexandria in the two centuries before Christ.

Revelation XII, 7–9
(Apocalypse)

b. *Deus creavit hominem ad ymaginem et similitudinem suam*
   (God created man in his own image and likeness)

In the medieval concept, Adam and Eve are at the origin of
Redemption, for without their sin no redemption would
be necessary. In the typological concept Adam prefigures
Christ, and Eve, Mary. In addition, Eve emerging from
the side of Adam was the symbol of the Church coming
from the body of Christ.

Genesis II, 22

c. *De omni ligno paradisi commedetis*
   (Of all the trees of paradise you may freely eat)

The scene shows the marriage of Adam and Eve, which is described in the text (Eve was given to Adam in marriage by the command of God), as found in Genesis II, 22–25. The verse of the caption referring to the trees is irrelevant to the text and comes from Genesis II, 16. In many manuscripts the caption is *copulatio ade et eve*, to relate to the marriage sacrament.

d. *Nequaquam moriemini sed eritis simultudine domini scientes bonum et malum*
   (Surely you will not die but you will be like God knowing good and evil)

Satan is portrayed here in the form of a basilisk to tempt Eve. This legendary winged creature had a human head and eagle feet, and was believed to poison fruit trees with its breath. The caption records Satan's words to Eve.

Genesis III, 4–5

mulier deapit vmī ut fecū comederet   angels expulit eos de padilo gladio igiiito

CHAPTER II

a. *Mulier decepit virum ut secum commederet*
   (The woman beguiled the man to eat with her)

The serpent has become a snake with a dog's head and Eve
has given Adam the fruit, which he is eating. Then the eyes
of both of them were opened and they knew they were
naked. According to the Bible story they sewed some fig
leaves into aprons. Eve is shown taking an apple from the
serpent's mouth.

Genesis III, 6–7

b. *Angelus expulit eos de paradiso gladio ignito*
   (The angel expelled them from paradise with a burning
   sword)

The Garden of Eden is enclosed with a heavy wall and a
portal. The Genesis story does not include the angel but he
is mentioned in the text of the *Speculum*, "holding the
sword of justice." The Bible states that God drove out the
man and woman and placed cherubims at the east of the
Garden and a flaming sword which turned.

Genesis III, 24

c. *Hic Adam operatur terram in sudore vultus sui*
   (Here Adam tills the soil in the sweat of his brow)

The concept of Eve spinning is drawn from a medieval
tradition of unknown origin, but the Bible story includes
the Lord God driving Adam out of Paradise to till the earth
from which he was taken. The *Speculum* text tells both of
Adam tilling and Eve spinning.

Genesis III, 23

d. *Archa Noe*
   (The Ark of Noah)

The Deluge was considered to be God's punishment for
man's wickedness, and in medieval historiography it
marked the end of the First Age. The ark is shown without
rudder or oars, in order for it to float freely. It is of typically
fifteenth-century Dutch construction, but the superstruc-
ture with its vaulted nave suggesting a reference to the ark
as the Church was a well-known equation in the Middle
Ages.

Genesis VIII, 10–11

CHAPTER III

a. *Hic annunciatur ortus Marie*
  (Here is announced the birth of Mary)

The annunciation by the angel who appeared to Joachim
to foretell the birth of the Virgin Mary does not appear in
the Gospels, but it is treated here as a New Testament event,
prefigured in the following three typologies. The story is
drawn from the *Legenda aurea*.

b. *Rex Astyages mirabile vidit sompnium*
  (King Astyages had a marvelous dream)

The King dreamt that from the breast of his daughter a
verdant and fruitful vine grew, signifying that her off-
spring, King Cyrus, would deliver the children of Israel
from captivity. This prefigured that the daughter of
Joachim and Anna would bear the child, Jesus, who would
redeem mankind. The story is from the *Historia scholastica*
of Petrus Comestor.

ortus conclusus fons signatus   Balaam pronunciavit ortum marie i stella

c. *Ortus conclusus fons signatus*
(The enclosed garden and sealed fountain)

Drawn from the Song of Songs, these symbols prefigure the virginity of Mary. The Middle Ages saw the Bride, in the biblical verses, as the Virgin Mary. St. Bernard applied all of its metaphors to her; she was the Burning Bush, the Ark of the Covenant, the Fleece of Gideon.

Song of Solomon IV, 12, 15
(Canticle of Canticles)

d. *Balaam pronunciavit ortum marie in stella*
(Balaam prophesied the birth of Mary in a star)

Balaam beat his ass with a whip of three cords when it turned away from the path on seeing the angel with a sword. As the text of the *Speculum* and the inscription state, Balaam saw a star and then prophesied the birth of the Virgin Mary. The prefiguration is that of Balaam's prophecy but the artist has omitted the star from the picture.

Numbers XXII, 22–34

natiuitas glofe virgis mane / egredietur virga de radice yeffe

CHAPTER IV

a. *Nativitas gloriose virginis Marie*
   (The glorious birth of the Virgin Mary)

The scene shows Joachim presenting the nude infant Mary, with a nimbus, to his wife Anna, in a fifteenth-century Netherlandish bedroom. He is dressed exactly as in Chapter III. This scene is not described in the Gospels but is drawn from the *Legenda aurea*.

b. *Egredietur virga de radice Yesse*
   (The branch rises out of the root of Jesse)

The symbolic interpretation of the Tree of Jesse as the lineage of kings goes back to the time of St. Jerome, when the verse in Isaiah was combined with the genealogy of Jesus. Toward the end of the Middle Ages it became the Tree of Mary, with the Virgin shown at the top holding the infant in her arms. The seven plants on the ground may refer to the description in the text of the *Speculum* of seven "good medicines" or Gifts of the Holy Spirit embodied in Jesus, the flower of Jesse's tree.

Isaiah XI, 1; Matthew I, 1–16
(Isaias)

c. *Clausa porta significat beatam virginem mariam*
   (The closed door signifies the blessed Virgin Mary)

Ezekiel saw this gate in a dream and only the Lord had entered through it. It prefigures the virginity of Mary.

> Ezekiel XLIV, 1–2
> (Ezechiel)

d. *Templum Salomonis significat beatam mariam*
   (The temple of Solomon signifies the blessed Mary)

The three towers surmounting the temples symbolize the triple crown of Mary, that of the virgins, of the martyrs, and of the preachers and doctors.

> I Kings VI
> (III Kings)

Maria est dño ín templo   Menfa aurea ín fabulo oblā ē ín tēplo folis

CHAPTER V

a. *Maria (oblata) est domino in templo*
   (Mary is offered to the Lord in the Temple)

The child Mary is standing on the altar with Anna at her
right. She gives one hand to her mother and the other to
the priest of the Law. Flemish painters of the period often
showed this event as the little Mary climbing the steps of
the temple. The story is drawn from the *Legenda aurea*.

b. *Mensa aurea in sabulo oblata est in templo solis*
   (The golden table in the sand is offered in the temple of
   the sun)

Here, composed like the preceding woodcut, is an altar in
an apse on which stands the statue of the sun god, Apollo.
At the right is the priest, at the left the two fishermen who
offer the golden table hauled up with their fishnet. This
episode originated in a legend of the seven sages of Greece,
which was read in the Middle Ages in Valerius Maximus
and retold by Plutarch.

c. *Jepte obtulit filiam suam domino*
   (Jephtha sacrificed his daughter to God)

Jephtha had made a vow to the Lord that if the Ammonites
were delivered into his hands, he would offer as a sacrifice
the first person who came out of his house to greet him on
his return from the battle. It was his virgin daughter who
did so, and this prefigures the dedication of Mary's virginity to God.

Judges XI, 30–39

d. *Regina persarum contemplabatur patriam suam in orto
   suspensili*
   (The Queen of Persia contemplated her land in a hanging garden)

The inscription has erroneously assigned to Semiramis the
country of Persia instead of Babylon, and she is shown not
in the hanging gardens, but in a tower in which the queen
was said to have been shut up. The subject prefigures Mary,
who spent her time in the temple contemplating the realm
of the divine. The scene is from the *Historia scholastica*.

CHAPTER VI

a. *Hic virgo maria desponsatur joseph*
   (Here the Virgin Mary is married to Joseph)

In the same apse as in Chapter V a and b, the marriage of
Mary and Joseph is shown. The Bishop in the center, wearing a mitre, holds their right hands. The other scenes of
marriage in the *Speculum* are identically composed.

Matthew I, 18

b. *Hic zara desponsatur thobie juniori*
   (Here Sara is married to young Tobit)

Ragyel, the father of Sara, takes her hand and gives it to
Tobit with the words, "I give her to you, as says the Law
and the decision written in the book of Moses . . ." The
angel leans over Tobit to protect him, for the seven previous husbands of Sara died before the wedding night. As
a result, Sara had remained chaste, as did the Virgin Mary.
The scene is from the Apocrypha.

Tobit VII, 13
(Tobias)

c. *Hec turris dicta baris significat mariam*
   (The tower called Baris signifies Mary)

On top of the tower are two soldiers on guard, one wearing armor, the other blowing a horn. The tower of Baris prefigured, by its impenetrable character, the virginity of Mary. The legend comes from the *Historia scholastica*.

d. *Hec turris david de qua pendebant mille clypei*
   (The tower of David from which hung a thousand shields)

Only ten shields suffice to represent the thousand, described in the text of the *Speculum* as references to the thousand protecting virtues of the Virgin. The verse from the Song of Songs was accepted in the Middle Ages as a description of the virginity of Mary, "Thy neck is like the tower of David builded for an armory, whereon there hang a thousand bucklers, all shields of mighty men."

Song of Solomon IV, 4
(Canticle of Canticles)

CHAPTER VII

a. *Hic annunciatur ihesus per angelum virgini marie*
(The annunciation of Jesus by the angel to the Virgin Mary)

The scene is portrayed in an interior as was commonplace in Flemish art of the fifteenth century. The banderoles read "Ave gracia plena dominus tecum" (Hail, full of grace, God is with you), and "Ecce ancilla domini fiat mihi secundum verbum tuum" (Behold the handmaiden of the Lord: be it unto me according to thy word).

Luke I, 28, 38

b. *Dominus apparauit moysi in rubo ardenti*
(God appeared to Moses in the burning bush)

As Moses tends the sheep of Jethro, God the Father appears amidst the flames of a bush which is not being consumed by the fire. The Bible states that God called out to Moses and told him to remove his shoes for he was on holy ground. The unconsumed bush prefigures Mary conceiving without losing her virginity, and also God descending to earth to deliver humanity from damnation. God, as elsewhere in the *Speculum*, appears in the form of Christ.

Exodus III, 2–5

c. *Vellus gedeonis repletus est terra sicca manente*
   (Gideon's fleece is soaked while the earth remains dry)

Gideon stretched out the fleece on the ground, stating that
if the dew fell on it and the soil around it remained dry,
then he would know that Israel would be delivered by his
hand, as God had promised. The drops of dew descend
from the clouds like giant hail. The scene conforms to the
iconography of Gideon established in the eleventh century,
and the fleece was a frequent prefiguration of the virginity
of Mary.

Judges VI, 37

d. *Rebecca nuncio abrahe potum tribuebat*
   (Rebecca gave drink to the servant of Abraham)

Abraham's servant, Eleazer, was sent to find a wife for
Isaac and asked the Lord to let this woman be the one who
would bring drink for him and his camels. This was
Rebecca who by her virginity and compassion prefigured
Mary.

Genesis XXIV, 14–19

CHAPTER VIII

a. *Nativitas domini nostri ihesu christi*
(The birth of our Lord Jesus Christ)

Christ, surrounded by a radiance, lies on the ground flanked by the kneeling figures of Mary and Joseph. At the left, the ox and ass observe from their stall.

Luke II, 7

b. *Pincerna pharaonis vidit in sompnis vineam*
(Pharaoh's cup bearer saw a vine in a dream)

Pharaoh's cup bearer had offended him and was put in the stocks. He dreamed that a vine was before him, with three branches which budded, blossomed, and bore grapes. He squeezed the grapes into Pharaoh's cup. Joseph interpreted the dream for him, wherein the cup bearer symbolized humanity captive in sin, the vine symbolized Christ who would redeem mankind, and the grape juice prefigured the blood of Christ.

Genesis XL, 9–11

c. *Virga aaron floruit contra naturam virtute divina*
(The rod of Aaron flowered against nature through
divine will)

Aaron's miraculous rod stands on a metal base on the altar
and bears leaves. In illuminated manuscripts of the *Speculum* the feet were shown as roots. The miraculous flowering
of the rod is another prefiguration of the Virgin Birth.

Numbers XVII, 10

d. *Sibilla vidit virginem cum puero*
(The Sibyl saw a Virgin with a child)

In this scene, drawn from the *Chronicon pontificum* of Martinus Polonus, the Sibyl shows to the emperor the Virgin
appearing in a cloud, telling him that at that moment
another king, more powerful than he, was born of a virgin.
Both the Sibyl and Augustus are kneeling in awe. This
event is often shown by early Flemish painters. In Roger
van der Weyden's altarpiece of the Nativity, now in Berlin, the Sibyl's annunciation to the Holy Roman Emperor
appears in the left wing of the triptych.

CHAPTER IX

a. *Tres magi adorant puerum cum muneribus*
   (The three Magi, with gifts, adore the child)

In front of the same shed as in Chapter VIII-a, Mary is
seated on a large bed. Following a tradition which goes
back to the twelfth century, the Magi are Kings of three
ages, one young, one middle-aged, and one old. Neither
the Book of Matthew nor the text of the *Speculum* refer to
the wise men as kings, but this detail is drawn from Psalm
LXXII which tells of the kings bringing tributes and gifts
to the Lord. The star which led the Magi to the Child
shines in the sky above the shed.

Matthew II, 11

b. *Tres magi viderunt novam stellam in oriente*
   (The three Magi saw the new star in the East)

This event, which preceded the adoration with gifts, is the
meeting of the three Magi, rarely shown in the art of the
fifteenth century. The oldest wise man, wearing a hat, is
riding a camel without a hump; the middle one, on horseback, wears a turban with a crown; and the youngest, also
mounted, wears a crown.

Matthew II, 10

c. *Tres fortes attulerunt david regi aquam de cisterna*
   (Three knights brought water from the cistern to King
   David)

Three brave warriors broke through the army of the
Philistines to draw water for King David from the well at
the gate of Bethlehem. They prefigure the three Magi with
their gifts. This scene was much popularized by the *Speculum* and appeared in other works of art.

> II Samuel XXIII, 15–16
> (II Kings)

d. *Thronus salomonis*
   (The throne of Solomon)

The author has drawn the episode from the Bible and
augmented it from the *Historia scholastica*. The Bible verses
describe the visit to King Solomon of the Queen of Sheba,
who brought gifts from afar, prefiguring the gifts brought
to Christ by the Magi. In the *Speculum* blockbook the artist
has entirely omitted the Queen.

> I Kings X, 18–20
> (III Kings)

CHAPTER X

a. *Maria obtulit filium suum in templo*
   (Mary presented her son in the temple)

The child Jesus is standing on the altar, held on one side by
the priest Simeon and on the other by the Virgin Mary.
Simeon wears a bishop's mitre. Behind Mary stands her
mother and a follower with the sacrificial offering.

Luke II, 22

b. *Archa testamenti significat mariam*
   (The Ark of the Covenant signifies Mary)

The Ark, in the form of a Gothic reliquary, is on an altar
supported by ten columns, an allusion to the Ten Com-
mandments. Twelve columns are dictated in the Scriptures,
to refer to the twelve tribes of Israel. Jesus embodies the
Law and is present in the Ark, which prefigures Mary containing the spirit of God.

Exodus XXV, 10–28

c. *Candelabrum templi Salomonis*
   (The candelabrum of the temple of Solomon)

The instructions for the making of the candelabrum, which is to be lighted in the temple for the glory of God, are very exact. The candelabrum is honored, in part, because candles are carried in the Feast of the Purification. According to the text of the *Speculum*, the seven branches signify the seven works of mercy within Mary.

Exodus XXV, 31–37

d. *Puer Samuel oblatus est domino*
   (The boy Samuel is dedicated to the Lord)

Hannah, who had been barren, vowed that if the Lord answered her prayers to bear a man child, she would consecrate him to the Lord for all his life. The presentation of Samuel is another prefiguration of the presentation of Jesus in the temple. A woman behind Hannah brings the calf to be sacrificed on this occasion.

I Samuel I, 24–28
(I Kings)

Oīa ydola coruerūt ītrāt ꝫ ihū in egiptū   Egiptī fecerūt ymaginē ūgīs aī puero

CHAPTER XI

a. *Omnia ydola corruerunt intrante ihesu in egiptum*
   (All the idols fell on the entry of Jesus into Egypt)

This legend of the idols that fell from their columns as the
Holy Family passed, on the flight into Egypt, is drawn
from Petrus Comestor and numerous other apocryphal
writings. It is also based upon a prophetic verse in Isaiah
which states that the Lord will ascend on a swift cloud into
Egypt, and that the idols of the Egyptians will be moved
at his presence.

Isaiah XIX, 1; Matthew II, 13–15
(Isaias)

b. *Egiptii fecerunt ymaginem virginis cum puero*
   (The Egyptians made an image of the Virgin with a
   Child)

In the familiar apse of other chapters, the Egyptians are
kneeling, their hands folded in prayer, in front of a statue
of the Virgin and Child seated on a throne on the altar.
Mary wears a crown and a nimbus. The event comes from
the *Historia scholastica* of Petrus Comestor.

c. *Moyses projecit coronam Pharaonis et fregit*
    (Moses threw down the crown of Pharaoh and broke it)

This legend is drawn from Comestor who gives its source
as the *Antiquitate judaica* of Josephus. At the feet of Pharaoh
is the shattered crown which the child Moses had thrown
down. A soldier prepares to slay him, but a servant holds
out hot coals, and Moses proves his favor with God by
putting one in his mouth without flinching or being
burned. After destroying the symbol of Egypt's sover-
eignty, the crown, Moses was saved by divine intervention
so that he could eventually lead the Israelites out of captivity. This parallels the destruction of the Egyptian idols
by the passage of the child Jesus, who was protected so that
he could live to redeem mankind.

d. *Nabugodnasur vidit statuam grandem in sompno*
    (Nebuchadnezzar saw a large statue in a dream)

The king is in a bed, wearing his crown, and dreams of a
column on which a young nude soldier stands with his
lance and shield. The statue was subsequently destroyed by
being hit with a stone which no hand had touched, prefiguring Jesus' destruction of the idols by his presence
alone. The untouched stone refers to the virginity of Mary.

Daniel II, 31–34

CHAPTER XII

a. *Jhesus baptisatus est a johanne in jordano*
   (Jesus is baptised by John in the Jordan)

Jesus is up to his knees in the river with his hands clasped in
prayer. The Holy Ghost in the form of a dove flies above
him. At his right kneels the angel holding the baptismal
robe, and at his left St. John lifts a goblet from which he
pours the water on the head of Jesus.

Matthew III, 13–17

b. *Mare eneum in quo ingressuri in templum lavabantur*
   (The brass vessel in which the entrants to the temple are
   washed)

God commanded Moses to make a laver of brass with feet,
to place between the Tabernacle and the altar. The description of the font, with its twelve oxen supporting it, is
explicit in the Bible. Symbolically, as the water is composed of many elements, the baptism can be said in many
tongues. The oxen represent the twelve tribes of Israel and
the apostles, but only seven are shown here.

II Chronicles IV, 2–5
(II Paralipomenon)

c. *Naaman leprosus (lavit) septies et nudatus (mundatus) est*
(The leper Naaman washed seven times and was cleansed)

As in the woodcut of Christ being baptised , Naaman is in the Jordan up to his knees. His escort waits on the bank where his cloak lies. His healing in the Jordan prefigures the purification by baptism of Christ.

II Kings V, 14
(IV Kings)

d. *Jordanus siccatus est in transitu filiorum dei*
(The Jordan is dry for the crossing of the children of God)

The priests carrying the Ark of the Covenant cross over the miraculously dry Jordan. The twelve stones on the dry bed signify the twelve tribes of Israel and prefigure the twelve apostles. The Ark in the middle of the Jordan prefigures Jesus baptised in that river.

Joshua III, 13–17; IV, 9
(Josue)

Cristus tripliater fuit teptatus a dyabolo / Daniel deftruxit bel eo mffrat dzacoñe

CHAPTER XIII

a. *Cristus tripliciter fuit temptatus a dyabolo*
   (Christ was tempted by the Devil in three ways)

The Devil, in the form of a monster with bird's feet, challenges Jesus to transform the stones into bread after his forty-day fast. In the background are the temple tower and the mountain where the other two temptations took place.

Matthew IV, 1–10

b. *Daniel destruxit bel, et interfecit draconem*
   (Daniel destroyed Bel and killed the dragon)

The Babylonian idol, Bel, had to be offered forty ewes, twelve measures of flour, and six measures of wine daily. Daniel mixed a concoction and formed it into balls which he threw into the mouth of the dragon. The creature swallowed them and burst. Nebuchadnezzar, in the background left, was a worshipper of Bel, who is shown as a statuette on the altar, with the offerings at his feet and one in his left hand. He is blowing on a horn. Originally Bel was biting a bone, but the tale was interpreted in many forms. Daniel also shattered the idol, and in killing two gluttons he prefigured Christ conquering the temptation of food. The story is taken from the Apocrypha.

Bel and the Dragon, 22–26
Daniel XIV, 21–27

c. *David superavit goliam philisteum*
   (David overcame the Philistine Goliath)

The giant Goliath is dressed in armor and helmet but the fatal stone is buried in his brow. In the background is David with his sling, wearing a crown although he was not yet the king. The scene prefigures Christ conquering the temptation of pride, for Goliath was proud of his strength and stature.

I Samuel, XVII, 48–50
(I Kings)

d. *David interfecit ursum et leonem*
   (David killed a bear and a lion)

David is shown with a raised club in the act of killing the bear and lion who took a ram from the midst of his flock. As the animals acted out of greed, this event prefigures Christ's triumph over avarice.

I Samuel XVII, 34–36
(I Kings)

CHAPTER XIV

a. *Magdalena penituit in domo symonis*
   (Magdalen repented in Simon's house)

Mary Magdalen washes the feet of Jesus with her tears of penitence and dries them with her hair. Jesus and Simon are seated at the table and an observer stands at the left to balance the composition. The three prefigurations in this chapter all demonstrate penitence and forgiveness.

Luke VII, 37–38

b. *Manasses egit penitentiam in captivitate*
   (Manasseh did penance in captivity)

This king of Judea, shown here in stocks, had built altars to false gods, and the Lord sent the army of the king of Assyria to capture him. They bound him and took him to Babylon as a prisoner. There he repented and prayed to God. The episode was traditionally considered a model of penitence.

II Chronicles XXXIII, 11–12
(II Paralipomenon)

Paterfamilias filiū p̄o:gū suscepit   Dauid de adulterio redargutus penituit

c. *Pater familias filium prodigum suscepit*
   (The father of the family welcomed the prodigal son)

The richly dressed father holds a ring in one hand and greets his penitent younger son with the other. The older brother watches and a servant stands nearby holding new clothing for the prodigal.

Luke XV, 11–22

d. *David de adulterio redargutus penituit*
   (David refuted, repented his adultery)

King David is depicted with his hands folded in prayer, repenting, and Nathan the prophet raises his right hand to express the Lord's pardon.

II Samuel XII, 13
(II Kings)

ᶜ Cristus flevit super ciuitatem ih̄rlin   ᴮeremias lamentabatur sup ih̄liū

CHAPTER XV

a. *Cristus flevit super civitatem jherusalem*
   (Christ wept over the city of Jerusalem)

While Jesus advanced on the ass, weeping, the people
spread out their cloaks on the road and strewed the way
with olive branches. The rich man, Zacchaeus, climbed the
tree to see Jesus passing.

Luke XIX, 2–4, 36–38, 41

b. *Jeremias lamentabatur super jherusalem*
   (Jeremiah lamented over Jerusalem)

Nebuchadnezzar had razed the city by fire and driven all
the inhabitants out. Jeremiah is shown in the top of a tower
lamenting the abandoned city.

Lamentations I, 1

c. *David susceptus est cum laudibus*
   (David is welcomed with praise)

The events of David's life have been somewhat confused
by the artist. Helmeted and crowned, he returns from
slaughtering the Philistines, not as a child, but as a knight,
wearing suitable fifteenth-century armor and carrying the
head of Goliath on his sword. On the standard of one of his
soldiers is the harp, his emblem. This prefigures Jesus' entry
into Jerusalem and his acclaim by the people.

I Samuel XVIII, 6
(I Kings)

d. *Helyodorus flagellabatur*
   (Heliodorus flagellated)

The text of the *Speculum* describes the scene in agreement
with the story in the Apocrypha, according to which
Heliodorus was struck down by an armored rider on horseback and then whipped by two strong men. Here the artist
shows what appears to be a battle between the armored
rider and the two men represented as angels. Heliodorus
himself is omitted. This is a prefiguration of Jesus driving
the money lenders from the temple.

II Maccabees III, 26–27
(II Machabees)

CHAPTER XVI

a. *Cristus manducat pascha cum discipulis suis*
(Christ eats the Paschal lamb with his disciples)

The scene is of the Last Supper. In the foreground is Judas without a halo and with a money bag over his shoulder. Christ raises his right hand, as if in blessing, over a plate with the dismembered parts of the Paschal lamb. This scene and the three others in this chapter are found, in similar compositions, in the altarpiece by Dirck Bouts at St. Pierre in Louvain (see p. 139).

Mark XIV, 22–23

b. *Manna datur filiis israel in deserto*
(Manna given to the Children of Israel in the desert)

Five people representing the Children of Israel are gathering manna and filling their jugs. They are wearing the costumes and headdresses of the Netherlands in the fifteenth century. The manna falls like giant hailstones, as does the dew in the picture of Gideon's fleece (p. 155).

Exodus XVI, 12–35

Judei mandumnmt agmi palchale

Melchisedech optilitabhe panet vini

c. *Judei manducaverunt agnum paschalem*
   (The Jews ate the Paschal lamb)

The composition recalls the Last Supper scene with the
Paschal lamb on a round plate at the center of a round table.
Each figure has a staff in hand, and all wear hats, except the
center figure, who prepares to cut the lamb. The Bible
says, "And thus shall ye eat it; with your loins girded, your
shoes on your feet, and your staff in your hand . . ." The
kneeling woman in the foreground is not identified in the
Bible or the text of the *Speculum*.

Exodus XII, 8, 11, 46

d. *Melchisedech optulit abrahe panem et vinum*
   (Melchizedek offered Abraham bread and wine)

Melchizedek, King of Salem, meets Abraham on his return
from battle and gives him bread and wine and his blessing.
He is wearing a bishop's mitre to accentuate the association
with the Eucharist. The event prefigures the Last Supper.

Genesis XIV, 17–18

CHAPTER XVII

a. *Cristus prostravit hostes suos unico verbo*
   (Christ prostrated his enemies with a single word)

The four soldiers sent to arrest Jesus of Nazareth drew back
and fell to the ground at his words, "I am he."

John XVIII, 6

b. *Sampson prostravit mille cum mandibula asini*
   (Samson prostrated a thousand with the jawbone of
   an ass)

Filled with the power of the Lord, Samson killed a thousand Philistines with the jawbone, out of vengeance for the
killing of his wife. This prefigured the divine power of
Jesus' words.

Judges XV, 15

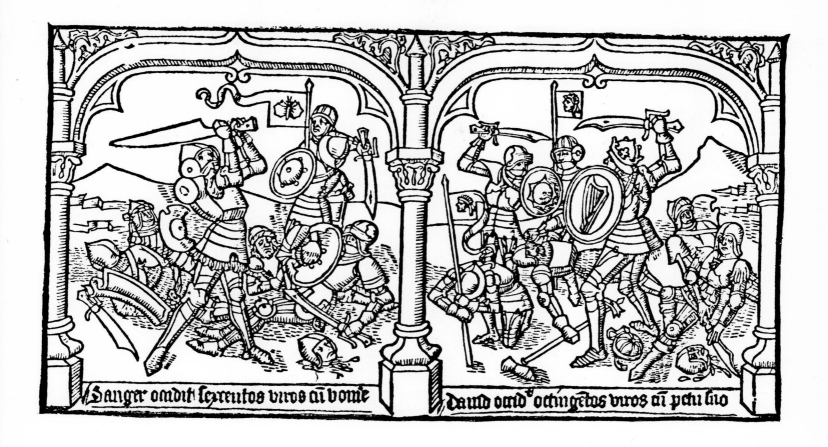

Sanger omdit sexcentos viros aī vome

Dauid ocid octingetos viros aī pchi lio

c. *Sanger occidit sexcentos viros cum vomere*
(Sangar killed six hundred men with a ploughshare)

Sangar defied the Philistines and killed six hundred men to
deliver Israel from its enemies. The ox goad with which
he slew them is here represented as a large sword or knife.

Judges III, 31

d. *David occidit octingentos viros cum (im)petu suo*
(David killed eight hundred men with his attack)

The author has given David the credit for killing eight
hundred Philistines, in error. In the Bible it was Adino the
Eznite, but in the *Speculum* text David "was like the most
tender little worm of the wood, who killed eight hundred
men at one onset." The scene shows David, crowned and
bearing a shield with his harp, defeating a group of soldiers
in battle. Compared to the effect of Jesus' words, these prefigurations seem exaggerated.

II Samuel XXIII, 8
(II Kings)

‖ Cristus dolose traditus ‖ Joab interfecit fratrem suum amasam

CHAPTER XVIII

a. *Cristus dolose traditus*
   (Christ grievously betrayed)

Jesus is surrounded by five armored soldiers while Judas kisses him. There is a flaming torch at the left. St. John's account of the arrest of Christ is the only one of the four Gospels which does not mention the kiss.

   Matthew XXVI, 47–50; Mark XIV, 45; Luke XXII, 47

b. *Joab interfecit fratrem suum amasam*
   (Joab killed his brother Amasa)

Joab grasps his brother's hand, instead of his chin as in the biblical account, to kiss him, and runs him through with his sword. Joab's kiss and the treacherous murder prefigure the kiss and betrayal of Christ by Judas.

   II Samuel XX, 9–10
   (II Kings)

c. *Rex saul reddidit david malum pro bono*
   (King Saul rendered to David evil for good)

Saul, out of envy of David, draws his sword (the text calls
for a spear) to murder him while he is playing the harp for
Saul. But God protects David, who dodges the thrust. This
episode, like the others in this chapter, prefigures the betrayal of trust.

I Samuel XVIII, 10–11
(I Kings)

d. *Caym dolose interfecit fratrem suum abel*
   (Cain grievously killed his brother Abel)

The artist has juxtaposed within the same frame the scene
of the offerings of Cain and Abel on the altar and the scene
of the murder. God's acceptance of Abel's offering is
shown by the flames rising toward heaven; those of the
rejected offering of Cain descend toward the earth. On the
right the jealous Cain kills Abel with the traditional jawbone of an ass.

Genesis IV, 8

Criſtus fuit velatus oſputus τ colaphiſatt̃   Hur vir marie fuit ſuffocatt̃ ſpnt̃o ⅲⅾⱬ

CHAPTER XIX

a. *Cristus fuit velatus, consputus et colaphisatus*
   (Christ was blindfolded, spat at, and beaten)

Jesus is shown seated but not blindfolded, while he is spat
upon and beaten. This is traditionally the "first derision";
the text of the *Speculum* is clear on this (line 42). St. John is
the only Evangelist who does not write of it. The second
derision is the placing of the Crown of Thorns, which is
much more often pictured, as in Chapter XXI. There is no
apparent explanation for the man in the left foreground
who kneels, touching (lifting?) his hat with his left hand
and proffering a letter (?) with his right.

Matthew XXVI, 67

b. *Hur vir marie fuit suffocatus sputo Judeorum*
   (Hur, the husband of Mary, was suffocated by the spit
   of the Jews)

The story of Hur, who refused to adore the Golden Calf
and was suffocated with spittle by the Jews, does not appear
in the Bible. It has been taken from the *Historia scholastica*
The composition repeats picture XIX a.

c. *Cam derisit patrem suum noem et alii ei condolebant*
(Ham derided his father Noah, and others felt pity for
him)

Noah, who planted a vineyard and became drunk on the
wine, is mocked by one of his sons, who views his nakedness, while the two respectful sons observe at the right.
According to the biblical text, these two had entered back-
wards into the tent in which Noah lay sleeping, in order to
cover their father without viewing his nakedness.

Genesis IX, 21–23

d. *Philistei sampsonem excecantes deriserunt*
(The Philistines mocked the blinded Samson)

Gathered in a polygonal building, the Philistines are making sport of Samson, who grips the central post. This re-
flects the passage in the Bible, but there, two columns
provide the support. Here the post is cracking before the
building collapses, killing the "three thousand men and
women" within, and Samson himself.

Judges XVI, 21, 27, 30

Jhesus ad columpnã ligatus ẽ et flagellatus
Achior princeps ligatg ẽ ad arbore a servus holofer

CHAPTER XX

a. *Jhesus ad columpnam ligatus est et flagellatus*
   (Jesus is tied to the column and whipped)

Christ, tied to a column at the center of the composition,
is flanked by two scourgers who whip him. Each scene of
this chapter has the same composition: a central figure between two others, one seen in profile and the other in
three-quarter face.

Matthew XXVII, 26; John XIX, 1

b. *Achior princeps ligatus est ad (a)rborem a servis holofernis*
   (Prince Achior is tied to the tree by Holofernes' servants)

This episode is taken from the Book of Judith in the
Apocrypha and parallels the other torments in this chap-
ter. Achior had told Holofernes of the Israelites' God who
performed miracles for them. Holofernes protested that
Nebuchadnezzar was the god of the earth, and he had
Achior taken prisoner.

Judith VI, 10–13
(Judith VI, 7–9)

c. *Lamech constringitur (confligitur) a malis suis uxoribus*
   (Lamech tormented by his bad wives)

This event is drawn from Comestor's *Historia scholastica*.
The Bible account of Lamech and his two wives, Ada and
Sella, does not tell of any torment or beating.

Genesis IV, 19

d. *Job flagellabatur a demone et ab uxore*
   (Job was whipped by the Devil and by his wife)

The biblical story states that Satan smote Job with boils
from head to feet, and Job sat down among the ashes with
a potsherd to scrape himself. Then his wife said to him
"Dost thou still continue in thy simplicity? Bless God, and
die." But Job's piety was not shaken. The Devil, as a
monster with a grimacing face on his back, raises a whip
to strike him. Job's faith, in the face of his torment, is expressed by the words written on the banderole, "sit nomen
domini benedictum" (Blessed be the name of the Lord).

Job II, 7–9

Cristus conatur spinea corona.   Concubina ipsius conam rgf acepta sibnipn ipo sint

CHAPTER XXI

a. *Cristus coronatur spinea corona*
   (Christ is crowned with a crown of thorns)

This is the second derision of Christ. The crown of thorns
is being pressed down on his head by the tormentors with
two staves. A third tormentor kneels, placing a reed in
Jesus' hand while he spits on him. They dressed him in a
purple robe and crowned him with thorns, saying "Hail,
King of the Jews" and they spat upon him. (See *Speculum*
Chapter XIX.)

Matthew XXVII, 27–30; John XIX, 2–3

b. *Concubina ipsius coronam regis acceptam sibi ipsi imposuit*
   (The concubine took the king's crown and put it on
   herself)

This event comes from the *Historia scholastica*. Apeme takes
the crown from the king's head with one hand and slaps
him with the other. King Darius' wrists are bound to
reflect Jesus' hands in XXI a. A figure stands at the right to
balance the composition in the same way as the others in
this chapter.

c. *Semey maledicit david*
(Semei curses David)

The Bible story relates that Semei came out of his house
and cursed David and threw stones at him. David's soldier,
Abisai, drew his sword to cut off Semei's head, but David
prevented him. This is a prefiguration of derision.

II Samuel XVI, 5–7
(II Kings)

d. *Rex amon dehonestavit nuncios david*
(King Ammon dealt dishonestly with the messengers of
David)

Two of King Ammon's servants seize the messenger of
David. The one at right cuts his clothes with a knife. The
Bible states that David's messengers had half their beards
shaved and their clothing cut up to the buttocks; again a
prefiguration of derision.

II Samuel X, 2–4
(II Kings)

CHAPTER XXII

a. *Cristus baiulavit crucem suam*
   (Christ bore his cross)

Jesus is bent under the weight of his cross. At the right a
soldier holds a rope tied around Christ's waist in his left
hand, and a hammer for the nailing to the cross in his right.
Simon stands behind Jesus helping to support the cross.

Luke XXIII, 26; John XIX, 17

b. *Ysaac ligna portat pro sua immolatione*
   (Isaac carries the wood for his sacrifice)

The oldest manuscripts of the *Speculum* show Isaac carrying
the wood for his sacrifice on his back, thus paralleling
Christ carrying the cross. The artist of the block has chosen
the more dramatic moment of the episode, when Isaac
kneels on the altar and the Angel stops the sword of Abraham. The wood is stacked beside the altar. There is thus a
weakening here of the typological parallel, but the mere
presence of certain characters is enough to imply the prefiguration.

Genesis XXII, 6–12

c. *Exploratores uvam in vecte portant*
   (The spies are carrying a cluster of grapes on a pole)

This caption belongs to XXII d and is misplaced, which suggests that the letter-cutter did not cut the picture. The *Speculum* text here states that the son who inherited the vineyard was killed by greedy servants, in a parable told by Jesus. The vineyard owner had sent his son, as God sent Jesus, and both were put to death. The allegory is drawn from Isidore of Seville.

Matthew XXI, 33–39

d. *Heres vinee prectus est extra vineam et interfectus est*
   (The heir of the vineyard is cast out and killed)

The correct caption is XXII c. The emissaries of Moses in search of fertile lands for the Israelites came to a brook and cut a branch with an enormous bunch of grapes which they carried on their shoulders. Jesus was symbolized by the grapes, of which the juice was the wine of the Eucharist. The bearers symbolize the two peoples who took Jesus out of Jerusalem, the Jews (the one with his back to the grapes) and the Gentiles (following the grapes). The grapes hanging from the branch allude to Christ on the Cross.

Numbers XIII, 24

Xpus cruafixus morte sua figuris pdixit   Inuetores artis ferarie et melodiaru

CHAPTER XXIII

a. *Xpus crucifixus mortem suam figuris predixit*
   (Christ predicted in figures his own death by crucifixion)

Christ is being nailed to the cross by three kneeling men,
one for each hand and one for the feet. In some manuscript
versions, a blacksmith is seen forging the nails of the Passion. This may show the influence of the blockbook in
which, adjacent to the Crucifixion, the forge of Tubalcain
is shown as a prefiguration. The nailing to the cross is not
described in the Bible.

b. *Inventores artis ferrarie et melodiarum*
   (The inventors of the arts of smithery and melody)

Tubalcain was the ancestor of all who worked in metal, and
Jubal was the father of all those who played the harp and
the organ. The *Speculum* text states that while Tubalcain
made sound resonate by hammering in his forge, Jubal
made a melody of the sound. This prefigures the prayer of
Jesus for his enemies at the moment of his Crucifixion.
Here they are shown at work hammering on an anvil. The
figure in the center may be their father, Lamech.

Genesis IV, 21–22

Ysaias ppha dividitur cũ sarra ligua   Rex moab invlavit filiũ suy murũ

c. *Ysaias propheta dividitur cum sarra lignea*
(The prophet Isaiah is cut in half by a wood-saw)

This legendary account of Isaiah's death is drawn from
Petrus Comestor. According to the text of the *Speculum*,
the division of Isaiah into two parts prefigures the separa-
tion of Jesus' soul from his body.

d. *Rex moab immolavit filium super murum*
(King Moab sacrificed his son on the walls)

King Moab is shown with a raised sword about to sacrifice
his son in order to save the inhabitants of his city from
famine during a siege. Although the biblical and *Speculum*
texts describe the sacrifice of the child on the walls of the
city, it takes place here in an interior.

II Kings III, 27
(IV Kings)

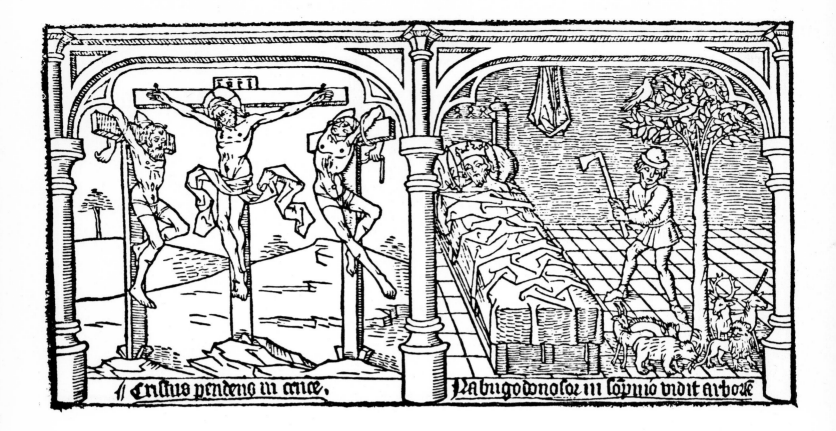

CHAPTER XXIV

a. *Cristus pendens in cruce*
(Christ hanging on the cross)

Christ on the cross is flanked by the two thieves who are
tied to their crosses. In crucifixion scenes by artists north of
the Alps, Jesus is shown nailed to his cross as in this woodcut, presumably indicating the cruelty of the Jews.

Matthew XXVII, 35; Mark XV, 25;
Luke XXIII, 33; John XIX, 18

b. *Nabugodonosor in sompnio vidit arborem*
(Nebuchadnezzar saw a tree in a dream)

Daniel interpreted the dream of Nebuchadnezzar of the
great tree whose branches sheltered the birds and shaded
the animals until a "holy one" came down from heaven
and felled it. The tree represented Nebuchadnezzar's great
power which must be humbled in the sight of the Lord.
This prefigures the death of Jesus to redeem mankind. Here
Nebuchadnezzar sleeps in a bed at the left while a man
raises an axe to cut down the tree, with birds in its branches
and animals at its foot, prophesying his downfall.

Daniel IV, 7–23

c. *Rex codrus dedit seipsum in exicium prosuis*
   (King Codrus gave himself to his destruction for his
   people)

Two armored soldiers with shields, one showing a dragon,
the other a sun, are killing the king at his own request, for
the sake of his people. The story is borrowed from Valerius
Maximus. In this scene Codrus wears royal clothes and a
crown, but according to the story he had changed his
clothing to a servant's attire in order to be killed by the
enemies who had declined earlier to kill the king. This
prefigures the willing sacrifice of Jesus, who dressed himself in human flesh in order to deliver us from our enemies.

d. *Eleazar confodiens elephantem ab ipso oppressus est*
   (Eleazar stabbing the elephant is crushed by it)

Eleazar is shown beneath an elephant supporting a tower
with two armed soldiers, as he runs his sword into its belly.
It collapsed and died, crushing Eleazar. The artist obviously
had never seen an elephant. The story comes from the
Apocrypha, and the event prefigures Christ's sacrifice of his
life for others.

> I Maccabees VI, 37, 43–46
> (I Machabees)

Dolor marie de filio   Jacob deflet filium suum ioseph

Chapter XXV of the manuscripts is omitted in the blockbooks, and at this point a new artist and/or woodcutter made the blocks. The compositions and the architectural framing, as well as the gestures of the figures, follow those of the first artist, but the form of the trees is rounded and the hatching for shadows is frequently diagonal rather than horizontal. The figures are generally larger in the frame.

CHAPTER XXV

a. *Dolor marie de filio*
   (Mary's sorrow for her son)

In this representation of the Descent from the Cross, the body of Christ divides the composition diagonally, with Joseph of Arimathea at the head, Mary Magdalen kneeling in the foreground, and the Virgin Mary supported at the left by St. John. One of the Virgin's hands is held to her face in sorrow, the other touches Jesus' foot. The texts of the Gospels do not describe the sorrow of the Virgin, but only the granting of the body, by Pilate, to Joseph of Arimathea, and his wrapping it and placing it in the sarcophagus.

Mark XV, 45–46; Luke XXIII, 53; John XIX, 38–40

b. *Jacob deflet filium suum joseph*
   (Jacob laments his son Joseph)

The jealous brothers of Joseph had cast him into a pit, and spotted his coat with goat's blood to convince their father that he had been killed. Here five of them show the coat to the grieving Jacob who is seated at the center. The banderoles have not been lettered and presumably were to be inscribed later. The text of the *Speculum* emphasizes the sorrow of Rachel, Joseph's mother, as a parallel to that of Mary. This is not present in the biblical account or in the illustration.

Genesis XXXVII, 31–34

Prothoplanstí lꝰꝛuút ueͨ abel   Noemy flet moꝛteͫ filioꝛ̅

c. *Prothoplansti luxerunt necem abel*
   (The first parents mourned the violent death of Abel)

Drawn from Comestor, who states that Adam and Eve
mourned for Abel one hundred years, this event is not described in the Bible. As in the other prefigurations of this
chapter, the subject is parental grief. Abel is stretched out
in the foreground, mourned by the kneeling figures of
Adam, who pulls his beard in grief, and Eve, who prays.

d. *Noemy flet mortem filiorum*
   (Naomi bewails the death of her sons)

The widow Naomi kneels in grief for the death of her two
sons. They lie side by side in winding sheets on the ground
before her. Naomi, wearing a large headdress, clasps her
hands in an attitude of prayer. In the background is the sil-
houette of a fifteenth-century city with its spires, as in the
preceding illustration.

Ruth I, 5, 20–21

Hora gpletonÿ datur sepulture   David flevit sup exequias abner

CHAPTER XXVI

a. *Hora completorii datur sepulture*
(At the hour of compline [the body] is given to the sepulchre)

Instead of being placed in a cave hollowed out of the rock, as described in the Bible, the body of Jesus is lowered into a rectangular sarcophagus. Nicodemus and Joseph of Arimathea hold Jesus. Mary and St. John are behind, the former bending over her son. Mary Magdalen and another holy woman are present.

Matthew XXVII, 60; Mark XV, 46;
Luke XXIII, 53; John XIX, 42

b. *David flevit super exequias abner*
(David wept at Abner's funeral)

Abner was killed by Joab because he had killed Joab's brother Asahel, but he was much loved by King David, who mourned for him. Here the coffin is carried to the left by two monks and two pages while the King follows, mourning.

II Samuel III, 32
(II Kings)

f Joseph missus vii cisternam ·   *f* Jonas a cete devoratus ·

c. *Joseph missus in cisternam*
   (Joseph cast into the well)

Joseph is thrown into the dry well by his jealous brothers because their father, Jacob, loved him most and gave him a coat of many colors. The artist has represented a round well with a brick wall conveniently broken away at the front to show Joseph being pushed in, naked, by his brothers. The event prefigures Christ's Entombment.

Genesis XXXVI, 24

d. *Jonas a cete devoratus*
   (Jonah devoured by the whale)

The boat is in stormy waters and Jonah, pictured like Joseph in the preceding image, is cast naked into the whale's mouth. There he remained praying for three days, prefiguring Jesus in the tomb.

Jonah I, 15; II, 1
(Jonas)

ŝm pꝛes libeꝛantur de ĩferno   Iſrahel liberatio a pharaone

CHAPTER XXVII

a. *Sancti patres liberantur de inferno*
   (The holy fathers are liberated from Hell)

The holy prophets and patriarchs who are in Hell, through
no fault of their own (they lived before the Christian era),
are delivered from Limbo to occupy a special section of
Heaven. The first two to emerge are Adam and Eve, delivered by Jesus and followed by the other rescued souls.
The entrance to Hell is commonly shown as the mouth of
a Leviathan. This is taken from the *Historia lombardica*.

b. *Israhel liberatio a Pharaone*
   (Israel's liberation from the Pharaoh)

Moses, staff in hand and two little horns on his head, leads
the children of Israel out of Egypt, represented by a city
gate at the left. The 600,000 of the Bible account are represented by eight people, including two children.

Exodus XII, 37, 51

Silvatio abraha de yr caldeoru   libratio loth a sodomis

c. *Liberatio abraham de yr caldeorum*
   (The liberation of Abraham from Ur of the Chaldees)

The story in Genesis is the origin of the legend as told in the
Historia scholastica, but the Bible does not tell of the flames
in which Abraham is kneeling when God appears in the
cloud.

Genesis XV, 7

d. *Liberatio loth a sodomis*
   (The liberation of Lot from Sodom)

Sodom is chastised for its wickedness by "hellfire and brim-
stone." An angel directs Lot to escape with his wife and
two daughters without turning back. But Lot's wife looks
back and is turned into a pillar of salt. In the *Historia scholastica*, Petrus Comestor quotes Josephus' *Antiquitate Judaica*
where the word used is "stele," and the artist has placed
the bust of salt on a short column.

Genesis XIX, 15, 17, 24

CHAPTER XXVIII

a. *Resurrectio domini nostri jhesu cristi*
   (The resurrection of our Lord Jesus Christ)

Jesus steps out of the sarcophagus with a cross standard in
one hand, and giving the sign of benediction with the
other. The Resurrection is not described by the Evangelists
nor found in the Passion plays. All four Evangelists tell, instead, of the holy women coming to the sepulchre and
finding the stone rolled back and Jesus gone. Angels appeared to tell them that Christ had risen. The text of the
Speculum states that the four guards were as if dead from
shock at seeing the miracle.

Matthew XXVIII, 1–3; Mark XVI, 1–8;
Luke XXIV, 1–8; John XX, 1–13

b. *Sampson tulit portas gaze*
   (Samson carried off the gates of Gaza)

Samson is a very large figure with one gate under his arm
and the other on his shoulder. His enemies had been lying
in wait for him at the gates all night to kill him in the morning. But Samson came in the middle of the night and
carried off the gates. This prefigures the strength of Jesus'
spirit in breaking out of the tomb among his enemies.

Judges XVI, 3

Exitus ione de ventre ceti.   lapis reprobatus factus est in caput anguli.

c. *Exitus ione de ventre ceti*
   (The emergence of Jonah from the whale's stomach)

Jonah prayed inside the belly of the whale, and after three
days and nights God spoke to the whale and it vomited
Jonah out "upon the dry land." The event is taking place
in a body of water bounded by rocky banks. In the background there are city towers and a boat with six figures sil-
houetted in it. This event is a prefiguration of the resurrection of Christ.

Jonah II, 11
(Jonas)

d. *Lapis reprobatus factus est in caput anguli*
   (The stone rejected is made into the head of the corner)

Jesus said to them "Have you never read in the Scriptures
that the stone which the builders rejected, the same is become the head of the corner? By the Lord this has been
done; and it is wonderful in our eyes." The parable is illustrated by four masons at work constructing the temple of
Jerusalem. According to the text of the *Speculum*, the building was completed with an irregularly shaped stone that
had previously been rejected. This prefigures Jesus resur-
rected, to become the cornerstone of Christianity.

Matthew XXI, 42; Psalm CXVII, 22–23

CHAPTER XXIX

a. *Extremum judicium*
   (The Last Judgment)

Christ is seated on a rainbow, his feet resting on a globe,
flanked by the figures of the Virgin and John the Baptist
who kneel and pray in intercession, the former by showing
her breast. Below, four nude figures of the dead emerge
from the ground to be judged. From the right side of Jesus'
head comes the lily of mercy and from the left the sword
of vengeance; his right hand, similarly, is held palm up for
the saved and his left palm down for the damned.

Revelation XX, 11–12
(Apocalypse)

b. *Nobilis reversus ex longinquis fecit rationem*
   (The noble returned from afar and made an accounting)

The scene is drawn from the parable of the ten talents, in
which the master settles accounts with his servants. The one
who buried the money (talents) instead of multiplying it is
thrown into "exterior darkness." This prefigures the division of the faithful from the wicked. Before the enthroned
master, two of the servants carry a third and prepare to
cast him into a hole or well in the left foreground.

Matthew XXV, 19–30; Luke XIX, 13–24

Regnū ccloꝛū lile decē virginibus   Aꝛanus dūi ſcrpſit ꝝ pariete·

c. *Regnum celorum simile decem virginibus*
(The kingdom of heaven is like the ten virgins)

Jesus told the parable of the ten virgins, five wise and five foolish, who took their lamps and went to meet the Bridegroom. The foolish virgins took no oil in their lamps, and the wise ones took vessels with oil. At midnight there was a cry "Behold, the Bridegroom cometh." The foolish virgins went off to buy oil, while the Bridegroom came and took the five wise ones into the marriage chamber and shut the door. When the others returned, saying "Lord, Lord, open to us," he answered "I know you not." Christ is shown standing at the top of a stairway receiving the wise virgins who approach from the left; at the right, the foolish virgins, with their empty lamps held upside-down, descend a stair into the jaws of hell. An angel leans out of a window of the church-like edifice at left to help welcome the wise virgins.

Matthew XXV, 1–12

d. *Manus domini scripsit in pariete*
(The hand of God wrote on the wall)

Daniel interpreted the miraculous handwriting on the wall for the kneeling King Belshazzar, whose father, Nebuchadnezzar, had stolen from the temple in Jerusalem the gold and silver vessels with which he had celebrated a great banquet. Daniel's interpretation is that God has weighed Belshazzar in the balance and found him wanting. The *Speculum* text is worded *Mane thetel phares* but the banderoles provided to be filled in by hand are blank. Literally, the words in the Bible "Mene, mene, tekel, upharsin" mean "numbered, weighed, divided," a prefiguration of the Last Judgment.

Daniel V, 5, 17, 25

The sixteen chapters of the full Latin manuscripts which are omitted from the blockbooks are listed below. Since the titles of the illustrations vary from copy to copy we have chosen to use those of The Pierpont Morgan Library, Ms. 766, as listed in the Karl W. Hiersemann Prospectus (Leipzig, 1933), adapted.

CHAPTER XXV

a. *Synagoga derisit Christum regem suum et deum*
(The Jews mocked Christ, their king and God)

b. *Michol subsannat virum suum david*
(Michal despises her husband David)

c. *Absalon confossus est tribus lanceis insuper invaditur gladiis*
(Absalom was pierced by three lances and two swords)

d. *Rex Elvilmoradach secuit corpus patris in trecentas partes*
(King Elvilmoradach cut up his father's corpse into three hundred pieces)

CHAPTER XXVIII

a. *Iste est infernus*
(This is Hell)

b. *Angelus domini refrigeravit tres pueros in igne*
(The Angel of the Lord kept the three boys cool in the fire)

c. *Angelus domini cibavit danielem in lacu leonum per abacuk*
(The Angel of the Lord fed Daniel in the lions' den by Habakkuk)

d. *Struthio liberavit pullum suum de vitro per sanguinem vermiculi*
(The ostrich freed his young from the glass with the reptile's blood)

CHAPTER XXIX

a. *Christus superavit hostem nostrum diabolum*
(Christ conquered our enemy the Devil)

b. *Bananias descendit in foueam ad leonem et occidit eum*
(Bananias descended into the pit and slew the lion)

c. *Sampson fortissimus dilaceravit leonem*
(Mighty Samson rent the lion asunder)

d. *Aioth perfodit eglon pinguissimum hostem filiorum israel*
(Ehud pierced Eglon, the fattest enemy of the Children of Israel)

CHAPTER XXX

a. *Maria superavit hostem nostrum diabolum*
   (Mary conquered our enemy the Devil)

b. *Judith decollavit holofernem hostem filiorum israel*
   (Judith decapitated Holofernes the enemy of the Children of Israel)

c. *Jahel perforavit sisarem per tempora*
   (Jael pierced Sisera through the temples)

d. *Regina thamarys decollavit cyrum regem*
   (Queen Thamarys decapitated King Cyrus)

CHAPTER XXXIII

a. *Ascensio domini*
   (The Ascension of the Lord)

b. *Jacob in sompnis vidit scalam*
   (Jacob saw the ladder in a dream)

c. *Christus ovem inventam reportat in domum suam*
   (Christ brings the lost sheep back to its home)

d. *Helyas translatus est in paradysum*
   (Elisha is taken up to paradise)

CHAPTER XXXIV

a. *Spiritus sanctus datur in specie diversarum linguarum*
   (The Holy Spirit is given in species of diverse languages)

b. *Turris babel ubi facta est divisio linguarum*
   (The tower of Babel where the division of many languages took place)

c. *Lex data est in monte syna*
   (The Law is given on Mount Sinai)

d. *Omnia vasa paupercule vidue impleta sunt oleo*
   (All vessels of the poor widow are filled with oil)

CHAPTER XXXV

a. *Consolacio beate virginis post ascensionem domini*
(The consolation of the blessed Virgin after the Lord's Ascension)

b. *Anna turbatur pro absencia filii sui sicut et Maria*
(Anna is perturbed by the absence of her son as was Mary)

c. *Mulier habens dragmas decem perdidit unam et querit eam*
(The woman having ten coins loses one and seeks it)

d. *Micol uxor david data alteri viro semper in luctu permansit*
(Michal, David's wife, having been given to another man, always remained in mourning)

CHAPTER XXXVI

a. *Christus rex celorum assumpsit mariam in celum*
(Christ, the King of Heaven, received Mary in Heaven)

b. *Rex david duxit archam testamenti in domum suam*
(King David brought the Ark of the Covenant into his house)

c. *Signum apparuit in celo*
(A sign appeared in the sky)

d. *Rex salomon posuit matri sue thronum ad dexteram suam*
(Solomon placed a throne for his mother at his right)

CHAPTER XXXVII

a. *Maria mediatrix nostra placat iram dei contra nos*
(Mary, our mediatrix, appeases God's wrath against us)

b. *Abigael placat iram regis david contra nabal stultum*
(Abigail appeases King David's wrath against the churlish Nabal)

c. *Mulier thecuites placat iram david contra absalonem*
(The Tekoah woman appeases David's wrath against Absalom)

d. *Mulier sapiens in abela placat iram ioab contra urbem*
(A wise woman of Abel appeases Joab's wrath against the city)

CHAPTER XXXVIII

a. *Maria est nostra defensatrix*
(Mary is our defender)

b. *Tharbis defendit urbem saba ab impugnacione moisi*
(Tharbis defended the city of Saba against Moses' attack)

c. *Mulier laudabilis in thebes defendit cives suos*
(A laudable Theban woman defended her fellow-citizens)

d. *Micol defendit david incidiis apparitorum*
(Michal defended David from the incursions of the armed servants)

CHAPTER XXXIX

a. *Christus ostendit patri suo vulnera*
(Christ showed his wound to his Father)

b. *Antipater ostendit julio cesari cicatrices suas*
(Antipater showed his scars to Julius Caesar)

c. *Mary ostendit filio suo ubera sua et orat pro nobis*
(Mary showed her son her breast and speaks for us)

d. *Hester orat pro populo suo regem assuerum*
(Esther speaks on behalf of her people to King Ahasuerus)

Chapter XL appears in the blockbook editions as Chapter XXIX

CHAPTER XLI

a. *Pene dampnatorum in inferno*
(The punishments of the damned in Hell)

b. *Sic punivit rex david hostes suos*
(Thus King David punished his enemies)

c. *Gedeon discerpens derisores suos*
(Gideon reviles his mockers)

d. *Pharao cum exercitu suo submersus est in mari rubro*
(Pharaoh with his army is drowned in the Red Sea)

CHAPTER XLII

a. *Regnum celorum erit retribucio beatorum*
   (The Kingdom of Heaven shall be the reward of the
   Blessed)

b. *Regina saba, rex salomon*
   (The Queen of Sheba, King Solomon)

c. *Convivium regis assueri*
   (The feast of King Ahasuerus)

d. *Convivium filiorum job*
   (The feast of Job's sons)

CHAPTER XLIII

a. *Miraculum de passione christi* (The Miracle of Christ's
   Passion)

b. *Hora vespertina* (The Washing of the Feet)

c. *Hora completorii* (The Judas Kiss)

d. *Hora matutina* (Christ before Caiaphas)

e. *Hora prima* (Christ before Pilate)

f. *Hora tercia* (The Flagellation)

g. *Hora sexta* (Christ Bearing the Cross)

h. *Hora nona* (The Crucifixion)

CHAPTER XLIV

a. *Miraculum de dolore christi et sue gloriose matris* (Miracle
   of the sorrows of Christ and his glorious mother).

b. *Prima tristitia beate virginis* (First sorrow of the blessed
   Virgin). The prophecy of a sword piercing Mary's soul.

c. *Secunda trisitia beate virginis* (Second sorrow of the
   blessed Virgin). The flight into Egypt.

d. *Tertia tristitia beate virginis* (Third sorrow of the blessed
   Virgin). Christ in the temple with the learned doctors.

e. *Quarta tristitia beate virginis* (Fourth sorrow of the blessed
   Virgin). The Capture of Christ.

f. *Quinta tristitia beate virginis* (Fifth sorrow of the blessed Virgin). The Crucifixion.

g. *Sexta tristitia beate virginis* (Sixth sorrow of the blessed Virgin). The Entombment.

h. *Septima tristitia beate virginis* (Seventh sorrow of the blessed Virgin). Mary surrounded by the symbols of Christ's life.

CHAPTER XLV

a. *Miraculum de septem gaudiis beate virginis* (Miracle of the seven joys of the blessed Virgin). Mary consoles a sick cleric.

b. *Primum gaudium* (First joy). The Annunciation.

c. *Secundum gaudium beate virginis* (Second joy). The Visitation.

d. *Tertium gaudium beate virginis* (Third joy). The Nativity.

e. *Quartum gaudium beate virginis* (Fourth joy). The Adoration.

f. *Quintum gaudium beate virginis* (Fifth joy). The Presentation.

g. *Sextum gaudium beate virginis* (Sixth joy). Christ in the temple.

h. *Septimum gaudium beate virginis* (Seventh joy). The Coronation.

VII-1.
Balaam and the Angel, Chapter III d.
The Resurrection, Chapter XXXII a.
Jacob's Ladder, Chapter XXXIII b.
Speculum humanæ salvationis, Günther Zainer, Augsburg, 1473.
Henry E. Huntington Library and Art Gallery, San Marino, California, 104027.

VII

Later Speculum Editions

The continued popularity of the *Speculum humanæ salvationis* is evident from the remarkable number of incunabula editions issued before the end of the fifteenth century. No less than sixteen were published by eleven printers, in Latin, Dutch, French, and German, all with wood-block illustrations.[1] The first of these was printed by Günther Zainer in the Benedictine Abbey of SS. Ulrich and Afra at Augsburg, together with another work intercalated into the chapters of the *Speculum*. The Latin text is printed beneath the woodcuts, followed by a translation of the chapter into German, and then by pages of the *Speculo Sanctae Mariæ Virginis*, a metrical summary, by Brother Johannes of the Abbey.

Günther Zainer, first known as a scribe, was a famous printer of Strassburg. About 1468 he moved to Augsburg, where the guild of woodcutters tried to prevent him from getting a permit to print, but then allowed him to do so if his books were not illustrated. Later, through the intervention of the powerful Melchior, the Abbot of SS. Ulrich and Afra, he received his regular license on condition that he use only woodcutters belonging to the guilds, although it is said that he was capable of cutting blocks himself. The Abbot set up a press in the monastery in order to avoid the control of the guilds, and there Zainer printed an illustrated edition of the *Speculum* in 1473. It included forty-five chapters, 192 fine new woodcuts (fig. VII–1), fifteen of which are repeated, and it was rubricated throughout. The unity of character between Zainer's type and the blocks has caused the book to be called one of the most beautiful of in-cunabula to be created in Northern Europe.[2] The inventory made about the middle of the

1. Arthur M. Hind, *An Introduction to a History of Woodcut* (1935; reprint New York, 1963),
   p. 811. To Hind's list must be added the 1498 edition, printed by André Bocard at
   Paris for Durand Gerlier; the two printed by Johann Schönsperger at Augsburg in
   1492 and 1500; and the edition of 1492, printed by Michel Greyff at Reutlingen.
2. Alan G. Thomas, *Great Books and Book Collectors* (London, 1975), p. 49.

century by Jean Schlipat, listing the books in the monastery, included a copy of the *Speculum* of forty-five chapters and it may be assumed that it was used by Zainer as printer's copy.

The enlightened Abbot Melchior invited a succession of Augsburg printers to direct and instruct his monks. Johann Baemler and Anton Sorg printed, with their own types, at the Abbey in the same year as Zainer, 1473, and in succeeding years. Zainer produced a number of other important illustrated books at Augsburg, many with blocks by the same artist who illustrated his *Speculum* edition. His blocks for the *Speculum vitæ humanæ* were used in Reinhard's Lyon edition of 1482 and in the Hurus edition of 1491 at Saragossa, which demonstrates how commonly the woodcuts for popular books travelled from one printer to another.[3]

The *Spiegel menschlicher Behältnis*, a German translation of the *Speculum* which issued from the press of Bernhard Richel in August 1476, was the most important early book to be printed at Basel. It had a new set of vertical woodcuts, partially derived from Zainer's blocks, but more directly influenced by the *Biblia pauperum*. They are placed in the double-column text wherever a new subject begins rather than at the head of the text columns (fig. VII–2).

In the same month and year, Anton Sorg in Augsburg printed an edition of the German translation with cuts also based on Zainer's blocks. Sorg was the most prolific of the printers in that busy center. He produced more than a hundred illustrated books between 1475 and 1493, but in the quality of cutting, their illustrations are below the standards of Zainer and Baemler.[4]

The first illustrated book to be printed at Lyon was a French translation of the *Speculum*, made by the Augustinian monk Brother Julien Macho from the Basel German edition. Entitled *Le Mirouer de la Redemption*, it was issued by Martin Huss in 1478 with the blocks of Richel's edition (fig. VII–3). The work must have been extremely popular in France, as elsewhere, for he republished it in 1479 and 1482, and his kinsman, Matthias Huss, printed editions in 1483 and 1484.

At Speier, Peter Drach printed three editions of the *Spiegel menschlicher Behältnis*, in 1478 (fig. VII–4), 1481, and 1495, using blocks whose design has been attributed to the Master of the Amsterdam Cabinet (the Master of the Hausbuch).[5]

3. A. W. Pollard, "The Transference of Woodcuts in the XV and XVI Centuries," in Bibliographica, II (1896), p. 343.
4. Hind, *op.cit.*, p. 295.
5. *Ibid.*, p. 346.

Lutzifers val

Lutzifer ſprach ich ſtige vff in den hymmel vnd wurde glich dē oberſten pſaie am riiij vnd apocalipſis am xij.

Das erſt capitel

In gottes nammen amen. Hie vohet an ein ſpiegel der menſchlichen behaltniſze. In dem geoffenet wurt dēr vale des menſchen vnd die ſpiſe. Oder die moſſe des wider bringendes. In diſem ſpiegel mag der mēſche erkennē vmb was ſache der ſchöpfer alle zū rote wart den mēſchen zū beſchaffende Vnd wie dēr mēſche von des tüfels trügniſze verdamnet wārt Vnd wie er mit der erbermde ſū wider brachte zū behaltniſz Lutzifer dēr öberhūp ſich wider ſinen ſchöpfer den ewigē got Dar vmb wart er ī eime ougenblicke verworfen von der höhede der hymmele īn die helle. Vmb die ſach wart got zū rote menſchlich kind zū beſchaffende. Das er mit dem menſchen möchte lutzifers vnd finre

geſellen val wider bringē. Dar vmb neit der tüfel den menſchen vnd ſtalte ſich dar vff wie er in dar zū brechte das er gottes gebot breche vnd vberginge Zū diſen ſachē erwelte dēr tüfel imme ſelbes einē ſlangen vs der wo zū mole vffrecht ging vnd einre megde houbt hette In den ſlāgen ſloff der tüfel vnd rette durch ſinē müt trügenliche wort zū der frowen eua Wēne ſū mynre fürſichtig was wen der man Vnd duchte im wie adā fürſichtiger wer denn das wip. Dar vmb ging er zū dem wibe wo ſū alleine was on den man. Vnd betroug vnſer müter euam Das ſū vber alles menſcheliches geſchlecht den ewigen tot brachte

Adam vnd eua wurden geſchaffen. Geneſis am ij vnd am iiij.

Man ſol nūn wiſſen das adam wart geſchaffen in eime acker der heiſſet damaſcenus vſzwēdig des paradiſes. Vnd wart võ got in das paradis gefürt Aber dz wip wart in dem paradiſe geſchaffen vs

VII–2.
The Fall of Lucifer, Chapter I a.
The Creation of Eve, Chapter I b.
Spiegel menschlicher Behältnis, Bernhard Richel, Basel, 1476.
Henry E. Huntington Library and Art Gallery, San Marino, California, 105168.

plaisant aux mondains mais les plaisances
z delectacions mondaines maimnēt lōme a
eternelle dāpnation Cōbien que les riches
ses ne sont pas touliours cause de la damp
naciō des hōmes car richesse est bōne a cel
luy qui en vse bien z iustemēt mais lamour
desordōne que les hōmes ont aux riches=
ses est cause de les mener a perdicion et a
dampnacion eternelle

    Comment adā laboura la terre au·iij·
et au·iiij·chapitre de genesis

Vant adam et eue furēt iettes
hors de paradis terrestre par
ce quilz avoiēt trespasse le cō
mandement de dieu ilz furent
moult dolens car leur createur estoit cou-
rouce cōtre eulx et ne attēdoient nul con-
fort Et les bestes et les creatures sus les
quelles dieu leur avoit dōne seignourie ne
les cōgnoissoiēt pl9 car ilz les virēt vestus
Et quant la seignourie leur fut donnee ilz
estoiēt nudz lozs fist adā vng tabernacle de
brāches darbzes pour luy z sa fēme gar-
der contre lardeur du soleil et aussi pour

eulx garātir cōtre les bestes sauuages et
et cōmenca a labourer la terre· Et quant
adā et eue eurēt este vng tāmps ensamble
adm cōgneut eue cōme nature lui enseigna
et engēdra vng beau filz Et pozta eue len
fant autāt de tēps q nostre seigneur lui e=
stablist et sen deliura et dist Jay hōme en
possession de par dieu Et lappellerēt adaz
et eue cayn Et son pere et sa mere neurēt
dequoy le couurir fozs que derbes et de
feulles mais il se pzint a la mamelle de sa me
re cōme nature lui amōnestoit z en pzint sa
soubstenāce Et apzes cōgneut adā eue sa
fēme et engēdza vng aultre filz le quel ilz
appellerēt abel moult aymerēt adā et eue
leurs enfās et les nourrirēt le mieulx quilz
peurent iusques a ce quilz furēt grans·

    Comment cayn occist abel son frere

Vant cayn et abel furēt grās
z hors denfāce cayn laboura
la terre et abel fut pasteur et
garda les brebis Et quant les
bzebis avoient angneaux abel pzenoit vng
des pl9 beaulx et le sacrefioit a dieu nostre

a iiij

VII-3.
Adam Toils and Eve Spins.
Cain Kills Abel. In the background they are at the altar with their offerings.
Le Mirouer de la Redemption, Martin Huss, Lyon, 1478.
Henry E. Huntington Library and Art Gallery, San Marino, California, 105169.

er folte fy nit laffen · warm fy hätt ein feucht empfangen von dem heiligen geyſt vnd von keinem menſchen·

℘Got erſchyne Moyſi in dem brynnendē buſch der doch grün belybe· Exodi am·iij·cap·

Diſe wunderbare empfängknuß die ward moyſi vorverkündet vn̄ erzeyget in dem feürin buſche· Der buſch der lydte das feüwer vn̄ verloze doch nit ſein grüne· Maria dy empfienge jren ſune· vnnd verloze doch nicht jren magtumb· Got der wonet durch den engel in dem brinnenden feürin buſch· vnd der ſelbig got wonet ſelbs in marie leyb· Er füre herab in den buſch vmb erlöſung der juden· Er kame auch herab in mariam·das er vns alle erlöſet von der helle· Do aber got meins jch werden wolt·do erwölet er jm ſelber mariam auß zů einer müter über alle weyber die jn der ganczen welt waren·

℘Gedeonis feel warde des hymels tawe vol·vnd belybe das erdtrich do bey truckē Judicum·das iſt·am̄ büche der Richter am ſechſten ca·

Vellus Gedeonis·

Diſe maria was auch vor bezeichnet bey Gedeonis feel·das do warde gefeüchtet mit dem hymeliſchen tawe· das ſchaff feel empfieng allein den hymeliſchen tawe vnd belybe das feld darumb vnnd dobey alles truckenn· Alſo warde maria allein mit dem hymeliſchen tawe erfüllet· Gedeon bate got das er jme ein zeychen gäbe an dem ſchaff feel ob er durch jn das volck von iſrahel von den feynden erlöſen woltt·vnd wär es das er das thůn wolte·ſo ſolt das feel das gedeon auff das feldt het geleget mit tawe gefeüchtet werden·vnd ſolt das feldt dobey all vmb vnd vmb trucken belybben· Do warde das feldt erfüllt

mit tawe·das was ein zeychen der erlöſung der juden· Alſo was auch marie empfängknuß ein zeychenn vnſer erlöſung· Das feel gedeonis bedeütet vnd bezeychnet die werde junckfrawen mariam· Von dē feel machet Jheſus criſtus einen rock do er wolt gekleidet werden mit dē rock vnſer menſchheyt· darumb dz er vns wolt kleyden mit dem kleyde der ewigen freüden· Gedeonis fel empfienge den tuw on verkerung ſeiner woll· Maria empfienge jren ſune vnuerſeeret jres magtumbs· Gedeon der drucket den tawe auß dem feel vnd füllet domit ein ſchal Maria gebare jren ſune der alle diſe welt hat erfüllet mitt dem tawe ſeiner genaden·

℘Rebecca gab Eliezer abrahams boten zetrincken·Geneſ̄ am·xxiiij·

Die empfängknuß marie beſchahe von gabriel dem enngel·das iſt bezeychnet bey abrahams knechtt·

vnd bey rebecca batuelis thochter· Abraham der ſchicket eliezer ſeinen knecht auß das er ſolte ſůchen ein maget die ſeinem ſun wol gezäme vnd gemeſſen wär zů einem gmahel· Des kame der bote abrahams knecht zů rebecca bey einem brunnen vnd hieſche von jr zetrincken· do gab ſy jm zetrincken· vn̄ darüb erwölet er ſy auß zů einem gmahel ſeines herren ſune· Zů gleych· erweyß der hymeliſch vater ſchickt ſeinen boten gabriel in diſe welt dz er ſolt ſůchen ein maget ſeinem ſun zů einer müter·do fand er die zymlichen magt mariam· die jm gabe den tranck·das was·das ſy jre gehell vnd jren willen gab zů ſeiner verkündung· Rebecca troncket nit allein den knecht·ſy gab auch ſeinen kämmelthieren zetrincken Alſo hat auch maria den engelen vñ den menſchen den brunnen des ewigen lebens geſchencktt·

℘Von vnſer lieben frawen tag in der faſten·

Hienach findeſtdu wie die heylig kirch diſen tag vnd diſe hochzeyt begeet·mit ewangelien vnd epiſtlen·vnd mit der legend·

℘Von vnſer frawe tag in der faſten die epiſtel· Yſaie am·xj·cap·

Diſes ſpricht der herre· Es wirdt außgeen ein růtte von der wurczel yeſſe·vnd ein blům wirt außgeen von ſeiner wurczel·vnd auff je wirt růwen der geyſt des herren·der geyſt der weyßheyt vnd der verſtändnuß·der geyſt des rats vnd d̄ ſtercke·der geyſt der kunſt vnd d̄ miltigkeit·vnd in jr erfüllet der geyſte

VII–4.
Moses and the Burning Bush, Chapter VII b.
Gideon's Fleece, Chapter VII c.
Rebecca at the Well, Chapter VII d.
Spiegel menschlicher Behältnis, Peter Drach, Speier, 1478.
Henry E. Huntington Library and Art Gallery, San Marino, California, 104026.

As for the woodcuts of the *Speculum* blockbooks, they were preserved, if our surmise is correct, at a community of the *Devotio moderna* near Louvain. It was at Louvain that Jan Veldener set up his original printing equipment and there issued the *Fasciculus temporum*, dated 29th December, 1475.[6] It was the first printed book, after the *Speculum*, with woodcut illustrations to be produced in the Low Countries.

6. Wytze and Lotte Hellinga, *The Fifteenth-Century Printing Types of the Low Countries* (Amsterdam, 1966), I, p. 18.

Veldener is also known to have supplied type and printing equipment to the Brethren of the Common Life in Brussels, and probably set up their press which was the first printing workshop in that city. Their community was known as Nazareth, or as the House of the Annunciation, and thirty-six editions were issued from it between 1474 and 1485.[7] It is an attractive thought that out of appreciation, if not obligation, perhaps the Congregation at Brussels or at Groenendael rewarded Veldener by turning over the *Speculum* woodblocks to him after the last edition was printed about 1479. In any case Veldener had moved to the bishopric of Utrecht in 1478 where he printed two editions of the *Epistelen en Evangelien*. For the third edition, in 1481, he used two of the *Speculum* blocks sawed in half, the cuts for the Last Judgment, and the Wise and Foolish Virgins.

Because of the ecclesiastical conflicts in Utrecht, he soon took refuge at Culemborg, and there, in 1483, printed a Dutch translation of thirty-two chapters of the *Speculum*, entitled *Dat Spieghel onser behoudenisse*, using the woodcuts from the blockbooks, cut in half, as noted earlier, and eleven more by the second artist/cutter of the *Speculum* (fig. VII–5). The source of the Dutch text for these three added chapters is unknown. Deviating from the pattern of the Latin manuscripts, Veldener substituted for the first half-block of Chapter XXV (properly the scene of the Synagogue deriding Christ) the Crucifixion scene, which he had also used in Chapter I in place of the Fall of Lucifer. Chapters XXVIII and XXIX of the manuscript texts, omitted in the blockbooks, are also included with their appropriate woodcuts. The sturdy blocks were not, however, laid to rest yet. In 1484, after his return to Louvain, Veldener used two of them in his edition of *Herbarius in dietsche*, or *Kruidboeck*.

At Lübeck in about 1483, Lucas Brandis printed a *Spiegel menschlicher Behältnis* with many crude and angular illustrations in woodblocks.[8] Another Augsburg edition of the *Spiegel* printed by Peter Berger appeared in 1489, with illustrations that follow the Richel subjects and are even more directly influenced by the *Biblia pauperum*.[9]

7. Elly Cockx-Indestege, "Les Frères de la Vie Commune à Bruxelles," in
   Le Cinquième centenaire de l'imprimerie dans les anciens Pays-Bas (Brussels, 1973), p. 196.
8. William Martin Conway, *The Woodcutters of the Netherlands in the Fifteenth Century*
   (1884; reprint Hildesheim, 1961), p. 13.
9. Hind, *op.cit.*, p. 364 and p. 326.

Angels in fornace pueros visitauit

die enghel visiteerde die kinderen in dat fornay

dse pijn is onspreckelic allen waerlike pinen gheliick
ds vuer ongheliicliic is de ghemaelde vuer also on
gheliic is dit vuer de vuer des vegeuiers Boue dse

Daniel in lacu leonu missus

Daniel inde put bide leeuwe gesent Danielis iiij

enghels verandt wort in soetichept Mocht die tege
woerdichept des engels der kinderen pijn verwelken
Veel meer soe mocht xpristus dan sijn vrienden in
die helle verbliden Dat die enghel tot dey kinderen

Struao pullu viniculo libeauit

Die strups verloste sijn ionc met ene worm

Dit staet inder ecclesiastica hystoria
Dit was voermaels mede ghefigureert in salomos
strups wyens ionghe salomon dede sluten in een gla

VII–5.
An Angel Visited the Boys in the Furnace, Chapter XXVIII b.
Daniel in the Lions' Den, Chapter XXVIII c.
The Ostrich Liberated Her Young from the Glass
with a Reptile's Blood. Chapter XXVIII d.
Dat Spieghel onser behoudenisse, Jan Veldener, Culemborg, 1483.
New York Public Library, Spencer Collection, NETH 1483.

Oer heilige geist ð erzeiget auch
das maria notturfftig were
vns alle da er vns ir geburt ge
lobet durch den munt des pro/
pheten Balaams. Wan er gelobte vns
vñ sprach das ein stern solt vff gan võ Ja
cob. By ðe vns bezeichet ward maria ein
kunfftige gottes zelle. Balaam der hette
des willen das er ðe volck von israel wolt
fluchen/ da verwandelte der heilige geist
ðe fluch in eine segen. Da by erzeigte der
heilige geist das vnser fluch solte verwan
delt werden in einen sege vñ solte geschehe
von einer megde der geburt. Vnd ir vff/
gang bezeichet was in einem sterne die da
ist allein ein forerin vñ ein leiterin vñ ein
helferin aller der die da wonen in den flu
ten disser welte. One dissen sternen mochte
wir nymmer syn gefaren vber das wuten
ðe mere. Noch mochten nit komen syn zu
ðe staden des hymmelschen vatters lande.
Darvmb hat got vor beteutet mit ðe ster
nen Marien geburtlichen vfgang. Wen
er hette das vor geordent das er vns mit
ir wolte widder füren zu dem hymmelsche

IN ðe vordern capitel han wir
gehort võ marien verkundüge
Nun so llen wir horen von irer
geburt oder võ irem vrsprüge
sagen. Marien geburt hette ein vrsprüg
von ðe geschlechte yesse der dauids vatter
was. Von dem Isaias durch den heilige
geist hat gewyssaget.
❦ Die rüte von yesse beteütet mariam.
Isaie am.xi.
Aaias wyssagunge ist also.
Ein rüte wirt vß gan von der
würtzele yesse/ vnd ein blume
wirt vff gan võ ð rüte würtze
len. Dar vff so wirt rugen die sieben formi
ge gnade des heiligen geistes Disse rüte ist
maria/ die da behafftig ward von dem
hymmelschen dauwe/ vnd vns gebare
die aller lustliche blüme. In der blümen
vindt man sieben güte artzenie/ by den
vns auch bedeüt werden die sieben ga/
ben des heiligen geistes. In disser blümen
so wirt funden berurde vñ geschmack vnd

VII–6.
Balaam and the Angel, Chapter III d.
The Birth of Mary, Chapter IV a.
Spiegel menschlicher Behältnis, Johann Schönsperger, Augsburg, 1492.
Henry E. Huntington Library and Art Gallery, San Marino, California, 101922.

Johann Schönsperger, another Augsburg printer, was one of the most prolific producers of illustrated books of the period, but many of his woodcuts were copied from, or had been used in other printers' issues of the same texts, not the least of which were his three plagiarized editions of the Nuremberg Chronicle (Koberger, 1493).[10] He printed two editions of the *Spiegel*, one in 1492 (fig. VII–6) and one in 1500, but the source of his blocks is unknown.

Very few editions of the *Speculum* were printed in the sixteenth century, for the change in religious and intellectual climate and the rise of Humanism and Protestantism gradually undermined the popularity of the typological treatises.

We have attempted to trace the steps in the metamorphoses of the *Speculum humanæ salvationis* from its fourteenth-century Latin manuscripts into the gloriously illuminated French translations for ducal courts, and their models; then, with the advent of the woodcut and of movable type, its appearance in the four editions of the blockbooks; and finally, its many letterpress editions with woodblocks and text printed in the press.

10. Adrian Wilson, *The Making of the Nuremberg Chronicle*, 2nd edition, revised (Amsterdam, 1978), p. 191.

The *Speculum* was also the source for works in many art forms, among them medieval tapestries at La Chaise-Dieu in the Auvergne; stained glass at Mulhouse, Colmar, Rouffach, and Wissembourg in Alsace; and sculptures at Vienne near Lyon.[11] In individual woodcut prints it appears in the form of a hand (fig. VII–7), presumably used as an aid to prayer. Four examples are preserved, each from a different woodblock.[12] At the top of the print reproduced here is an almost indecipherable text from the Bible, above a large hand with an inscription at the joint of each finger and a banderole at each tip. On either side of the wrist is the Latin text, translated as follows:

If you know the will of God	The thumb signifies the will of God
Recognize evil so you may avoid it	The index finger signifies knowledge
If you acted evilly, be sorry	The middle finger (means) contrition
If you are truly sorry, confess	The ring finger (means) confession
If you have confessed, be content	The little finger (means) contentment

The fingers are flanked by Maria Magdalena with an ointment jar, and Maria Martha using an aspergill which is attached by a rope to a bulldog (or dragon?). This is presented here as a final benediction to our study.

11. Robert A. Koch, "The Sculptures of the Church of Saint-Maurice at Vienne, the *Biblia Pauperum* and the *Speculum humanæ salvationis*," in Art Bulletin, XXXII (1950), pp. 151–55.
12. Hind, *op.cit.*, p. 111.

VII–7.
Speculum humanæ salvationis in the form of a hand, 1476.
Germanisches Nationalmuseum, Nuremberg, H. 60.

Selected Bibliography

Alexander, J. J. G. *The Decorated Letter* (New York, 1978).
———. "Scribes as Artists" in *Medieval Scribes, Manuscripts and Libraries: Essays Presented to N. R. Ker*, edited by M. B. Parkes and Andrew Watson (London, 1978).

Attwater, Donald. *The Penguin Dictionary of Saints* Harmondsworth, 1965).

Barrois, Joseph. *Bibliothèque prototypographique* (Paris, 1830).

Bing, Gertrud. "The Apocalypse Block-Books and their Manuscript Models," in Journal of the Warburg and Courtauld Institutes, V (1942).

Blum, Shirley Neilsen. *Early Netherlandish Triptychs, A Study in Patronage* (Berkeley and Los Angeles, 1969).

The Book Through 5000 Years. Edited by H. D. L. Vervliet (London and New York, 1972).

Boon, K. G. "Een Utrechtse schilder uit de 15de Eeuw, de Meester van de Boom van Jesse in de Buurkerk," in Oud Holland, LXXVI (1961).
———. "Nieuwe Gegevens over de Meester van Katherin van Kleeve en sijn atelier," in Bulletin van de Koninklijke Nederlandsche Outheidkundige, XVII (1964).

Bossuat, R. "Jean Miélot, traducteur de Cicéron," in Bibliothèque de l'Ecole des Chartes, XCIX (1938).

Bradley, J. W. *A Dictionary of Miniaturists, Illuminators, Calligraphers and Copyists* (New York, 1958).

Bradshaw, Henry. "List of the Founts of Type and Woodcut Devices used by Printers of Holland in the Fifteenth Century," in *Collected Papers of Henry Bradshaw* (London, 1889).

Breitenbach, Edgar. *Speculum Humanæ Salvationis. Eine typengeschichtliche Untersuchung*, Studien zur deutschen Kunstgeschichte, no. 272 (Strasbourg, 1930).

Briquet, C. M. *Les Filigranes*. Edited by Allan H. Stevenson (Amsterdam, 1968).

British Museum Catalogue of Books Printed in the XV Century, Vol. IX (London, 1962).

Bühler, Curt F. "A Note on Zedler's Coster Theory," in Papers of the Bibliographical Society of America, XXXVII (1943).
———. *The Fifteenth Century Book* (Philadelphia, 1961).

Byvanck, A. W. *Principaux manuscrits à peinture de la Bibliothèque Royale des Pays-Bas et du Musée Meermanno-Westreenianum à La Haye* (Paris, 1924–25).

Cahn, Walter, and Marrow, James. "Medieval and Renaissance Manuscripts at Yale: A Selection," in The Yale University Library Gazette, LII, no. 4 (April, 1978).

Calkins, Robert G. "Parallels between Incunabula and Manuscripts from the Circle of the Master of Catherine of Cleves," in Oud Holland, XCII (1978).

Carter, D. G. "The Providence Crucifixion: its Place and Meaning for Dutch Fifteenth Century Painting," in Bulletin of Rhode Island School of Design Museum, XLVIII, no. 4 (1962).

Carter, T. F. *The Invention of Printing in China and its Spread Westward*, 2nd edition, revised by L. Carrington Goodrich (New York, 1955).

Le Cinquième centenaire de l'imprimerie dans les ancien Pays-Bas, Catalogue of Exhibition, Bibliothèque Royale Albert Ier (Brussels, 1973).

Conway, William Martin. *The Woodcutters of the Netherlands in the Fifteenth Century* (1884; reprint Hildesheim, 1961).

Cornell, Henrik. *Biblia Pauperum* (Stockholm, 1925).

Cust, Lionel. *The Master E. S. and the Ars Moriendi* (Oxford, 1898).

Daniels, L. M. Fr., O.P. *De Spieghel der menscheliker Behoudenisse*, Studien en tekstuitgaven van Ons Geestelijk erf, IX (1949).
———. "Ludolphus van Saksen en Henricus Suso," in Ons Geestelijk erf, XX, 1–2 (1949).

Delaissé, L. M. J. *La Miniature Flamande: le mécénat de Philippe le Bon* (Brussels, 1959).
———. *Le siècle d'or de la miniature flamande* (Brussels, 1959).

——. *A Century of Dutch Manuscript Illumination* (Berkeley and Los Angeles, 1968).

Delen, A. J. J. *Histoire du livre et de l'imprimerie en Belgique des origines à nos jours*. Deuxième partie (Brussels, 1930).

Doudelet, C. *Le Speculum Humanæ Salvationis à la Bibliothèque Nationale de Florence* (Ghent and Antwerp, 1903).

Doutrepont, Georges. *Inventaire de la 'Librairie' de Philippe le Bon, 1420* (Brussels, 1906).

——. *La littérature française à la cour des ducs de Bourgogne*. 2 Vols. (Paris, 1909).

Dressler, Fridolin. *Scriptorum Opus: Schreiber-Mönche am Werk* (Wiesbaden, 1971).

Durrieu, Paul. *La miniature flamande au temps de la cour de Bourgogne (1415–1530)* (Paris-Brussels, 1927).

The Early Illustrated Book: Essays in Honor of Lessing J. Rosenwald, edited by Sandra Hindman (Washington, 1982).

Even, Edward van. *L'ancienne école de peinture de Louvain* (Brussels, 1870).

Febvre, Lucien, and Martin, H. J. *The Coming of the Book: the Impact of Printing, 1450–1800*, translated by David Gerard (London, 1976).

Flanders in the Fifteenth Century: Art and Civilization, Exhibition catalogue, edited by E. P. Richardson (Detroit, 1960).

Friedländer, Max J. *Early Netherlandish Painting* (Leiden, 1968).

Frocheur, F. "Inventoire de Viglius," in *Catalogue des manuscrits de la Bibliothèque Royale des Ducs de Bourgogne* (Brussels/Leipzig, 1842).

Gaspar, C., and Lyna, F. *Les principaux manuscrits à peinture de la Bibliothèque Royale de Belgique* (Paris, 1937).

Geisberg, Max. *Die Kupferstiche des Meisters E. S.* (Berlin, 1926).

Giliodts-van Severen, L. *L'Oeuvre de Jean Brito* (Bruges, 1897).

Gilissen, Léon. *Prolégomènes à la codicologie* (Ghent, 1977).

Goffin, Arnold. *Thierry Bouts* (Brussels, 1907).

Goldschmidt, E. P. *Gothic and Renaissance Bookbindings*, 2 Vols. (London, 1928).

Gorissen, Friedrich. *Das Stundenbuch der Katharina von Kleve, Analyse und Kommentar* (Berlin, 1973).

Gravell, Thomas L., and Miller, George. *A Catalogue of American Watermarks 1690–1835* (New York and London, 1979).

Hadrianus Junius. *Batavia* (Leiden, 1588).

Hartz, Sem L. "Notes on the 'Types Lyonnais Primitifs,'" in Quaerendo, IV, 4 (1974).

Harvard College Library. *Illuminated and Calligraphic Manuscripts*, Exhibition catalogue (Cambridge, 1955).

Heireman, Kamiel, S. J. "Le Prétendu atelier Malinois," in *Le Cinquième centenaire de l'imprimerie dans les anciens Pays-Bas*, Exhibition catalogue (Brussels, 1973).

Hellinga, Wytze Gs. *Copy and Print in the Netherlands* (Amsterdam, 1962).

——, Wytze and Lotte. *The Fifteenth-Century Printing Types of the Low Countries*, 2 Vols. (Amsterdam, 1966).

——, Lotte. "Further Fragments of Dutch Proto-typography," in Quaerendo, II, 3 (1972).

——, Lotte and Wytze. "Die Coster-Frage," in *Der gegenwärtige Stand der Gutenbergforschung*, edited by H. Widmann (Stuttgart, 1972).

——, Lotte. "Prototypographie" in *De vijfhonderdste verjaring van de boekdrukkunst in de Nederlanden*, Exhibition catalogue (Brussels, 1973).

Hessels, J. H. "A Bibliographical Tour," in The Library (Cambridge, 1908).

——. "Typography," in *The Encyclopaedia Britannica*, 11th edition (London, 1911).

Hind, Arthur M. *An Introduction to a History of Woodcut* (1935; reprint New York, 1963).

Hindman, Sandra. *Text and Image in Fifteenth-Century Illustrated Dutch Bibles* (Leiden, 1977).

Hindman, Sandra, and Farquhar, James Douglas. *Pen to Press*, Exhibition catalogue (College Park, Maryland, 1977).

Hintzen, Johanna. *De Kruistochtplannen van Philip den Goede* (Rotterdam, 1918).

Hobson, Anthony. *Great Libraries* (London and New York, 1970).

Hodgkins, John Eliot. "The Evolution of the Type-Mould," in *Rariora*, II (London, 1902).

Hollstein, W. H. *Dutch and Flemish Etchings, Engravings and Woodcuts ca. 1450–1700*, XII (Amsterdam, 1949).

Holtrop, J.W. *Monuments typographiques des Pays-Bas au XVᵉ siècle* (The Hague, 1868).

The Hunterian Museum Library in the University of Glasgow. *Catalogue of Manuscripts*, edited by John Young and P. H. Aitken (Glasgow, 1908).

Huth, Alfred. "*The Miroure of Man's Salvacienne*," a Fifteenth-Century Translation of the "*Speculum Humanæ Salvationis*" (London, 1888).

James, M. R., and Berenson, Bernard. *Speculum Humanæ Salvationis* (Oxford, 1926).

Kessler, Herbert L. "The Chantilly Miroir de l'humaine salvation and its Models," in *Studies in Honor of Millard Meiss*, I, edited by Irving Lavin and John Plummer (New York, 1977).

Kloss, Ernst. *Speculum Humanæ Salvationis. Ein niederländisches Blockbuch* (Munich, 1925).

Koch, Robert A. "The Sculptures of the Church of Saint-Maurice at Vienne, the Biblia Pauperum and the Speculum Humanæ Salvationis," in Art Bulletin, XXXII (1950).

———. "New Criteria for Dating the Netherlandish Biblia Pauperum Blockbook," in *Studies in Honor of Millard Meiss*, I, edited by Irving Lavin and John Plummer (New York, 1977).

Kristeller, Paul. *Kupferstich und Holzschnitt in vier Jahrhunderten*, 4th ed. (Berlin, 1922).

Laborde, Alexandre de. *Histoire des Ducs de Bourgogne*, I (Paris, 1849).

Lebeer, Louis. *Spirituale Pomerium* (Brussels, 1938).

Lehmann-Haupt, Hellmut. *Schwäbische Federzeichnungen* (Berlin and Leipzig, 1929).

Lehrs, Max. *Late Gothic Engravings of Germany and the Netherlands* (1908; reprint New York, 1969).

La Librairie de Bourgogne, Exhibition catalog. Introduction by Léon Gilissen (Brussels, 1970).

La Librairie de Philippe le Bon, Exhibition catalogue, edited by Georges Dogaer and Marguerite Debae (Brussels, 1967).

Lieftinck, G. I. *Manuscrits datés, conservés dans les Pays-Bas. Les Manuscrits d'origine étrangère (816–c. 1550)* (Amsterdam, 1964).

Loo, G. Hulin de. "Sur la biographie de Dieric Bouts avant 1457," in *Mélanges d'histoire offerts à Henri Pirenne* (Brussels, 1926).

Lutz, J., and Perdrizet, P. *Speculum humanæ salvationis*, 2 Vols. (Leipzig, 1907).

Mâle, Emile. *The Gothic Image* (1913; reprint New York, 1958), translated from *L'Art religieux du XIIIᵉ siècle en France* (Paris, 1898) as *Religious Art in France of the Thirteenth Century*.

———. *L'Art religieux de la fin du moyen âge en France* (Paris, 1949).

———. *Religious Art in France, the Twelfth Century: A Study of Medieval Iconography* (Princeton, 1978), translated from *L'Art religieux du XIIᵉ siècle en France* (Paris, 1953).

Marrow, James H. "Dutch Manuscript Illumination before the Master of Catherine of Cleves," in Nederlands Kunsthistorisch Jaarboek, XIX (1968).

———. "A Book of Hours from the Circle of the Master of the Berlin Passion: Notes on the Relationship between Fifteenth-Century Manuscript Illumination and Printmaking in the Rhenish Lowlands," in *Art Bulletin*, LX, 4 (1978).

Marston, Thomas E. "The Speculum Humanæ Salvationis," in The Yale University Library Gazette, XLII, no. 3 (1968).

Masai, François, and Wittek, Martin. *Manuscrits datés conservés en Belgique*. Vol. III: *1441–1460* (Brussels/Ghent, 1978).

Meerman, Gerard. *Origines Typographicæ* (The Hague, 1765).

Merguey, J. *Les Principaux manuscrits à peinture du Musée Condé à Chantilly* (Paris, 1930).

La Miniature Hollandaise, Exhibition catalogue. Introduction by Albert Brounts (Brussels, 1971).

Mortet, Charles. *Les Origines et les débuts de l'imprimerie* (Paris, 1922).

Musper, H. Th. *Die Haarlemer Blockbücher und die Costerfrage* (Mainz, 1939).

———. *Die Urausgaben der holländischen Apokalypse und Biblia pauperum* (Munich, 1961).

———. "Xylographic Books," in *The Book Through 5000 Years*, edited by H. D. L. Vervliet (London and New York, 1972).

Needham, Paul. *Twelve Centuries of Bookbinding, 400–1600* (New York/London, 1979).

Neumüller, Willibrord (Kommentar). *Speculum Humanæ Salvationis. Vollständige Faksimile-Ausgabe des Codex Cremifanensis 243 des Benediktinerstifts Kremsmünster* (Graz, 1972).

Obbema, Pieter F. J. "Writing on Uncut Sheets," in Quaerendo, VIII, 4 (1978).

———. "Van schrijven naar drukken" in *Boeken in Nederland*, edited by Ernst Braches (Amsterdam, 1979).

Ottley, William Young. *An Inquiry Concerning the Invention of Printing* (London, 1863).

Painter, George D. "Gutenberg and the B-36 Group," in *Essays in Honour of Victor Scholderer*, edited by D. E. Rhodes (Mainz, 1970).

Panofsky, Erwin. *Early Netherlandish Painting*, 2 Vols. (Cambridge, Massachusetts, 1953).

Paris, Paulin. *Les Manuscrits Français de la Bibliothèque Royale de Paris*, 7 Vols. (Paris, 1836–1848).

Pen to Press, Exhibition catalogue by Sandra Hindman and James Douglas Farquhar (College Park, Maryland, 1977).

Perdrizet, Paul. *Etude sur le Speculum humanæ salvationis* (Paris, 1908).

Pierron, Sander. *Histoire illustrée de la Forêt de Soignes*, 4 Vols. (Brussels, 1935).

Plummer, John. *The Hours of Catherine of Cleves* (New York, 1966).

Pollard, Graham. "The *pecia* system in the medieval universities," in *Medieval Scribes, Manuscripts and Libraries: Essays Presented to N. R. Ker*, edited by M. B. Parkes and Andrew Watson (London, 1978).

Post, R. R. *The Modern Devotion: Confrontation with Reformation and Humanism* (Leiden, 1968).

Praet, J. B. B. van. "Bibliothèque de Louis de la Gruthuyse" in *Recherches sur Louis de Bruges*, VI (Paris, 1831).

Reau, L. *Iconographie de l'art Chrétien*, II (Paris, 1956).

Reiffenberg, F. A. F. T. *Bulletin du Bibliophile Belge*, II (Brussels, 1845).

Samaran, Charles, and Marichal, Robert. *Catalogue des manuscrits en écriture Latine*, Vol. I (Paris, 1959).

Schreiber, W. L. *Manuel de l'amateur de la gravure sur bois et sur métal au XVᵉ siècle*, 8 Vols. (Berlin, 1891–1910).

Schretlen, J. J. *Dutch and Flemish Woodcuts of the Fifteenth Century* (1925; reprint New York, 1969).

Sheppard, L. A. "The Speculum-Printer's Editions of Donatus," in *Gutenberg-Jahrbuch*, edited by Aloys Ruppel (Mainz, 1954).

Smeyers, Maurits. "De invloed der blokboekdeditie van de Biblia Pauperum op het getijdenboek van Maria van Vronensteyn," in *Bijdragen tot de geschiedenis van de grafische kunst opgedragen aan Prof. Dr. Louis Lebeer* (Antwerp, 1975).

Smits, Carolus. *De iconographie van de Nederlandse primitieven* (Amsterdam/Brussels, 1933).

Sotheby, S. Leigh. *Principia Typographica* (London, 1845).

Stevenson, Allan H. "Paper as Bibliographical Evidence," in The Library, 5th Series, XVII (1962).

———. "The Problem of the Blockbooks," unpublished notes of lectures given at the University of Amsterdam, 1965, now in the Haarlem Stadsbibliotheek.

———. "The Quincentennial of Netherlandish Blockbooks," in British Museum Quarterly, XXXI (1966–67).

———. "The First Book Printed at Louvain," in *Essays in Honour of Victor Scholderer*, edited by D.E. Rhodes (Mainz, 1970).

Stilwell, Margaret Bingham. *The Beginning of the World of Books, 1450–1470* (New York, 1972).

Tanselle, G. Thomas. "The Bibliographical Description of Paper," in Studies in Bibliography, XXIV (1971).

Terlinden, Charles de. "Les Origines religieuses et politiques de la Toison d'or," in Publications du Centre Européen d'Etudes Burgondo-Médianes, V (1963).

Thomas à Kempis et la Devotio moderne, Exhibition catalogue, edited by Herman Libaers (Brussels, 1971).

Thomas, Alan G. *Great Books and Book Collectors* (London, 1975).

Turner, Eric G. *The Typology of the Codex* (Philadelphia, 1977).

Verougstraete, Hélène. *Un incunabule flamand: le Speculum humanæ salvationis*. Mémoire présenté pour l'obtention du grade de licenciée en archéologie et histoire de l'art (Université Catholique de Louvain, 1968, unpublished).

Verougstraete-Marcq, H., and Schoute, R. van. "Le Speculum humanæ salvationis considéré dans ses rapports avec la Biblia pauperum et le Canticum canticorum," in De Gulden Passer, LII (1975).

De vijfhonderdste verjaring van de boekdrukkunst in de Nederlanden, Exhibition catalogue, edited by H.D.L. Vervliet, Bibliothèque Royale Albert Iᵉʳ (Brussels, 1973).

Weale, W. H. James. "Documents inédits sur les enlumineurs de Bruges," in Le Beffroi, IV (1872–73).

Wilson, Adrian. *The Design of Books* (1967; reprint Salt Lake City, 1980).

———. *The Nuremberg Chronicle Designs* (San Francisco, 1969).

———. *The Making of the Nuremberg Chronicle*, 2nd edition, revised (Amsterdam, 1978).

Winkler, Friedrich. *Die Flämische Buchmalerei des XV. u. XVI. Jahrhunderts* (Leipzig, 1925).

Woodberry, George E. *A History of Wood-Engraving* (London, 1883).

Zedler, Gottfried. *Von Coster zu Gutenberg* (Leipzig, 1921).

———. *Die neuere Gutenberg-Forschung und die Lösung der Coster-Frage* (Frankfurt, 1923).

———. *Der älteste Buchdruck und das frühholländische Doktrinale des Alexander de Villa Dei* (Leiden, 1936).

Index

Numbers printed in italic type refer to the page on which an illustration appears.

Brussels, 23, 93, 97, 137, 212
  Bibliothèque Royale :
  Ms. 7619, *103*, pl. IV-2 following p. 100;
  Ms. 9092, pl. III-5 following p. 64;
  Ms. 9243, pl. III-6 following p. 64;
  Ms. 9249-50, *51-54, 56-58*;
    pls. III-1, III-2 following p. 48;
  Ms. 12070, *96*;
  Ms. II 239, *72*
Bruyère-Chalabre sale, 81
Burgundian library, 60, 78, 79, 81, 91
Burgundy, Duke of, 17, 19, 79

Cain, 32, 177; *177, 210*
Calvary, Providence painting, 102; *104*
Cambridge, Houghton Library, Harvard:
  Ms. Lat. 121, 42; *42, 43*
Cambridge University Library, 112; Inc. 3300, *113*
Campin, Robert, 93
Candelabrum, 161; *161*
Canons Regular of St. Augustine, 19
Canticum canticorum blockbook, 89, 106; *107, 108*
Carthusian order, 88
Casting type, 112, 126
Catherine of Cleves, Hours, 19; *18*
Chaise-Dieu, tapestries, 28, 216
Chalice and Host, 73
Chantilly, Musée Condé:
  Ms. fr. 139, 81; *82*; pls. III-11, III-12 following p. 80
  Apocalypse blockbook, 132
Charles the Bold, 59
Charles V of France, 49
Chicago, Newberry Library:
  Ms. 40, 77-79, 81; *77, 80*; pl. III-9 following
    p. 76, pl. III-10 following p. 80
Chronicon pontificum, 157
Clairmarais, Abbey, 85
Cleppinck *Speculum*, 40
Cloister of Clarissa, Clarenberg, 40
Closed door (Mary), 149; *149*
Codrus, King, 189; *37, 189*
Cologne Chronicle, 112
Comestor, Petrus. See *Historia scholastica*
Common Life, Brethren and Sisters of, 19, 21
Communion, 73, 136, 137
Concubine crowned, 182; *182*
Conradus of Altzheim, 26
Coornhert, Dirck Volkertsz, 112
Copenhagen, Kongelike Bibliotek: 70,
  Apocalypse blockbook, 96, 132; *90, 92*
Cornerstone of Christianity, 197; *197*
Coronation of the Virgin, 97
Cosimo de' Medici, 49
Coster, Laurens Janszoon, 111, 112; *110*
Creation, 97
Creation of Eve, 25, 142; *29, 34, 39, 53, 62, 75,*
  142, 209; pl. III-9 following p. 76

Cross, bearing of, 73, 184; *47, 184*;
  pl. IV-1 following p. 100
Crucifixion, 27, 102, 188, 212; *36, 104, 188*
Crusade, 55
Culemborg *Spieghel*, 134, 212; *213*
Cyrus, 201

Daniel, 166, 199, 200; *47, 166, 199, 213*
Darius, 182
Darmstadt, Hessische Landes- und Hochschulbibliothek, 20:
  Hs 2505, pls. II-1, II-2, II-3 following p. 40;
  Hs 720, *41*; pl. II-4 facing p. 41
Dating of blockbooks, 89, 91, 97, 98, 101, 106, 109,
  112, 116
David, 143, 159, 167, 169, 171, 175, 177, 183, 192,
  200, 202, 203; water brought to, pl. II-1 following
  p. 40; punished enemies, *41, 54*, pl. III-8 following
  p. 76; killed Goliath, *44, 167*; tower of, *153*; killed
  bear and lion, *167*; repented adultery, *169*; wel-
  comed, *171*; killed 800 men, *175*; played harp, *177*;
  cursed by Semei, *183*; messengers to King Ammon,
  183; mourning Abner, *192*
Debat de noblesse, 55
Decorated initials, *51, 56, 57, 58, 67, 68, 69, 71, 72*;
  pls. III-1, III-2 following p. 48
Deluge, 26, 70
Deposition, 190; *89, 190*
Devil tempted Jesus, 166; *166*
Devotio moderna, 19, 93, 137, 211
Doctrinale of Alexander de Villa Dei, 112; *113*
Dominican Order, 27, 34
Donatus, 112, 114; *115*
Drach, Peter, 207; *211*
Dutch printing. See Prototypography

Ecce panis angelorum, 114
Eglon, 200; *76*
Egyptian image, 162; *41, 162*; pl. II-2 following p. 40
Ehud, 200; *76*
Eleazar, 189; *189*
Elisabeth, Visitation of, 120
Elijah, pl. IV-1 following p. 100
Elisha, 201
Enclosed garden (Mary), 147; *147*
Entombment, 192; *192*
Entry into Egypt, 162; *41, 162*;
  pl. II-2 following p. 40
Epistelen en Evangelien, 112, 212
Epistre de Cicéron à son frère Quintus, 66, 70
Esther, 203
Eucharist, 73, 136, 137; *138, 139*
Eve, 25, 142-145, 191, 194; *23, 30, 31, 32, 34, 35,*
  39, 42, 75, 77, 142-145, 191, 194; pl. III-4
  following p. 60
Evilmoradach, 200
Exercitium super pater noster, 21, 89, 93, 97, 137; *94, 95*

Exodus, 194; *194*
Explicit, 59, 77; *74*
Expulsion from Eden, 26, 144; *31, 64, 144*
Ezekiel, 149

Fall from Grace, 26, 101, 144; *31, 64, 144*
Fall of Lucifer, 25, 50, 83, 142, 212; *29, 34, 52, 62,
  75, 142, 209*; pl. III-9 following p. 76
Fasciculus temporum, 132
Fiery furnace, 200; *213*
Flavius Josephus. See *Antiquitate judaica*
Flémalle, Master (Robert Campin), 93
Flight into Egypt, 162; *41, 162*; pl. II-2 following p. 40
Florence, Biblioteca Laurenziana, 134
Font of Moses, 165; *165*
Frans Hals Museum, 88

Gaddi, Taddeo, 35
Gaignat sale, 73
Genealogiæ deorum, 211
Germanisches Nationalmuseum. *See* Nuremberg
Gerson, Jean, 98
Getty, J. Paul Museum, 84; *84*
Ghent-Bruges school, 19, 81
Gideon, 155, 203; *46, 155, 211*; pl. III-8 following p. 76
Girdle book *Speculum*, 38; *38, 39*
Glasgow, University, Hunterian Museum Library, 74;
  Ms. 60: 73, 74, 77, 79, 81; *74, 75, 76*; pls. III-7, III-8
  following p. 76
Gleeson Library. *See* San Francisco
Golden table, 150; *150*
Goliath. *See* David
Groenendael, 21, 93, 97, 137, 212

Haarlem, 23, 111-112; Gemeente Archief, 132
Haarlem Stadsbibliotheek, 111; *110*;
  Ms. II 17, *124*; Inv. II 14 and Inv. II 15, 126
Hadrianus Junius, 112
Hainaut, Chroniques de, pl. III-6 facing p. 65
Hannah, 161
Heavenly Bread, 136
Heidelberg *Biblia pauperum*, 101
Heir of the Vineyard; 185; *185*
Heliodorus, 171; *171*
Hell, 194, 200; *194*. *See also* Pain of the Damned
Hellinga, Lotte and Wytze, 112, 116, 132
Hendricksdr, Mechtelt, 101
Hennequin de Bruges, 91
Henricus ex Pomerio, 97
Henricus Suso, 26, 27
Herbarius in dietsche (Kruidboeck), 212
Hessische Landes- und Hochschulbibliothek.
  See Darmstadt
Hind, Arthur M., 23, 101
Histoire du mors de la pomme, 66, 70
Historia destructionis Troiæ, 79
Historia lombardica, 194

Historia scholastica, 17, 25, 141, 146, 151, 153, 159,
  162, 178, 182, 195
Holy Ghost, 106, 148, 201
Holy Scripture, 61. *See* Bibles
Horlogium sapientiæ, 27
Houghton Library. *See* Cambridge
Hours, Books of: Catherine of Cleves, 19; *18*;
  Queen Mary, 78; Mary van Vronensteyn, 78,
  101, 102; *103*; pl. IV-2 following p. 100
House of the Annunciation, 212
Humanism, 215
Hundred Years' War, 17
Hunterian Museum. *See* Glasgow.
Huntington Library. *See* San Marino
Hur derided, 178; *178*
Hurus, Pablo, 208
Huss, Martin, 208; *210*
Huss, Matthias, 208

Initials, decorated. *See* Decorated initials
Ink, 89, 126
Invention of printing, 111, 112
Isaac, 184; *47, 184*; pl. IV-1 following p. 100
Isaiah, 187; *187*

Jacob, 190, 201; *25, 39, 87, 190, 206*
Jacoba van Loos-Hensberghe, 114
Jacobus de Voragine, 25
Jael, 201
Jan van den Berghe, 23
Jan van Zuren, 112
Jean, Duke of Berry, 49
Jean le Tavernier, 60; pl. III-5 following p. 64
Jean the Fearless, 49, 55
Jean Wauquelin, pl. III-6 following p. 65
Jephtha's sacrifice, 151; *151*
Jeremiah, 170; *33, 170*
Jerusalem, entry of Jesus, 170, 171; *170*
Jesse, tree of, 102, 148; *105, 148*
Jesus Christ: 24, 26, 28, 61, 101-106, 142, 148;
  Nativity, 46, 96, 156; Conquered the Devil, *76*;
  Presentation, 160, *160*; Entry into Egypt, 162,
  41, 162, pl. II-2 following p. 40; Baptism, 164,
  164; Temptations, 166, 167, *166*; with Mary
  Magdalen, 168; *168*; Weeping over Jerusalem,
  170, *33, 170*; Last Supper, 136, 138, 139, 172;
  pl. II-3 following p. 40; Prostrating Enemies,
  174, 175, *174*; Derision, 178, *178*; Torture, 180,
  180; Crown of Thorns, 182, *182*; Bearing Cross,
  184, *184*, pl. IV-1 following p. 100; Nailing of,
  186, *186*; Crucifixion, 102, 188, 189, *36, 104, 188*;
  Deposition, 190, *87, 190*; Entombment, 192, *25,
  192*; in Limbo, 194, *194*; Resurrection, 196, 197,
  38, 196, 206; Last Judgment, 198, 199, *198*
Joab, 176, 192, 202; *176*
Joachim, 26, 146, 148; *146, 148*
Job, 181, 204; *82, 181*; pl. III-12 following p. 80

New York Public Library, *KB+1471, 131, 134; Spencer Collection, NETH 1483, *213*

Nicholas V, Pope, 49

Nicodemus, 192; *192*

Noah, Ark of, *32, 42, 77, 145*; pl. III-4 following p. 60; shame of, 135, 179; *18, 103, 179*

Nuremberg, Germanisches Nationalmuseum, 217; *217*

Nuremberg Chronicle, 215

Ostrich, 200; *213*

Ottley, William Young, 112

Oxford, 30, 46; Bodleian Library, Auct. D4.17, 91; Ashmolean Museum, 98

Pain of the damned in Hell, 200, 203; *41, 54*; pl. III-8 following p. 76

Paper, 22, 109, 126, 129, 130-132

Paris, Bibliothèque de l'Arsenal, Ms. lat. 593, 26, 30; *33*

Paris, Bibliothèque Nationale, 101; Ms. fr. 6275, 60, 61, 74, 79; *16, 62, 63, 64, 65*; pls. III-3, III-4 following p. 60

  Ms. lat. 9584, 26; *29, 30, 31, 32*;

  Ms. fr. 17001, 66, 70; *67, 68, 69, 71, 72*;

  Ms. fr. 188, 83; *83*;

  Ms. fr. 460, 84; *84*;

  Xyl. 31, 93; *94*

Paschal lamb, 136, 172, 173; *138, 139, 172, 173*

Passion, Christ's, 204

Persia, Queen of, 151; *151*

Pharaoh, 156, 163, 203; *156, 163*

Philip the Good, 49, 55, 59, 60, 73, 81, 83; pls. III-5, III-6 following p. 64, pl. III-7 following p. 74

Plutarch, 150

Pontanus, *Singularia*, 132

Prado, altarpiece, 97

Presentation miniatures, 49, 70, 73; *71, 72*; pl. III-5 following p. 64, pl. III-7 following p. 76

Printer of the Text of the *Speculum*, 114, 132; *113*

Printing, fifteenth century methods, 128, 129

Printing press, *127*

Prodigal son, 169; *169*

Prophets in Limbo, 194; *194*

Protestantism, 215

Prototypography, 109, 112

Providence, Rhode Island School of Design, Museum of Art, No. 61.080, 102; *104*

Raephorst, Maria van, 101

Rebecca, 155; *155, 211*

Redemption, 26, 101; Master of the, 97

Red Sea, 203, pl. III-8 following p. 76

Reformation, 26

Resurrection, 196; *38, 196, 206*

Reuwich, Erhard, 102

Richel, Bernhard, 208; *209*

St. Anna, 26, 148, 202; *148*

St. Augustine, 24

St. Bernard, 106, 147

St.-Bertin, Abbey of, 85

St. Foillan, 66; *69*

St. Foursy, 66; *68*

St. John the Baptist, 164; *164*

St. Luke, 70; *72*

St. Matthew, 70; *72*

St.-Omer, Bibliothèque Municipale, 85, Mss. 182, 183, 184, 236; *85*

St. Thomas Aquinas, 25, 27

SS. Ulrich and Afra, Abbey of, 207, 208

St. Ultain, 66; *69*

Saliceto, 114, 132; *113*

Samson, 174, 179, 196, 200; *54, 76, 174, 179, 196*

Samuel, 161; *161*

San Francisco, University of, Gleeson Library, *34, 35, 36, 37*

Sangar, 175; *175*

San Marino, California, Henry E. Huntington Library and Art Gallery, 126; 104685, *127*; 104026, *211*; 105168, *209*; 105169, *210*; 101922, *214*

San Pedro de Roda monastery, 42

Saul, 177; *177*

Schlipat, Jean, 208

Schöffer, Peter, 102

Schönsperger, Johann, 215

Script, 20, 32, 40, 42, 49, 73, 77, 86, 87

Scriverius, Petrus, 112

Sculpture, 28, 216

Semei, 183; *183*

Semiramis, 151; *151*

Sept-Fontaines, 21, 93, 137

Seth, 32

Seven Sorrows and Seven Joys of Mary, 26, 27, 204, 205

Sheba, Queen of, 159, 204; *86*; pl. II-1 following p. 40

Sibyl, Tiburtine, 29, 157; *157*

Sign appeared in the sky, 202; pl. III-10 following p. 80

Simeon, 160; *160*

Simon, 168; *168*

Singularia in causis criminalibus, 114

Sisera, 201

Sisters of the Common Life, 19

Solomon, 149, 159, 161, 202, 204; *86, 149, 159, 161*; pls. II-1 following p. 40, III-10 following p. 80

Song of Songs, 106, 147; *107, 147*

Sorg, Anton, 208

Speculo Sanctæ Mariæ Virginis, 207

Speculum humanæ salvationis, blockbook editions, 89, 106, 109-137, 141; *117, 118*

Speculum humanæ salvationis woodcuts, 89, 109, 134-137, 141-199; *122, 123, 125, 127, 138, 142-199*; in the form of a hand, 216; *217*

Acknowledgments for Illustrations

The authors and publisher would like to thank the following institutions and individuals for permission to reproduce illustrations and for supplying photographs:

Archivum Artis Lovaniense, Louvain
(photo: P. Stuyven)

The Bancroft Library, University of California, Berkeley

Bayerische Staatsbibliothek, Munich

The Beinecke Rare Book and Manuscript Library, Yale University, New Haven

Bibliothèque de l'Arsenal, Paris

Bibliothèque de l'Université de l'Etat à Mons

Bibliothèque Nationale, Paris

Bibliothèque Royale Albert Ier, Brussels

The British Library, London

Cambridge University Library, courtesy of the Syndics, Cambridge, U.K.

Germanisches Nationalmuseum, Nuremberg

The J. Paul Getty Museum, Malibu, California

The Gleeson Library, University of San Francisco

Haarlem Stadsbibliotheek (photo: Tom Haartsen)

Hessische Landes- und Hochschulbibliothek Darmstadt

The Houghton Library, Harvard University, Cambridge

The Hunterian Museum Library, Glasgow

The Henry E. Huntington Library and Art Gallery, San Marino, California

Det Kongelige Bibliotek, Copenhagen

The Library of Congress, Preservation Office, Washington

Musée Condé, Chantilly (photos: Lauros-Giraudon, Paris)

Museum of Art, Rhode Island School of Design, Providence

The Newberry Library, Chicago

The New York Public Library, The Research Libraries, Rare Books and Manuscripts Division, and Spencer Collection, New York

The Pierpont Morgan Library, New York

Photographie Bulloz, Paris

Rijkdienst voor de Monumentenzorg, Zeist

Rijksmuseum Meermanno-Westreenianum, The Hague (photo: B. Frequin)

Ruusbroecgenootschap, Antwerp
(photo: P. D. van der Poel)

Staatsbibliothek Preussischer Kulturbesitz, Berlin

Designed by Adrian Wilson, San Francisco.

Typesetting by Mackenzie-Harris Corp. in Bembo for the text, and by the designer in Palatino Italic for the headings.

Production supervision by Czeslaw Jan Grycz with the assistance of Ellen Herman.

Printed and bound by Dai Nippon Printing Co., Ltd., Tokyo, Japan.

The publishers wish to acknowledge with gratitude the contribution provided from the Art Endowment Fund of the Associates of the University of California Press, without whose generous assistance this book would have been more difficult to finance appropriately.